GREENLAND

ICELAND

HUDSON BAY

ATLANTIC

OCEAN

A.

N
W E
S

THE ANIMAL BOOK

American Mammals North of Mexico

By DOROTHY CHILDS HOGNER
and NILS HOGNER

HENRY Z. WALCK, INC.

Preface

What is it about? The Animal Book is a book about native American animals which live on the North American continent or in adjacent waters, north of Mexico. The members of the animal kingdom included in the book are all mammals (class *Mammalia*).

What is a mammal? Deer and Bears are mammals although in everyday life we usually speak of them as animals. As in common usage we will use the word animal frequently in place of the more specific name. Strictly speaking, an animal may be any creature which has the power to move about at will, as opposed to plant life, or it may mean any beast, as opposed to man. A mammal is a form of animal life which is separated from all other classes of animal life by a unique characteristic, the presence of mammary or milk glands. The mother secretes milk for her young ones and suckles them for some time after birth. This is true of every member of the mammal group from Wapiti to Whale.

Mammals are the highest class in the animal kingdom. They are varied in form and habits. Some have tusks, some have no teeth; some fly like birds, others cannot leave the sea and live. Man is of course the most highly developed of the group. His intelligence places him far above the wild mammals.

Mammals are all warm-blooded. They have lungs and breathe air. A very important distinction is the hair which covers their bodies while fish and reptiles have scales and birds are feathered. In some mammals hair is scant, and in a few it disappears in the adult animal but most mammals are very hairy beasts.

How are mammals classified? It is not always possible to identify an animal by its common name because the same name is sometimes given to two different animals. For example the Thirteen Lined Ground Squirrel is often called a Gopher although he is not the least bit like a true Gopher. Dolphins are called Porpoises and vice versa.

Scientists have developed an elaborate system to classify animal life in its proper relationship. They have divided the mammals into many different groups. They began with major differences. These divisions they call orders. There are eleven orders of North American mammals and each order is treated in a separate chapter in this book. The orders are again divided into suborders, then into families. There are thirty-eight native American animal families. Each family is divided into genera. Each genus is further split into species, each species into subspecies, all according to important, less important, then very slight differences such as variation in skull shape or tooth formation. The method works like steps in a stair, thus:

order *Carnivora* (Flesh Eaters)
family *Mustelidae* (Weasel)
genus *Mephitis* (bad odor)
species *nigra* (black)

and you have the common Eastern Skunk.

We have brought the classification down to the genus step to give the key to the species. Species differences are frequently so slight that they are of no major importance in field identification. For example, the Red Fox may be easily identified as a Red Fox whether he is the golden species which lives on the northern plains or the slightly different and redder species which lives in the northeastern states. On the other hand, some species do differ greatly in external appearance. In these cases we have described each one.

In the Appendix will be found a list of every

order, family, and genus of every animal found in North America north of Mexico. All these animals are described in *The Animal Book*.

What are the sources of animal material? Travel with a tent and camp kit over many sections of the continent has been our fortunate experience. In America today we find the lives of the wild creatures very much disturbed by man. Fencing the Great Plains and cutting the primeval forests has affected the habits of big game and small Rodents. Large farms offer Gophers, Mice, and Hares a new source of food supply but at the same time bring them a powerful enemy, the farmer. Fur bearers, oil bearers, and animals of prey also play an important part in the economy of life on the continent today. For these reasons the United States government has made exhaustive studies of the habits of American animals, and the books and leaflets published by the Department of the Interior have been an invaluable help in preparing the material for *The Animal Book*. The studies such as Vernon Bailey's *The Mammals and Life Zones of Oregon* (1936) and *Mammals of New Mexico* (1931), published in the series "North American Fauna" under the direction of the Department of Agriculture, Bureau of Biological Survey, and the leaflets more recently published under the Fish and Wildlife Service are very important contributions to the field.

A second very important source is the *Journal of Mammalogy*. I regret that space does not permit a detailed list of articles and books consulted but no book about mammals would be complete without mention of a few highlights in the study of animal life. The *Field Book of North American Mammals* (1928) by H. E. Anthony is the most thorough study ever made of every mammal form within our borders. Charles M. Scammon's classic book on Whales, *The Marine Mammals of the Northwestern Coast of North America* (1874), Glover Allen's scholarly and very readable volume, *Bats* (1939) are both entertaining as well as informative. W. J. Hamilton, Jr.'s *American Mammals* (1939) has the most thorough bibliography.

We are grateful to Dr. Claude W. Leister, Curator of Mammals and Educational Activities at the New York Zoological Park, for a critical reading of the manuscript. We also wish to thank James L. Clark, director of the Department of Preparations at the American Museum of Natural History in New York, for his liberal assistance and for his constructive comments on the illustrations; Dr. Goodwin of the Natural History Museum staff for helpful information and the staff of the Museum library for their kind assistance.

DOROTHY CHILDS HOGNER
NILS HOGNER

New York, 1942.

Contents

Illustrations

THE ANIMAL BOOK

Chapter 1
Under the Forest Floor

THE INSECT EATERS
(order *Insectivora*)

Under the leaf mold of the forest live the Insect Eaters. All are small, some are among the tiniest of living mammals. Their teeth are formed for catching and chewing insects, their favorite food. Here we find the source of the scientific name of their group, from the Latin *insectum* (insect) and *vorare* to devour, order *Insectivora*.

There are two families of Insect Eaters found in North America north of the Mexican border, the Shrew Family and the Mole Family.

THE SHREW FAMILY
(family *Soricidae*)

Members of the Shrew Family differ in size from very small to the very smallest of living mammals. All have soft, silky, molelike fur, tiny eyes, inconspicuous ears, long narrow heads terminating in sharply pointed noses. The upper front teeth are large and project forward.

Several Shrews look mouselike but are most frequently mistaken for Moles. From a Mole a Shrew may easily be distinguished by its tiny delicate front feet.

These little creatures live in all parts of North America except very arid country where but one rare species is known. There are a confusing number of species and subspecies. Many of these are of interest only to anatomists since the species differ mainly in the formation of their skulls. Others are easily distinguished on sight but are rarely seen because of their secretive habits. Some years they are rare, other years abundant. In spite of their tiny size Shrews are fierce and sometimes eat their own kind.

Their family name *Soricidae* comes from the Latin word *sorex* which means a shrew.

There are six main genera or groups in the Shrew Family north of Mexico, the Common Shrew, the Short-tailed Shrew, the Water Shrew, the Little Shrew, the Gray Shrew, and the Pygmy Shrew.

Smallest Living Mammal

PYGMY SHREW
(genus *Microsorex*)

Shrew Family

The rare Pygmy Shrew is the smallest mammal living today. The tiny creature measures but a fraction over three inches from the tip of his pointed nose to the end of his short tail. He lives in the region around the District of Columbia. Slightly larger cousins inhabit northern North America south to Virginia. Their brownish coats with white or grayish under parts blend with their surroundings. While Common Shrews like moist country, Pygmy Shrews like dry clearings. Otherwise their habits are thought to be similar.

Not much bigger than a large grasshopper, these tiniest of mammals are classified in genus *Microsorex*, *micro* meaning very small, *sorex* meaning Shrew.

The Shrew Whose Name is Given to Scolding Women

COMMON SHREW
LONG-TAILED SHREW
SHREW MOUSE
(genus *Sorex*)

Shrew Family

This mouselike Shrew and its many cousins has a very small body, not much bigger than the Pygmy Shrew, and a rather long hairy tail. He has characteristic small delicate forefeet and a pointed snout.

He behaves like a large animal of prey. He is nervous but brave, his temper is vicious. A gluttonous appetite sometimes leads the tiny creature to turn cannibal.

The famous experiment of Dr. C. Hart Merriam with these Common Shrews is frequently quoted. He put three of the tiny animals under a tumbler. Soon there were but two. They had killed and eaten the third. Before the night was ended there was but one survivor. He had eaten his companion. For one tiny Shrew to eat so much in such a short period of time means that the process of digestion in this family is amazingly fast. A Shrew is forever hungry.

If captive Shrews are well fed they are not cannibals. Their favorite food is insects and their larvae, and snails. Active by night as well as by day trying to satisfy their ravenous appetites they search for prey under the leaves in moist, densely vegetated country. They are frequently found scurrying along burrows of other small animals or under old logs. Should they meet a Mouse they show enormous courage, often attacking prey larger than themselves. Their eyes are tiny and weak, and can probably distinguish only light and darkness, but like Moles they feel their way around.

These Long-tailed Shrews are prolific. They have two or three litters in the spring and summer. The four or five young in a litter are nearly grown in a month.

A large dusky species of Long-tailed Shrew lives in the tundra of Labrador and the Hudson Bay region. Others are found in the damp, heavily vegetated country from Canada to North Carolina. In color they are dark brown above, gray beneath. The Smoky Shrew which lives in the mountainous regions of New England, New York and the Alleghenies is slate-colored above, lighter below. The southern Long-tailed Shrew of North Carolina has a larger snout and skull. Fisher's Shrew is found in the Dismal Swamp of Virginia and another species lives in the Adirondacks and the Catskills. The latter may be recognized by his very thick tail with long hairs at the tip. He has a dark-gray coat, lighter under parts.

The Common Shrews belong to the main genus *Sorex* meaning a Shrew.

A Burrowing Shrew

SHORT-TAILED SHREW
MOLE SHREW
(genus *Blarina*)

Shrew Family

This little mammal is large for a Shrew, often reaching five inches in length from the end of its short tail to the tip of its pointed snout. He is called Mole Shrew because he digs his own burrows like a Mole. His front feet are small and delicate, like other Shrews, but his snout is strengthened by cartilage and acts like a drill as he pushes up the earth.

The Short-tailed Shrew feeds on worms, insects and their larvae, centipedes, slugs, and some vegetable matter. He also likes meat. When he meets smaller Shrews and Mice in his burrow he often attacks, conquering them with his sharp front teeth. Like all of his kind he has a voracious appetite, has been said to devour more than his weight daily. Nervous and shy, he shows great courage.

These Shrews do not shun the sun as Moles do. They may come out of their burrows by night or by day but are infrequently seen because of their shy habits. They often run under fallen logs or stone walls, or scutter under the leaf mat of the forest. They enjoy a damp, dark habitat.

They do not hibernate, nor do they dig tunnels beneath the frost line when winter comes. They are active all during the cold months, seeking dormant insects under the leaf mold beneath snow drifts, often devouring leftovers from meals

of meat-eating animals of the forest, to satisfy their enormous hunger.

The fur of the common Short-tailed Shrew is sooty. His front teeth are chestnut-colored at the tips. His range is from southern Canada over most of the eastern half of North America. Several species and geographic races occur in the south. A brown Short-tailed Shrew, ashy below, is found from New Jersey west to Nebraska and southward in the lowlands. One, dark-slate-colored, is found in the Everglades of Florida, another in the Dismal Swamp of Virginia.

Blarina is a coined word.

Short-tailed Shrew

A Shrew That Swims

Shrew Family

WATER SHREW
Marsh Shrew
(genus *Neosorex*)

This Shrew has a smaller body than his Short-tailed cousins, but his long tail gives him a greater all-over length and places him among the largest of the family. His nose is typically shrewish, long and sharp, his hind feet are relatively large and broad and stiff hairs grow between the toes.

These hairs act like webs, helping the little semiaquatic animal to swim.

The Water Shrew frequents small streams, lake shores, and marshes in the colder parts of North America from Alaska and Labrador southward over the high mountain regions throughout the United States. The color of the two species and the several subspecies varies from light reddish brown to dark gray above, from white to yellowish below. A sprinkling of light-tipped hairs on the back gives a hoary appearance.

The Rocky Mountain Water Shrew has a slate-colored velvety coat. A rather uncommon, high-altitude species, his habits have been observed in captivity. He searches for food underwater. He dives straight down, paddling with all four feet to submerge his body. Air bubbles are caught under his outer guard hairs. They give his coat a silvery sheen and at the same time make his body buoyant. He kicks constantly to keep his nose on the bottom of the pool and to stay upside down looking for snails. His long whiskers seem to be sensitive and help him find prey. Like all Shrews he has weak eyes but his hearing seems acutely atuned to small, squeaky sounds. He remains underwater but a few seconds at a time, a quarter of a minute at most, but he dives frequently.

Water Shrews have typical shrewish appetites. They are said to eat their own weight in food in a day. Yet in spite of their rapid digestion and continuous hunger, they have been kept in captivity for two days unfed without being harmed.

They are fond of snails, insects, Mice, and in some place are called Fish Mice. They eat fish eggs and some say they can catch tiny fish.

Their genus name *Neosorex* comes from the Greek *neos* (new [form]), plus *sorex* (Shrew).

LITTLE SHREW
(genus *Cryptotis*)

Shrew Family

The Little Shrew is much like the Long-tailed Shrew in appearance but is smaller and his tail is short. He is a southerner, not common north of the Rio Grande, but species do appear in the eastern states and as far west as the previously-mentioned river in Texas.

The genus name of this tiny creature comes from the Greek word *kryptos* meaning hidden.

GRAY SHREW
CRAWFORD'S SHREW
(genus *Notiosorex*)

Shrew Family

There is but one species of this very small Shrew known, and unlike his relatives he lives in an arid country ranging from eastern Texas to southern California. He is rare within this range.

The genus name *Notiosorex* comes from the Latin words *notius* (southern) and *sorex* (Shrew).

THE MOLE FAMILY
(family *Talpidae*)

Moles rarely see the sun. They spend their lives tunneling beneath the surface of the earth, emerging only at night when the earthworms rise.

The form of a Mole is greatly modified to meet the needs of life underground. All parts which might interfere with quick passage through a tunnel are reduced. External ears are absent. The soft, delicate fur pushes backwards as easily as it pushes forward, letting the Mole slip rapidly back and forth through holes which he digs just large enough for his own body. His eyes are tiny and degenerate, in some species sealed. His nose has sensitive nerves which help him feel his way around in the dark.

The skull is long and narrow, ending in a pointed snout. The neck is so short that the animal appears neckless. The bones of the hip region are so reduced that there is no room for internal organs to pass through them as they do in the skeletons of most animals. These organs lie on the undersurface of the pelvic bones. Thus narrow-hipped, the Mole turns easily in his burrow. His hind feet are relatively small but strong enough to push earth behind him.

Most important is the specialized form of the shoulders, forelimbs, and front paws. They are tremendous. They are the tools of a digger. The broad paddle-shaped, heavy-clawed front feet immediately distinguish a Mole from his dainty-footed cousin, the Shrew. The scientific family name *Talpidae* comes from the two Latin words *talus* (an ankle) and *pes* (a foot), meaning club-footed.

The following are the five main genera or groups of our Moles: Brewer's Mole, the Common Mole, the Star-nosed Mole, the Oregon Mole, and Gibbs' Mole.

In Forest Subways

Mole Family

BREWER'S MOLE
HAIRY-TAILED MOLE
(genus *Parascalops*)

This is a woods Mole. He is at home in southeastern Canada, in most of New England, New York, Pennsylvania, and northeastern Ohio, and ranges south along the Allegheny Mountains into northern South Carolina. Among the largest of the Insect Eaters in the United States and Canada, he reaches a length of over five inches. He usually lives beneath the leaf mold in the forest or in old pasture land where he digs his burrow with his long tough snout and his huge paddle-shaped forefeet. The hills and ridges which he makes are not so conspicuous as those of the Lawn Mole because the leaf mold conceals them.

Usually found in less cultivated places than the Lawn Mole he also differs in size, color of fur, and hairiness of tail. Brewer's Mole is smaller. He is dark gray in color, his very short tail is furred, giving him the name Hairy-tailed Mole. Old Moles become light gray, almost white, about the snout and feet and tail.

Moles are forever hungry like their Shrew cousins. One authority states that this Hairy-tailed Mole will eat his own weight in food within twenty-four hours, although others say this is a slight exaggeration. All agree that he has a tremendous appetite which keeps him very busy.

In the summer he digs a great series of near-surface tunnels, looking for insects. Sometimes at night he follows the earthworms to the surface world. Awkward aboveground, he moves slowly around searching for food. His vision is very poor and he does not come out in the sunlight. His tiny eyes are only one millimeter in diameter. Although all the basic elements of a good eye are crowded into this small space, they are modified in the adult Mole, and he cannot see well.

Sensitive hairs on his snout guide him through the underworld. By pressing his great paws against the sides of his tunnels he probably shoves himself forward and backward with considerable speed.

Like all of his kind, the Hairy-tailed Mole lives by himself. He does not associate even with other Hairy-tailed Moles except during the mating season. In late March or early April these Moles mate. The male takes no interest in the welfare of the young Moles which are born from four to six weeks later. He goes away to live by himself. The mother Mole keeps the dry grass and leaf nest and the tunnels clean and neat. Her four or five young are born hairless and helpless but she does not have a long period of family responsibility. The baby Moles soon grow hair on their bodies, dark-brown hair on their feet and tails. Their snouts are black. They are full grown in a month or two when they become independent, leaving the mother Mole alone in the eerie quiet of the underworld of roots and narrow runways and heavy earth.

All alone she seeks food and meets none of her own kind except by chance. By chance too she may meet a little Shrew which has entered her runways. She and her kind have few enemies. Perhaps the hungry little Short-tailed Shrews prey on the young, and a Red Fox or a Gray Owl may pounce on an adult which has ventured out onto the forest floor at night.

When winter comes Moles do not hibernate. In October or November or when the surface ground is frozen Brewer's Moles burrow deep into the earth beneath the frost. Here they make new tunnels over an area from fifty to eighty feet in diameter. Alone in this dark underworld each solitary Mole lives like a hermit in his own series of tunnels. There is no evidence that these little mammals ever live in pairs. During the cold months they come to their surface runs only during thaws.

Winter and summer, earthworms are a favorite food. Hairy-tailed Moles also eat insect larvae and pupae. They like beetles and ants, and sometimes eat millepedes and centipedes, a slug, snail, or sow bug.

Hairy-tailed Moles sometimes make tunnels under lawns causing damage but the harm they may do in this way is perhaps offset by their fondness for cutworm larvae and other injurious insects. The genus name *Parascalops* comes from the Greek *para*, near (a variety of), and *skalops*, a Mole, literally a digging animal.

Lawn Mole

COMMON MOLE
Naked-tailed Mole
Eastern Mole
(genus *Scalopus*)

Mole Family

What country-home owner in the eastern lowlands from southern Canada to Florida has not deplored the ridges and the small fresh heaps of earth which suddenly appear in his lawn? This damage is caused by a blind little animal, the Common Mole. His eyelids are sealed shut, but loss of sight does not hinder him from making long tunnels in his earnest search for worms and grubs. His life forever dark, he feels his way with his sharp sensitive nose, scooping out narrow passages usually about five or six inches under the surface of the ground. He digs the earth with his great forepaws, kicks it behind him with his rear feet until a pile has collected. Then he turns and with tremendous energy breasts the pile toward the last outlet. Becoming discouraged he will stop, break through the surface, and make a new "molehill" which is really no more than a pile of discarded dirt.

All this activity is to satisfy a voracious appetite which is typical of his family but quite out of keeping with his size. He reaches but a fraction over seven inches long but he may consume from one third to two thirds of his body weight in one day.

His favorite food is earthworms which he kills by crushing them against the side of his burrow with his great clawed "hands." He often piles loose earth over his victim to hold it until he has time to finish it. He likes white grubs as well as earthworms and also eats larvae of many kinds and adult insects. In captivity he has shown a taste for corn, ripe tomatoes, and apples as well as Irish potatoes, even when offered quantities of his normal insect food. How much vegetable matter this Mole eats in the wild state is not known.

His appetite for many injurious insects makes him valuable when he confines his digging to uncultivated areas, but when, as frequently happens, he invades lawns and cultivated fields he is a pest.

He may be distinguished from Brewer's Mole by his larger size, and by his tail which instead of being furry like the woods Mole's is very short and naked. His fur is smoky brownish gray.

His habits are similar to his cousins. He lives alone except during the mating season. In the winter he retires to deep burrows which he digs below frost line. There he hunts for worms and grubs in the depth of the underworld, seeking to satisfy the constant gnawing of his appetite.

The genus name *Scalopus* comes from the Greek *skalops*, a Mole.

Star-nosed Mole

Swamp and River Mole

STAR-NOSED MOLE
(genus *Condylura*)

Mole Family

This Mole lives in bogs or along small streams in northeastern North America. His peculiar fleshy pink nose has growths on it resembling those of a sea anemone. Like his cousins the Lawn and Brewer's Moles he has large front paws with which he tunnels through the dark peaty soil of swamps and into the muddy banks of small meadow brooks and ponds, searching for worms and grubs and the larvae of water insects.

His holes often open in the banks on small rivers, sometimes are submerged. This Mole has no fear of water. He is a good swimmer, dives into streams after water beetles and small crustacea. One authority states that he also catches small fish.

The cylindrical tail of the Star-nosed Mole is stout, a little constricted at the base. It is longer than the tails of Common Moles and very hairy, serving as a rudder in the water. The color of this Mole's fur is dark smoky brown; his eyes are little dots.

His activities are all underground, underwater, or perhaps in the winter months also under ice like a Muskrat. During most severe weather he is sometimes seen abroad when the rivers are ice-bound.

The mother Mole makes her nest of grassy material in a chamber in one of her burrows. In marshy and swampy areas she selects her nesting place with care, choosing ground above high-water level.

There is only one species of Star-nosed Mole. He is easily recognized by the odd growths on his nose which give the genus name *Condylura*, meaning wartlike growth on the skin. This word is derived from the Greek *kondylos*, meaning literally a knuckle or knob, and *oura,* meaning tail.

Oregon Mole

In the West

OREGON MOLE
WESTERN MOLE, TOWNSEND MOLE
(genus *Scapanus*)

Mole Family

The Oregon Mole lives in the humid regions of the Cascade Range in Washington and Oregon and northwestern California. Related species range south along the coast into Mexico, north into British Columbia. This is a large American Mole having velvety, nearly black fur.

The Western Mole prefers to live in open meadows and damp canyon bottoms but will also be found on the floors of cone-bearing forests. He is an active burrower like his eastern cousins, persues earthworms and grubs underground. He also eats butterflies and moths, bees, wasps, centipedes, and beetles as well as ants, crickets, and grasshoppers and flies and some vegetable matter.

Tulip growers of Oregon complained that these big Moles were destroying their bulbs. In the year 1929 an experiment was conducted at Hillsboro, Oregon, to discover whether or not the Moles were guilty. Mice were excluded from a quarter-acre tract. Six hundred Darwin tulips were planted and a male Oregon Mole placed in the enclosure. There were plenty of earthworms in the ground. But although the Mole had a plentiful supply of his favorite worms, within about a month he had eaten eleven tulip bulbs and had injured eleven more bulbs.

Three hundred feet of garden peas and wheat were planted in the same enclosure. The Mole ate twenty-six feet of peas, about as much of the wheat.

This experiment along with the examination of the stomach contents of several small coastal Moles, small Western Moles, convinced the tulip growers that Moles in tulip country are a pest. When these animals confine their activity to uncultivated land they are harmless.

During the humid weather which is common on the north Pacific coast, Western Moles work near the surface, reserve their deep tunnels for dry periods and cold weather and for making a nest for the young. Three or four babies are born. They grow quickly, give their mother no trouble after the first few weeks. They are full grown and independent in one or two months.

The genus name *Scapanus* comes from the Greek *skapane*, a digging tool.

GIBBS' MOLE
(genus *Neürotrichus*)

This is a little Mole which lives in the humid regions from British Columbia to northern California. He has an annulated hairy tail. His fore- legs are not so overdeveloped as those of his cousins.

The genus name *Neürotrichus* comes from the Greek *neuron* (nerve) plus *thrix, trichos* (hair).

Chapter II
In the Air

THE HAND-WINGED
(order *Chiroptera*)

The Bat group is named from two Greek words *cheir*, meaning hand, and *pteron*, meaning wing. A Bat's wings are membranes of skin spread between its body and legs and the extraordinarily long toes of its front feet. Bats are at home in the air. On the ground they flop awkwardly because their hind limbs rotate outward on the wing, causing the knee to bend backwards. They are mammals of the twilight and the night, not often observed other than as a scuttering shadow. On unfeathered wings they fly swiftly, as skillfully as Night Hawks.

When day comes Bats seek a secluded spot, hang themselves upside down on the long curved claws of their hind feet which form natural hooks. Folded in the hammock of their wings, they sleep until dusk calls them out again to search for food.

None of the Fruit Eaters, the Fish Eaters, or the blood-drinking Vampires come north of the Mexican border. Our native Bats live on insects.

No Bat builds a real nest. Our Bats build no shelter of any kind for their young, nor do the fathers take interest in the welfare of their offspring. The mother Bat feeds her babies as all mammals do, with milk secreted from her breasts. She lets her little ones cling to her while she is asleep. When they are very small she takes them with her on night flights, the babies clinging to her body while she chases insects. When the young are larger she hangs them up on the limb of a tree, hidden among the leaves, or in a cave while she hunts food.

If a young Bat falls to the floor of a cave his cries bring adults swooping down, but it is doubtful if mother Bats are able to rescue their young. In caves lighted for sight-seers the babies may fall so often that they have to be removed by the shovelful.

Contrary to the old saying "as blind as a Bat," Bats can see. But their eyes are small, not nearly as big as in Mice of their size. Although most of the elements present in a normal eye are found in a Bat's eye, the cells which see color are lacking. The animal is perhaps color-blind. It has long been thought that some sixth sense guides his flight. Many experiments have been made to discover what this other sense was.

In the latter part of the eighteenth century an Italian named Spallanzani reported that Bats which he had blinded flew without hitting silk threads which he had suspended in their path. Early in the twentieth century Hahn experimented in America with thin black wires instead of threads. It was easier to record the number of "hits." The wires twanged when struck. At first Hahn used forty-seven normal Little Brown Bats in over 2000 trials.

He recorded twenty-five per cent hits. He then covered the eyes of twelve of these Bats with a mixture of glue and lampblack and gave them 600 trials. They made only twenty-two per cent hits, a better average than the Bats which could see! In another experiment Hahn plugged the Bats' ears with plaster of Paris. They flew into the wires many more times than the blinded Bats, which seemed to prove that the sixth sense was in the inner ear of the animals. Extremely sensitive to small sounds like the hum of insects the Bat is perhaps guided in flight by the little vibrations he alone can hear.

Others suggest that the nose leaves, the wattles and warts on the heads of some Bats are sensitive to air vibrations.

Whatever the answer to this puzzling question, the theories have led to an invention of an instrument of great value to man, a delicate device which sends out low tones from the prow of a ship and by recording the echoes on a sensitive membrane warns of obstacles in the ship's path, directing a vessel through fog and darkness as the Bat is supposed to be directed in his night flight.

In America Bats have few enemies. Owls, particularly the Barn Owls, eat some. Hawks catch them less frequently. Some species of snakes, the chicken snake and the rat snake and black snake, hunt Bats in barns and caves. Large trout sometimes catch Bats when they dip to the surface of water to drink and occasionally a Skunk or Opossum picks up a fallen Bat.

The odor of Bats may be disagreeable to animals as it is to man. Several species have scent glands with a musky odor so strong that they make very undesirable attic tenants. The purpose of these glands is not surely known. It probably is perfume to the opposite sex during the breeding season or it might aid the well-developed homing instinct which guides Bats back to their roosts.

Bats are queer ancient creatures. For sixty million years their tribe has lived. During that great period of time there have been no important changes in their form. Before Eocene, dawn time, their ancestors were perhaps little primitive Shrewlike animals which lived in trees and with flattened bodies learned to leap, then to sail, at last developed skin wings and learned to fly from tree to tree. This is supposition. There is no proof.

Of the seventeen families of the enormous Bat group, only three families inhabit our continent north of Mexico. They are the Common Bat Family, the Leaf-nosed Bat Family, and the Free-tailed Bat Family.

THE COMMON BAT FAMILY
(family *Vespertilionidae*)

This large family includes most of the well-known species of North America as well as Europe. Of the forty-one genera, ten make their homes from the limit of tree growth on our continent south to the Mexican border.

Common Bats are small and with one exception have no outgrowth on their noses or mouths. Their ears are well developed, their long tails are caught in the wing membranes between their hind legs. In several species this tail wing helps the Bat catch food. The animal seizes an insect, turns his tail down to form a net into which he bends his head, and, while holding the prey therein, gives it several quick bites to cripple it. Then he chews it with his sharp-cusped grinding teeth.

Insects are the food of this family. Formerly they were supposed to live almost entirely on mosquitoes. Some authorities urged that Bat towers be erected so that Bats would come and live in mosquito country. Aside from the fact that these flying mammals do not flock to Bat houses as birds do to houses built for them, recent experiments have proved that mosquitoes are not a major part of a Bat's diet. Swarms of Bats in malarial country have not been found to reduce malaria which is carried by mosquitoes.

Common Bats are among the highest of their kind, the farthest removed from ground animals in form. Their wing structure is very specialized for flight, the bones of their forelegs are fused, a complex shoulder joint has been developed.

The scientific name of this family, *Vespertilionidae*, comes from the Latin word *vespertilio* meaning a Bat.

The ten genera or groups of Common Bats found in the United States and northward are the Little Brown Bat, the Pipistrelle, the Big Brown Bat, the Twilight Bat, the Big-eared Bat, the Red Bat which is in the same genus with the Hoary Bat, Large Pale Bat in the same genus with the Cave Bat, the Silver-haired Bat, the Yellow Bat, and the Jackass Bat.

Little Brown Bat

A Cave Bat

LITTLE BROWN BAT
(genus *Myotis*)

Common Bat Family

The Little Brown Bat is a small mammal with a furry brown back, yellow belly, and long slender ears. In the air he may be distinguished by his size from all other Bats except the Pipistrelle. His tiny body reaches but four inches in the largest species. Most are smaller. The many species and subspecies of Little Brown Bats may be distinguished from one another only by a study of specimens. They are identified by a slight variation in color of fur, in shape of skull, and in ear structure.

Members of this large genus are the most primi-

tive of the Common Bat Family but the most widely distributed and the most ancient. They range over North America from the limit of trees in Alaska and Labrador southward. Other species live in Europe and parts of temperate Asia and North Africa while fossil forms are found in the Eocene and Oligocene deposits of France.

Most Little Brown Bats are social with their own kind. Also they are among the few wild animals which welcome settlers. They make use of buildings. In summer, during the day, they gather in small groups behind the blinds of empty rooms, creep under the eaves into attics, or hang up under the rafters of barns.

They are true hibernators. In northern latitudes they make ready for the long sleep of winter when fall comes. In limestone districts they seek caves.

By the time the temperature has fallen to zero outside, the Little Brown Bats of New England are safely hung up below frost level, sound asleep. Most species huddle close together. Members of one chestnut-brown species hang so close together that they are called Cluster Bats. In a cave in Vermont as many as a thousand Cluster Bats have been found in one mass, their little heads and shoulders covered with dew drops from the moist air, their bodies warmly touching their neighbors'.

A few species of Little Brown Bats are unsocial. The Keen Bat and the Long-legged Western are Little Brown Bats which are usually found alone or in small groups; and the Least Little Brown Bat, also known as Leib's Bat, hibernates all by himself. A rather uncommon little Bat with yellowish fur, black face and ears, and weak little feet, he will be found in caves where other species of his kind are sleeping close together. He will be tucked away alone or at most with one companion in a rock cranny where he lies flat on his abdomen as if afraid that his feet are not strong enough to hold him in a proper Bat position, upside down, during the long winter sleep.

All during the winter while the snows are deep and winds cold the Little Brown Bats sleep. A few individuals may remain hung up in one spot for three or four months but most of them wake up from time to time, shift their positions, fly about. Perhaps they drink a drop of water from the cave wall but they have not been observed eating during this period. In the spring they become more restless and are said to move nearer the cave entrance as if testing the air for signs of the changing season.

During the warm months in New England the Bat caves are deserted. The little animals fly over the near-by countryside, many of them returning to the same cave the following winter. In Missouri and Indiana some Bats may stay in the caves all year round.

One member of this large genus of Bats is the Yellowstone Bat, a mountain and forest dweller sometimes found by day in buildings or in caves. Within the Yellowstone National Park some spend their daylight hours asleep in "Devil's Kitchen", a cave at Mammoth Hot Springs and a very hot spot. They leave "Devil's Kitchen" in the fall to hibernate in some cooler place. One summer a colony of them chose the Yellowstone Hotel for a summer home.

Little Brown Bats mate in the fall before hibernation although females which are immature in the autumn may mate in the spring. In the north they become active in April and soon leave the caves. Three months later the young are born. There is only one baby, rarely two except in the Florida species which generally has twins.

In the far west the males of three species of Little Brown Bats leave the females after hibernation and fly to the high mountains to hunt insects. The females stay below and take care of their young which in the typical species do not learn to fly for three or four weeks.

The genus name *Myotis* is derived from the Greek *mys,* a Mouse.

Smallest Bat

PIPISTRELLE   **Common Bat Family**
(genus *Pipistrellus*)

Pipistrelles are very small Bats. The largest does not reach quite three and a half inches. The tiny Canyon or Western Bat is the smallest of this group and the smallest of all our Bats. It is frequently called the Pygmy Bat, being a fraction under three inches long. It dwells in the canyons of New Mexico.

Pipistrelles range over a wide area but prefer

warmer climates than do the Little Brown Bats and are not found as far north. It is very difficult to distinguish these two in the air. Comparison of specimens show that the Pipistrelle has broader ears and is more of a uniform yellowish brown all over. There are few different forms.

These little Bats are rather unsocial. In Vermont caves they may be seen hanging up during winter in small groups apart from the others.

Pipistrelles which live in the caves of Missouri have been seen mating in the autumn, but perhaps the individuals which are immature in the autumn may breed in the spring. They almost always have twins.

The genus and common name are both taken from the Italian *pipistrello*.

A City Bat

BIG BROWN BAT   Common Bat Family
(genus *Eptesicus*)

The Big Brown Bat ranges over a large part of North America but does not live as far north as the Little Brown Bat. Members of the group are among the few wild animals which enjoy town life. They frequently summer in large cities, including New York. Since they fly at about the height of a third-story window, they often fly into rooms, uttering squeaky cries. At other times they may shoot down chimneys.

They are usually seen singly or in pairs, sometimes in small groups. In New England and similar latitudes the urge to hibernate comes with the cold weather. Some seek caves but quite commonly they hang up in city buildings. The air is not moist as in a cave and the Bats dry out. Perhaps this explains why they often wake up and fly about.

Careful studies of these Bats have been made during their curious long sleep. They were observed in their natural habitat, a cave. When the air temperature in the open stayed below from fifty to fifty-four degrees, the Big Brown Bats of the vicinity flew into a cave, hung up below frost level where the temperature was forty-four degrees. When they were sound asleep their temperature was tested with a thermocouple, an electric instrument made especially for the purpose of taking Bats' temperatures without disturbing them. Interesting facts about hibernation were discovered.

When active in summer a Bat's temperature may be as high as 104 degrees or even a little higher, a dangerous fever temperature in man. The sensitive thermocouple showed that during hibernation the Bat's temperature tumbled until it equaled that of the surrounding air (forty-four degrees)! This curious cooling of the body is suggestive of reptiles or other cold-blooded animals which are unable to keep a constant body temperature. More primitive in form, cold-blooded animals change their body temperature to suit the air or water they live in.

When dormant, Bats breathe very slowly and irregularly, sometimes ceasing to breathe for periods of from three to eight minutes, averaging not quite five breaths in a half-hour, then quickening for two or three minutes to as often as forty-eight respirations a minute. Only when breathing at the rate of two hundred breaths a minute can they fly!

These Big Brown Bats with two species of Little Brown Bats were observed asleep in a cave in Minnesota one winter. A few Bats were flying about but when any sleeping individuals were disturbed they bared their teeth and tried to bite. But if knocked off the wall they could not fly. They fell to the ground where they crawled slowly about for about a half-hour when they could use their wings.

Big Brown Bats mate before hibernation. Perhaps some mate in the spring.

For food they are fond of beetles, flying ants, ichneumon flies, May flies, stone flies, caddis flies, lacewings, and some other insects.

TWILIGHT BAT
EVENING BAT
(genus *Nycticeius*)

This is a brownish Bat with short thin fur, short ears. In size he is halfway between the Little and the Big Brown Bats. He is rather common in the Gulf and Atlantic states from the southern border of Pennsylvania southward.

Twin babies are born to the mother.

The root word in genus *Nycticeius* is the Greek *nyx* meaning night.

Big-eared Bat

BIG-EARED BAT
LUMP-NOSED BAT
(genus *Corynorhinus*)

This is a low-flying Bat which ranges from Virginia to the Pacific coast. He may be seen skimming over the ground but three feet in the air and has a very unbatlike habit of descending to the ground to catch insects. In this manner he catches June beetles, Jerusalem crickets, grasshoppers, and scorpions.

Rather large Bats, they are named for their big ears which are longer than their heads and meet over their foreheads. Their second common name comes from the wartlike lumps on their noses. Their fur is wood brown above, pinkish buff below, with slaty gray basal hairs.

Sometimes they live in buildings, more often in caves where they hibernate during the winter in their northern range.

The genus name *Corynorhinus* aptly describes this Bat. It is formed from the Greek *koryne*, a club, and *rhis, rhinos*, nose.

A Tree Bat

RED BAT
(genus *Lasiurus*)

This Bat is known to have more than two young. Sometimes the mother Red Bat has twins, frequently three, sometimes four babies. Many Bats have but one.

One might expect this mammal with a rather large family to be social. On the contrary, the Red Bat is a hermit. By day instead of hiding in caves or under eaves he usually hangs up all alone in full sunlight on a limb of a tree. Like many tree Bats he is bright-colored, having red fur tipped with white. This fur covers not only his back but also the upper side of the tail membrane.

Unlike his cave-dwelling companions he does not hibernate. When cold weather comes he migrates like a bird. From late August into November these Bats take off in small groups from their summer range in New England, the Great Lakes region, and beyond. They fly southward and coastwise. By mid-September the migration is at a height, the Red Bats flying away from winter on their long, narrow wings. They are powerful fliers. They have frequently been seen landing on ships far off the eastern coast, indicating that they follow the shore line some distance out at sea.

One subspecies of these Bats lives in California. In the summer the males fly to high altitudes to feed while the females stay below to care for their families.

The Red Bat, hairy both on his back and upper tail membrane, is appropriately included in genus *Lasiurus* which is from the Greek word *lasios,* meaning hairy.

Hoary Bat

Another Tree Bat

HOARY BAT
(genus *Lasiurus*)

Common Bat Family

Close cousin of the Red Bat is the Hoary Bat, another solitary tree dweller. Both belong to the same genus, both have hairy tail membranes. The Hoary Bat is well camouflaged with brownish-gray, hoary fur, looking truly like a leaf as he hangs by day, usually all alone, upside down among the foliage of a convenient tree.

Like his cousin he has long narrow wings, is a powerful flier, and migrates when winter comes. He summers in the northern United States and Canada, moving southwest and southeast in winter. In January Hoary Bats have been reported

in South Carolina and Georgia; in February they have been reported in Florida. Occasionally they have been seen in the Bermuda Islands over six hundred miles southeast of New York. Like the Red Bats they undoubtedly fly over water in part of their birdlike migrations.

Twins are reported to be the usual number of young, but like the Red Bat the Hoary Bat has four mammae, or breasts. The average Bat has only two mammae. Perhaps the Hoary Bat raises a larger family than has been observed.

A Desert Bat

LARGE PALE BAT
(genus *Antrozous*)

Common Bat Family

The Large Pale Bat inhabits the hottest arid land of the United States from eastern California through Nevada, Arizona to western Texas and

as far east as Kansas where he is known as the Cave Bat. During the heat of day these Bats hang up in buildings, caves or hollow trees.

They are large Bats with a wing spread of more than a foot. They may easily be recognized by their size and by their very long ears which, when turned forward, extend beyond the tip of the nose. The ridge on their noses and their color is also characteristic. Their fur is pale buff, their wings light brown.

They are low flying Bats, frequently descending to catch crickets and other insects on the ground. Few Common Bats have this habit.

The genus name *Antrozous* comes from the Greek *antron* (cave) and *zoön* (animal).

SILVER-HAIRED BAT
(genus *Lasionycteris*)

This black Bat is silvered with white hairs. He is often found sleeping in hollow trees or under shaggy bark. He ranges over most of North America but is found mostly in high meadows or along streams in forests.

He migrates like the Red and Hoary Bats and has been reported offshore where he probably follows the coast line, going south over water. His flight is slightly weaker although he has been reported occasionally in Bermuda.

Genus *Lasionycteris* is from the Greek *lasios* (hairy) plus *nycteris* (Bat).

YELLOW BAT
(genus *Dasypterus*)

This is a southern Bat which occasionally comes over our borders into Texas and Florida, sometimes Louisiana. He is very much like the Hoary Bat in appearance but his color is more yellowish brown. His long hair covers part of his tail membrane and is sparsely scattered under the membrane of the forearm. Therefore, he is grouped in genus *Dasypterus*, from the Greek *dasys* (shaggy) and *pteron* (wing).

JACKASS BAT
SPOTTED BAT
LONG-EARED BAT
(genus *Euderma*)

This very rare Bat has such big ears that they meet over his forehead and he is therefore called the Jackass Bat. He is so dark brown in color that he is almost black. There are white spots on his shoulders and on his rump.

He has been found in the very arid parts of the southwest but he is so uncommon that little is known of his habits.

The genus name *Euderma* comes from the Greek words *eu* (good) and *derma* (skin).

FREE-TAILED BAT FAMILY
(family *Molossidae*)

The Free-tailed Bats are southern Bats. Only two species range north of the Rio Grande into the United States. They may be identified by their tails which extend beyond the wing membrane. The family name *Molossidae* comes from the Greek *Molossos*, the Molossian Hound or Mastiff. The family includes the Bulldog Bats whose faces look like those of Mastiffs.

House Haunter

COMMON GUANO BAT   Free-tailed Bat Family
(genus *Tadarida*)

The Common Guano Bat is rather large, has a wingspread of about a foot and a tail which extends three quarters of an inch below the tail membrane. He is called Guano Bat because his guano, Bat manure, is of great commercial value. The short velvety fur is sooty in color.

These Bats frequently haunt houses. Hundreds of them may crawl beneath the eaves and their strong musky odor makes them unpleasant tenants.

They are, however, mainly cave Bats, found in the southeastern states and in large numbers in the southwest. They are the famous Bats of Carlsbad Caverns in New Mexico. Here such multitudes of them have made their home that by 1901 they had deposited a layer of guano a quarter of a mile long, a hundred feet wide in places and in some places nearly as deep. During the following twenty years this enormous deposit was shoveled into sacks and shipped to California for fertilizer. Each ton brought from twenty to eighty dollars. Approximately 100,000 tons were removed. The present supply is exhausted.

The Bats are still there. They haunt the caverns in incredible numbers. In late summer or early fall the evening flight of these winged mammals is like a black cloud visible two miles away. By rough estimate a little less than nine million Bats pass out of the caves at twilight at this season. They leave the neck of the cave in a column about twenty feet thick. The great mass is gone within twenty minutes but they continue to exit for two hours.

Some of the Bats stay in Carlsbad Caverns all summer. Many leave in April, go out over the countryside, and sleep by day in town and country houses. They return to the caves in August and September.

They have a very short period of laying up for the winter because they are tropical animals. They breed in March. One young is born in May or June. The baby is large, weighs, at birth, about a quarter of the weight of its mother, grows rapidly, and can fly before it is full grown.

The favorite food of the Guano Bats is moths. Moths form about ninety-five per cent of their diet. They also catch a few crane flies, beetles, and other insects.

A colony of one other species of this group was reported living in a crevice in a cliff in Texas. They were reddish brown in color. They were so high above the ground that little could be observed of their habits. They are rare, at least within our borders.

Largest Bat

CALIFORNIA MASTIFF BAT   Free-tailed Bat Family
(genus *Eumops*)

This is the largest Bat found north of the Mexican border. Species reach six and a half inches in length. Their bodies are large but their wings short and narrow. Their ears are very large and broad and join over the forehead. In color they are sooty brown. Their large size immediately identifies them.

The California Mastiff Bats are tropical Bats which range locally into southern California, Arizona, and Texas. They are social and when found are usually seen in groups.

Like all tropical animals they lay up for only a short period in winter. They have but one young.

LEAF-NOSED BAT FAMILY
(family *Phyllostomidae*)

The members of this odd family may be identi-fied by the leaf-shaped growth of flesh on the tips of their noses. They are rarely seen north of the Mexican border. They are tropical mammals which occasionally fly into extreme southern Cali-fornia and Arizona. An enormous family with fifty or more genera, or groups, only three or four forms ever enter the States. Although many are found in the West Indies, they do not reach Florida except when an occasional stray such as *Artibeus* gets blown into Key West. A very pale species of another genus (*Macrotus*) appears during winter in the hot, dry regions of the south-west. This is known as the California Leaf-nosed Bat.

The family name *Phyllostomidae* is formed from the Greek word *phyllon,* a leaf, and the Greek *stoma,* mouth.

The genus *Macrotus* is based on the Greek *makros,* long or large.

Chapter III
Ancient Animal

THE STRANGE-JOINTED
(order *Xenarthra*)

Members of this group are tropical mammals. They include Sloths, Ant-eaters, and the Armadillos. Only the Armadillo crosses the Mexican border into the United States. None of the Anteaters or Sloths come that far north.

Formerly scientists called the group *Edentata*, the toothless. Recently these strange animals have been classified as order *Xenarthra*, meaning strange-jointed. This is an especially appropriate name for the Armadillo.

ARMADILLO FAMILY
(family *Dasypodidae*)

A Mammal With a Shell

NINE-BANDED ARMADILLO
(genus *Dasypus*)

Armadillo Family

The Armadillo looks prehistoric. Many of his relatives are fossils. His cousins, huge armadillo-like Glyptodonts, reached a length of twelve feet. They roamed over the United States in early Pliocene times, several million years ago.

The Nine-banded Armadillo of today is a rather small mammal. An adult male will weigh approximately thirteen pounds. The bodies of both males and females are primitive in form. They are encased in a skin of horny shell which makes them look like elongated turtles. They have few hairs. The only species which comes into the United States is called Nine-banded because of the number of shell rings that are hinged together to form his armor.

Originally this strange mammal was a border animal, more properly classified as a Mexican or a South American although he did enter southern Texas. Recently he has been on the march, journeying northward and eastward, suddenly appearing in places where thirty years ago Armadillos were unknown. In many of these places he is now common. Today he is found in most parts of Texas, parts of Louisiana and some of Oklahoma. Very rarely he appears in the southeastern corner of New Mexico. He is still extending his range which is limited only by frost. He cannot stand freezing weather.

Several explanations have been offered to account for his sudden appearance in new country. The destruction of a great number of the animals of prey which were enemies of Armadillos is perhaps the cause. Another explanation is the cutting of forests. The Armadillo likes low thickets, thorny cactus patches, scrub oaks under which he can make hidden paths.

However, his favorite homeland is limestone country where there are numerous caves and ledges. He likes small holes in rocky walls of river gulches where large animals cannot follow him into his den.

When he goes out along the ledges to hunt insects he drags his short, horny tail. This marks his path through dust or mud from clump to clump of bushes. He is frequently seen because he himself is nearsighted and also very intense. He keeps his mind on his business, often his small eyes are hidden under the leaves where he is rooting for bugs. When he sights an enemy he dashes away with considerable speed, but if overtaken he curls up in a ball, the flexible plates of his armor protecting his body. He is hard to uncurl.

This queer little southerner has been accused of many crimes such as robbing hens' nests, eating game birds, stealing garden vegetables. Recently the United States Biological Survey made a study of the diet of the Armadillo and found that angleworms were a favorite food. Ants, beetles and their larvae, the larvae of cockroaches, an occasional brown cricket, a few spiders, and millepedes and other insects were eaten. One day in the month of May an Armadillo had one hundred and twenty caterpillars, mostly cutworms, in his stomach as well as other insects.

When Armadillos appear in gardens they apparently are not looking for vegetables but for insects. Their long claws are useful for digging worms. Their small toothless mouth openings are not suited for grasping or eating hens' eggs.

These harmless creatures are killed in large numbers for their shells which are made into baskets for curios. With a little protection they should continue to extend their range.

They have large families, from four to eight young. The mother Armadillo gives birth to four young at a time. The quadruplets are all of the same sex and identical, even to the number of hairs in a given skin area. They are born very large with tough, leathery skins.

The family and the genus name come from the Greek *dasys* (thick) plus *pous, podos* (foot).

Nine-banded Armadillo

Chapter IV

By the Millions

THE GNAWERS or RODENTS
(order *Rodentia*)

This group includes an enormous number of species of small mammals. None of them are very large. All have a set of fierce-looking gnawing teeth.

Among the Rodents are important fur bearers, several harmless creatures, and many pests. Their habits differ greatly. Some live in burrows, some in trees, some swim, and one, the Flying Squirrel, can glide through the air.

At first glance Rodents do not all appear related. Close inspection will show a marked similarity in form not only of teeth but of body.

The gnawing teeth are called incisors. They are the two front teeth in each jaw. They are wonderful tools. Unevenly covered with enamel they sharpen themselves to chisel-like points as they are used. The owner rapidly grinds these teeth down with his incessant gnawing but they never wear out. A Rodent's incisors continue to grow as the fingernails of people do.

Should a member of this group have the misfortune to break a chisel tooth, he is often doomed to death. The broken tooth fails to meet the tooth opposite, both teeth grow unhindered. Since they are no longer ground off against each other they grow wildly, sometimes circling the victim's face, locking his jaw, and causing starvation.

Unless such an accident occurs, the teeth of the Gnawers are useful as weapons as well as tools. The scientific name of the group, order *Rodentia*, comes from the Latin word *rodere* which means to gnaw.

There are eight native American families of Gnawers. They are the Squirrel and Marmot Family, the Beaver Family, the Mountain Beaver Family, the Porcupine Family, the Pocket Gopher Family, the Native Rat and Mouse Family, the Jumping Mouse Family, and the Pocket Mouse Family.

THE SQUIRREL AND MARMOT FAMILY
(family *Sciuridae*)

The Squirrel Family is enormous. Little tree animals and little ground animals of many different forms as well as the large squirrel-like Woodchuck and the Whistling Marmot all belong to it. The scientific family name *Sciuridae* comes from *sciurus*, meaning Squirrel.

A Tree Squirrel

RED SQUIRREL
CHICKAREE, PINE SQUIRREL
(genus *Sciurus*)

Squirrel and Marmot Family

The chatter of this small tree Squirrel is familiar to town dwellers as well as to woodsmen over most of forested America. His size and color make him easy to identify. He is about half as big

Red Squirrel

as the Gray Squirrel. In color he is reddish on his upper parts, paler in summer than in winter. Under parts are grayish. During the cold months these Squirrels grow tufts on their ears. Albino Red Squirrels occur.

Active little creatures, they do not hibernate in winter. During very cold spells they stay in their homes and eat food they have stored. They prefer to live in evergreen forests because spruce and pine and other cones are among their favorite foods. They store great quantities of these cones, sometimes piling as much as from six to ten bushels at the base of their home tree. They hide single cones under the ground. When they seek these hidden cones again they seem to locate them by smell.

Red Squirrels are also found in woods where evergreens are scarce. Here they feed on beechnuts, maple and other seeds in the fall; maple and beech and other buds in the spring. When the flowers of the trees are gone they gnaw the twigs. In areas where chestnuts were once plentiful, and

in cut-over woodland where their normal food supply is gone, they may do serious damage, especially in winter when they may eat the buds of Norway spruce and white pine and other trees.

Another favorite food of the Red Squirrels is mushrooms. They dry mushrooms in the crotches of trees where they leave them until they are hungry or store them in secret spots. They also eat some insects and a great many birds' eggs.

Home lovers, they apparently live for long periods in one tree, leaving many bushels of refuse, shucks of cones, at the base. Since they are about in the day, their scolding may be frequently heard. They appear to be angry much of the time. During the mating season they fight. However, when they are undisturbed they may be heard uttering a churring note which has been compared to the song of a bird. When the sun sets they generally retire but are sometimes seen scurrying about in the moonlight.

Red Squirrels make their nests of leaves and twigs built on the limbs of trees, in knotholes, in holes in the ground, under roots, or in a similar location. In the late spring four or five young are born. When the mother wants to move her young she takes them in her mouth as a Cat would. There is but one litter a year.

These little Squirrels have many enemies among the smaller animals of prey such as Martens, Foxes, and the larger birds such as Hawks and Owls. Man is their enemy because they are harmful to nesting songbirds. They also get into traps set for large animals.

Recently they have been trapped in Canada for their own fur. Over a million pelts of various kinds of Squirrels have been sold each season in recent years on the Canadian fur market. Most Squirrel skins used for coats come from Asia.

In spite of their numerous enemies, Red Squirrels remain abundant. Like many other mammals they have periods of scarcity. When food becomes scant in their home country they may migrate, often swimming wide rivers and lakes to reach better feeding grounds.

The Douglas Chickaree is a Red Squirrel which lives west of the Rocky Mountains. In winter he has a rusty-red back and grayish to reddish under parts and tail edged with whitish or yellow. In summer he changes to an olive-brown coat with a reddish abdomen and a dark line separating the two colors. Like most animals living in the humid evergreen forests of the northwest he is rather dark. There are several subspecies of this Chickaree known as the California Chickaree, the Red-wood Chickaree, the Cascades Chickaree. They differ slightly in color. Their habits are similar. They store great quantities of cones and nuts. When gathering hazel nuts they lift them to their noses, apparently discarding wormy nuts which they detect by scent.

Another species of Red Squirrel is Fremont's Chickaree. He is found in the southern Rockies. He is small, short-eared, and differs in color from the above. His under parts and the edge of his tail are always light gray or white. In winter his back is dark olive gray; in summer more yellowish brown or grayish on the back, under parts white with a black line along either side.

The Arizona Chickaree is quite reddish in summer and at this time his face and paws are often smeared with pitch from his home trees; his flesh tastes of turpentine. He lives among spruce and firs. When spruce cones are not in season he varies his diet with mushrooms, birds, seeds, berries. For the winter he stores food in holes under rocks or logs or buries seeds under the ground. Since Chickarees have many enemies among the Weasel Family, the Foxes and Coyotes and large birds, they often fail to return to eat their stores, and the buried nuts grow. Thus the little Squirrel helps plant forests to replenish the quantity of food he eats.

The other forms of Red Squirrel vary but slightly from the above. They are all closely related and belong to the same genus *Sciurus* which is the Latin word meaning Squirrel.

A Tree Squirrel

GRAY SQUIRREL   **Squirrel and Marmot Family**
(genus *Sciurus*)

The big brother of the Red Squirrel is a familiar figure in parks where he lives on peanuts and other food he receives from kindly visitors. He is so well known that he scarcely needs description. Gray, with some brownish hairs, he is about twice as big as the Red Squirrel from whom he differs in temperament. He is not as quarrelsome, does not scold continually, is easily tamed although in the wilds he is wary and clever. When frightened he flattens himself out on a branch. By circling the branch he keeps it between him and an intruder.

Like their cousins the Red Squirrels, the Grays are active by day, all year. Sometimes during the harvest season they are seen in the moonlight gathering nuts. They are very agile, make won-

FOX SQUIRREL
(genus *Sciurus*)

Squirrel and Marmot Family

The Fox Squirrel has many distinctions. He is the largest, exhibits the most varied coat colors, and is found in the most widely different kinds of forests of any species of Tree Squirrel.

The southern Fox Squirrel may be recognized by his white nose and ears. The color of the rest of his body varies from blackish to gray buff. He is found living among the southern pines where he feeds on the seeds of the cones. He is equally at home among the live oaks draped with Spanish moss or in the jungle of a cypress swamp. His range is from the southeastern states and Florida along the Gulf coast in Louisiana and Mississippi. He reaches over two feet in length from the tip of his white nose to the end of his bushy tail. Melanistic (black) phases are not uncommon.

The Fox Squirrels which live in the Mississippi Valley from Wisconsin to northern Louisiana are smaller and never have white noses and ears. The color of their coats is usually rusty red. They live among hickory trees, beech trees, and other hardwoods in the upland forest of the northern part of their range. Here they enjoy the nuts of these trees as well as pecans and walnuts. They also eat mushrooms, eggs of birds and their young, and some insects.

The form which lives eastward through Virginia to Pennsylvania is reported sometimes to have a white nose. One subspecies appears in western Texas.

Like all Tree Squirrels, Fox Squirrels store food for winter. They do not hibernate. They are active by day hiding nuts and seeds in hollow stumps or some other secret place, or burying single nuts underground where they find them again by their keen sense of smell.

They make large nests, nearly three feet by three and a half feet, circular or oval globes placed in tree crotches or hollows in trunks. The winter nests in which they later raise their young are expertly made of twigs and leaves and lined with shredded bark. The leaves in these strong nests are apparently gathered green. When they dry they form a water and wind proof shelter. They also build loose summer nests, perhaps in the same tree. This nest they use in fine weather.

In early spring from two to four young are born. It is not known whether there is more than one litter a year.

Their soft churring note or hoarse bark is now infrequently heard. Never as abundant as Gray Squirrels, the Fox Squirrel was a common species before forests were cut and before he became popular as a game animal. Large and waxing fat in the fall, he is considered good eating as well as good sport. Today he is a scarce species. He is the rarest of the Squirrels which belong to the genus *Sciurus*, Latin word for Squirrel. The abundant members of this genus are the Red and Gray Squirrels.

THE KAIBAB SQUIRREL and the ABERT SQUIRREL
(genus *Sciurus*)

Squirrel and Marmot Family

These large handsome Squirrels look much alike and are close neighbors but they never meet. They live on opposite sides of the Grand Canyon of Arizona. They are the only American Squirrels which have long ear tufts like those of Squirrels in northern Europe, Asia, and Japan. In

winter the tassels are an inch or two in length.

The Kaibab Squirrel has an extremely small range. He lives on the north rim of the Grand Canyon in a "land island" of yellow pine. When food is scarce he may venture down into the piñon and oak area or up into the firs, but his

Abert Squirrel

range is largely between 6000 and 9500 feet in altitude, plateau and mountain slope within a territory about thirty-five miles wide and seventy long. This is the only place in the world that the handsome Kaibab Squirrel is found. The area is within the Kaibab forest on the Kaibab plateau.

There these Squirrels have lived in isolation ever since the deepening gash in the earth cut them off from their cousins, the Abert Squirrels. Some years they are abundant, other years scarce.

The beautiful Kaibab Squirrels are about the size of a Gray Squirrel but heavier built. Their coats are gray with a reddish band along the back, black under parts, and nearly pure-white feathered tail which waves like a plume in the sunlight. In spite of their chunky build they leap expertly between tree limbs. On the ground they walk awkwardly but run with graceful bounds.

Their principal food is the seed of the yellow-pine cones and the bark of the twigs. When cones are gone they cut off the ends of pine twigs where the needles grow and nibble the bark. They often drop piles of twig ends on the ground where they eat.

These Rodents build large nests of twigs and leaves and pine needles, lined with shredded bark and grass. They place their nests high in tree branches or in holes in the trunks. Three or four young are born and there are probably two litters a year.

Like other Tree Squirrels they store food for winter. When a bitterly cold spell comes they may stay in their nests for a long time but they do not hibernate.

Sometimes they scold intruders as a Red Squirrel does. At other times they utter a soft churr or bark like a Fox Squirrel. If alarmed they are clever at hiding behind limbs of trees, circling the limb to keep it between them and the enemy.

Fifteen miles away on the south rim of the

Grand Canyon lives the Abert Squirrel. He is undoubtedly descended from the same ancestor as the Kaibab Squirrel. He looks like his cousin but his under parts are white, his tail has more black hairs, his ear tufts are blacker. In winter his back is colored bright brown and bordered with a black line, his ear tufts are long. In summer his back coat is gray with a dark-brown patch. Melanistic (black) or partly black Abert Squirrels are common.

The habits of this Rodent are like those of his cousin. His main food is yellow pine. From August when the cones begin to ripen and until the cones are gone, he feeds on the seeds. In May the diet is varied. He eats the bark of twigs of yellow pine and like the Kaibab Squirrel he often nips off the tips of the pine branches to get the bark. The feeding grounds are frequently littered with bushels of discarded tips. These Squirrels sometimes eat enough bark to injure the trees.

Between May and the time when the new cones ripen, they eat mushrooms, acorns, buds, birds' eggs, young birds. When the young first leave the nest they like the male flowers of the yellow pine. Some seeds of Douglas pine and white spruce and corn grains are also eaten.

In the fall they store quantities of pine cones and acorns. They bury each cone or nut by itself in a hole in the ground. Since these Squirrels have many enemies, a great number never return to use their stores. The seeds sprout. Thus the little

Rodents help plant forests which makes up for the seeds they eat.

Abert Squirrels nest in forks in trees thirty or forty feet aboveground. Their nests are very large, almost as big as a bushel basket. They are lined with plant and bark fibers. Sometimes they nest in hollow trees but since hollow pines are rare they do not find many shelters of this kind within their range.

Like their cousins', their range is largely determined by the yellow-pine zone, but they are found over a far greater territory than are the Kaibabs. Not only do they live on the south rim of Grand Canyon but also from Colorado south through Arizona and New Mexico into old Mexico, usually at an altitude of from 6000 to 9500 feet above sea level.

Like others of their kind they are polygamous, but each Squirrel has its own section of trees for feeding and storing food. This territory he or she protects, chasing away all others.

From two to four young are usual and sometimes there are two litters a year.

There is but one form of Kaibab Squirrel. The one species of Abert Squirrel is represented by two slightly different subspecies. Although both of the Tassel-eareds look startlingly different from the common Tree Squirrels they are so closely related that they are classified in the same genus *Sciurus* which means Squirrel.

The Glider

FLYING SQUIRREL
(genus *Glaucomys*)

Squirrel and Marmot Family

This small mammal is rarely seen. Unlike other American Squirrels he comes out by day only if disturbed. Sometimes a Flying Squirrel may be scared out of a hollow tree during daylight by rapping on the trunk. They come out willingly only during the night.

During the hours of darkness in most of the forests of North America from the arctic to the Mexican border these little animals glide from

tree to tree with the grace of a hawk sailing. They cannot truly fly as a bird flies. But they can glide great distances.

They spend little time on the ground. When one of these beautiful, soft-furred, large-eyed little woods animals wants to visit a neighboring tree he climbs up high in his home tree and leaps. As he leaps he spreads the fold of skin which extends on either side of his body from ankle to wrist. His tail, usually carried over his back, is jerked down, his front feet extend, and he is off. With his natural sail set he glides to a distant tree trunk. As he glides he gradually descends and if his destination is far away he lands rather low on the trunk. However, as he nears the end of the glide he can turn slightly upward. He frequently travels in this manner between trees fifty yards apart. On downhill slopes glides of more than a hundred yards have been reported.

The mother Squirrel makes her nest in a woodpecker's hole or in a natural hollow in a tree; sometimes in a bird box or a remodeled bird or Squirrel nest. From two to six young are born and there is thought to be only one litter a year. The father takes no interest in the family but the mother Squirrel is devoted to her young. Sometimes she takes them gliding with her as a mother Bat takes its young flying. If routed out of her nest she will try to rescue her babies and carry them in her mouth to another tree hole.

Usually but one family is found in a single tree but cases have been reported of from fifteen to fifty Squirrels being seen in one nest.

Flying Squirrels do not hibernate. Small species may den up for short periods during severe weather. But so active are the northern ones in the winter that they become pests to trappers. They get into traps set for Marten and other fur bearers. Abroad at the same time as Owls, they are sometimes caught by the big night birds. Prowling Cats also catch them.

Like all Squirrels they are fond of nuts. They eat acorns and hickory nuts in the fall, blossoms of the sugar maple in the spring. They also enjoy berries, seeds, corn, the catkins of birch, birds and their eggs. They like insects, particularly moths, night fliers like themselves.

There are two species of Flying Squirrel with several subspecies. The Flying Squirrels which make their home in the woods of the eastern United States and southward are smaller than those which are found in the west and in the forests of the farther north.

These little animals have reddish-brown or brownish-gray coats, white or very light underneath. Their ordinary voice is like that of other Squirrels but they also squeak and chirp.

Genus *Glaucomys* comes from two Greek words, *glaukos* (light gray) and *mys* (Mouse). The color probably refers to these Squirrels' very light under parts.

Mump-faced

EASTERN CHIPMUNK
(genus *Tamias*)

Squirrel and Marmot Family

Inside the cheeks of this little bay-colored, striped Squirrel are pouches for carrying seeds and nuts. Always active and nervous he is well known for his flickering tail, the body stripes running like paint splashes down his back, and for the mumpy look of his face when he is gathering food. He is constantly stuffing his cheeks with ragweed seeds, corn, hazelnuts, beechnuts, acorns, wheat and many other grains until they look ready to burst. Then he scurries down his hole which is under a tree root or an old pasture fence or a rock ledge. There is usually little or no dirt piled at the main entrance.

The Eastern Chipmunk lives from the Great Lakes region to Nova Scotia, south through New England to Georgia and west as far as Oklahoma. He ranges from sea level to the summit of Mount Washington. A forest animal, he is not a Tree Squirrel, although he is occasionally seen high up in beech or other trees, gathering nuts, and when chased by Dogs he will take refuge up a tree. His real home is on the ground. He likes to climb as high as the top of a stump and flee from danger down his burrow.

Very shy and wary he is constantly on the lookout for Weasels, Martens, Canadian Lynx, House Cats, and other animals against which his only defense is alertness. When unalarmed he chirps

Eastern Chipmunk

and clucks but he will scold intruders. He is willing to make friends with man if he is sure that he is safe and he likes to live near barns or houses, often making his home under a tree root a few yards away, sometimes even daring to live under a porch.

From the time and energy spent in storing food one would think that the tiny animal was preparing to stay awake in his burrow all winter and feast. He puts as much as half a bushel of hickory nuts away and is very well provisioned for a stormy day. He does not become very fat in the fall as true hibernators do. Nevertheless, he is overcome with sleep in the middle of winter. He does not usually go into his leaf- and grass-lined nest in the northern states until mid-November. He is a light sleeper, up and about during thaws. He rarely remains in his den much longer than

WESTERN CHIPMUNK
(genus *Eutamias*)

There are too many species and subspecies of Western Chipmunk to be described here. These little Squirrels have a different shade of fur to suit every environment in which they live. The differences in most cases are very slight. Whether they are large and dark as they are in the humid forests of the Pacific coastal belt, or small and pale as they are in the desert and arid regions of the southwest, they are easily recognized as

three months.

Eastern Chipmunks are fond of many kinds of foodstuffs including mushrooms, fruits, insects, young birds and their eggs. They hide many kinds of food in summer. In Minnesota they have been known to steal a whole nest of grouse eggs and hide them, unbroken. They are careful not to store food for winter which will spoil.

They are fond of one home area and often garner food from a small territory. Some years they are abundant, others scarce.

The young, from four to six in number, are born in the spring and grow slowly but there may be more than one litter. Sometimes a melanistic (black) individual is born.

The translation of the scientific classification, genus *Tamias*, means very appropriately the steward. *Tamias* is a Greek word.

Squirrel and Marmot Family

Chipmunks. Their backs are all marked with five dark lines interspersed with four light lines. The stripes are narrower than those of the Eastern Chipmunk. The bodies of the western species are more slender than their eastern cousins'. Their habits are similar but suited to life in the extremely different homeland in which they are found.

The Gray-collared Chipmunk or Arizona Chipmunk makes his home in the spruce and yellow-pine forest of the mountains of central Arizona and New Mexico and is found as high as 10,000 feet in altitude. He is rather dull in color, has broader black stripes and ash-gray neck and shoulders. He is very shy and lives in the thick forest or on the edge of clearings where he likes to dig under log piles. He may den aboveground in a fir stump. For food he takes the cones of Douglas spruce, acorns, berries of shad-blow, currants, gooseberries, as well as mushrooms.

A close relative, the Gray-footed Chipmunk, also lives in the forest and the deep thickets or on rocky slopes of mountains in New Mexico and southwestern Texas. He is fond of acorns and the cones of fir and spruce.

Another species lives in the humid coastal region from southern British Columbia into Washington and Oregon. This is called the Townsend or Oregon Chipmunk. Like most animals found in a dark and damp environment he is dark-coated and large for his kind. He is the very largest of the Western Chipmunks. Shy and alert, he is always watching for enemies, always looking for food. He stuffs his inside cheek pouches with acorns, hazelnuts, and a variety of seeds and berries. He likes raspberries, blackberries, elder-berries, blueberries, dogwood seeds, and many other foods. He is very busy in the fall storing for bad weather.

Among the pale and small Western Chipmunks is the Painted or Sagebrush Chipmunk. He lives on the sagebrush plains of the Great Basin and the northwestern states where he is often found far from any water supply. Like many desert animals this little Chipmunk is able to get water from his food. He digs his burrows under clumps of sage or under rocks. When settlers enter his chosen land he raids their grainfields. In his native haunts he lives on seeds of cactus and sage. When the sage is attacked by webworms, this little Squirrel makes his meals on the worms and their larvae, no doubt doing great good to the plant which would otherwise be stripped. He likes to climb sagebushes and he can run across the tops as Tree Squirrels travel in trees.

Another pale Chipmunk is the Cliff or Gila Chipmunk which lives in the mountains among pines and junipers in the dry country of Arizona and New Mexico. He likes the nuts of piñon pines, juniper berries, and the fruit of prickly pears. He lives among cliffs and rock ledges and can climb sheer rock walls as easily as most Squirrels climb trees. These Chipmunks have from four to six young, sometimes as many as eight, and perhaps two litters.

The Golden or Hopi Chipmunk is found up to 7000 feet in altitude in southwestern Colorado, southern Utah, northeastern Arizona, and in the yellow-pine forests of northern New Mexico. He is said to be a good climber and has been seen in the very tops of trees. He is fond of piñon nuts, acorns, berries, and seeds of plants and bushes. Like all of his kind he is very shy.

Many other varieties of Western Chipmunk are found from the headwaters of the Yukon River through British Columbia, Ontario, and the Rocky Mountain region of the United States.

All these Chipmunks hibernate in the colder parts of their range. They curl up in a tight ball in their nests but sleep lightly, moving about drowsily when disturbed. They curl up again as soon as left alone.

Eutamias, the genus name, comes from the Greek *eu* and *tamias* and means good steward.

Prairie Ground Squirrel

STRIPED GROUND SQUIRREL
THIRTEEN-LINED GROUND SQUIRREL
SPERMOPHILE, STRIPED GOPHER
(genus *Citellus*)

Squirrel and Marmot Family

Among the numerous Spermophiles is the Striped Ground Squirrel. The name Spermo-phile comes from two Greek words *sperma* (seed) and *phile* (loving).

Striped Ground Squirrel

Small and slender, reaching not quite a foot in length, the Striped Ground Squirrel might at first glance be confused with a large Chipmunk. However, he may at once be distinguished from the latter by the number of stripes on his back. This Ground Squirrel has thirteen stripes or lines of spots, the Chipmunk but nine. Dark-brown lines with white spots alternate with white lines. The under parts are yellowish. The coloring of the several geographic races varies, sometimes being redder, sometimes much lighter as in the case of the very pale Striped Ground Squirrel which ranges over the Llano Estacado, the Staked Plains of Texas, and northwest over the short grass plains. In all cases the pattern on the coat of this little animal serves to camouflage him against the background where he lives.

These Squirrels are misnamed Gophers. Their appearance and habits are entirely different. While a Gopher spends his entire life under ground, the Striped Ground Squirrel comes out of his burrow by day.

The prairies of the middle west are the homeland of many of these abundant little Rodents. They range from southern Alberta nearly to the Gulf coast and from southern Michigan and northern Indiana west to Utah. Adaptable animals, they are found in different environments such as the semiarid mountain valleys of Arizona and up to 10,000 feet in altitude in Colorado but not in forests.

Like their cousins the Prairie Dogs they are constantly alert for danger. They warn each other by trilling and chirping when anyone approaches. Then they duck into their holes which are usually dug under clumps of grasses. The burrows go straight down for several inches, then turn horizontally, branching many times into tunnels which lead to the surface. Many of the entrances are kept closed with plugs of earth.

Grass-lined nests and storage dens are located off the main tunnels. Striped Ground Squirrels have large families. From six to ten, sometimes as many as fourteen, young are born in a very undeveloped state, blind and hairless. They grow slowly and one litter is usual.

True Spermophiles, they often do great damage to crops. In the spring they eat the greens of sprouting plants, later eating corn and other grains. They also eat grubs, insects and their larvae, a little meat, sometimes killing Mice and birds. When grasshoppers are abundant they eat little else, thus contributing some good to their homeland, but they are considered pests because they are so fond of cultivated grains.

Although these Squirrels store food for emergencies, they sleep during the period when food is scarce. In arid country when plants begin to dry and grains to ripen, they become very fat. After eating little for about a week they crawl into chambers a foot or more underground, curl up in tight balls, squeeze their eyes tight shut. Soon they are in a sleep which is like hibernation but is known as estivation. This sleep is brought on by hot dry weather and lack of food. Later as the weather turns cold they sleep on into true hibernation. Their temperature falls until it is nearly that of the surrounding air. The heart beat is slower and slower until at last it seems almost to stop. It throbs but five times per minute. When awakened from an ordinary nap, the hearts of these Squirrels beat from one hundred to two hundred times per minute.

They are hard to arouse from the deep sleep. They are in a state of torpor which seems very near death. They do not eat or drink. In early spring they wake up thin and hungry, having lost as much as forty-one per cent of their weight.

They cannot stand freezing temperature and sometimes die if their den gets too cold during the winter but they usually awaken when the temperature drops below freezing point.

These Ground Squirrels have many enemies. The Badger finds them good food. Other members of the Meat Eaters such as Coyotes, Foxes, Wolves, and large birds prey upon them. Their worst enemy is man. Farmers make war on them because they do much damage to crops. In one middle western state a bounty was offered for Ground Squirrels' tails. The tail was considered evidence that the Squirrel was dead until it was discovered that some boys were catching the animals alive, cutting off their tails and letting them go free to raise more Squirrels.

Poison is the more common method of exterminating these cunning but injurious Rodents.

In Mountain Meadows

COLUMBIAN GROUND SQUIRREL
(genus *Citellus*)

Squirrel and Marmot Family

The Columbian Ground Squirrel is among the worst pests of its kind. Found in the mountain meadows of western and southern Alberta and southern British Columbia through eastern Oregon and Washington to western Montana, he is a social animal, living in groups of from a dozen to over a hundred. A true Spermophile, he loves seeds. Rather large, he has a good appetite, has been credited with nearly destroying whole fields of grain.

In early March the Columbian Ground Squirrels come out of hibernation and feed on the green shoots of winter wheat. Later they eat the wheat heads. One of these Rodents which reaches but fifteen inches from the tip of nose to tip of tail may destroy as much as fifty-six pounds of wheat.

Not only do they eat crops but they may bring disease to man. They are among the animals attacked by ticks which transmit the serious illness Rocky Mountain spotted fever.

Their appearance is quite handsome. Above they are grayish and yellowish with brighter reddish-yellow legs and head and yellowish to buff under parts. In habits they resemble other Ground Squirrels, eating insects as well as seeds. They too live in underground holes and hibernate for a long period. When the plants dry and grains ripen they go into estivation, the state of torpor resulting from heat and dryness. They may estivate as early as mid-August. Those which live in the northwest may go to sleep as early as mid-June. They curl up in tight balls in their underground nests and sleep on through winter, waking up thin in the spring. They lose about a gram of fat a day while they are asleep.

They have large families, from five perhaps even to fourteen young.

Several species closely related to the Columbian Ground Squirrel live from Mexico to Alaska and from the Mississippi River valley to the Pacific coast. Those which are found in the far north are very large, the Yukon Ground Squirrel reaching a foot and a half in length.

The Flickertail is a small, grayish or yellowish Ground Squirrel with mottled coat. This close cousin to the Columbian Ground Squirrel is credited with great injury to crops. He lives from North Dakota and Montana to Alberta and southern Saskatchewan. He begins pestering farmers the moment he wakes up in the spring. First he feasts on the seeds of the wheat, rye, barley, or flax which have been sown in the fall. As soon as spring sowing starts he digs up the newly planted grains. Then he attacks the sprouting grain and ends by carrying off as much of the ripened grain as he can't eat on the spot.

DESERT GROUND SQUIRREL
SAND SQUIRREL
(genus *Citellus*)

Squirrel and Marmot Family

This small spotted Ground Squirrel is about the size of a big Chipmunk, and is found in a waterless land, the arid plateau country and the sandhills of the prairies from western Nebraska into Colorado and Utah, Arizona, New Mexico, and Texas. He also makes his home on desert Mustang and Padre Islands off the Gulf coast.

These shy little Squirrels get water and food from the juicy pulp of cactus plants. Agriculture has not been much developed in their arid homeland. Except when pursued by animals of prey they lead undisturbed lives, eating the seeds of desert plants such as saltbush, cactus, wild gourds and sunflowers, the beans of mesquite, as well as insects and fresh meat.

They dig their holes under clumps of cactus or creosote in sand dunes or sand washes and frequently live in holes deserted by Kangaroo Rats or Prairie Dogs.

They have one or more litters a year. Each family consists of at least five young.

Forest Ground Squirrel

GOLDEN-MANTLED GROUND SQUIRREL
SAY'S GROUND SQUIRREL, BIG-STRIPED
GROUND SQUIRREL, GOLDEN CHIPMUNK
CALICO SQUIRREL
(genus *Callospermophilus*)

Squirrel and Marmot Family

This Ground Squirrel looks like a large heavy Chipmunk. In winter his coat is brownish gray with buff and black stripes along each side. In summer his head and shoulders are overlaid with a bright chestnut mantle which gives him one of his common names. The mantle is much less noticeable in winter.

This Squirrel lives in the yellow-pine and fir forests of the western mountains of New Mexico, Arizona, and California, north into British Columbia, and may be seen in the same woods with the Western Chipmunks from which he may at once be distinguished by his larger size, his heavier build, lesser stripes, and the golden mantle.

These Spermophiles live in forests but are not so active as Chipmunks, rarely climb trees but are frequently seen perched on top of rocks or logs. Underneath they make their burrows. They also dig holes under barns or cabins and steal into camps to plunder. They are fond of berries, nuts, and, like all of their kind, particularly of grains. They are active only by day. In the fall they store food, carrying away hundreds of kernels of wheat, barley, or other grain which they find planted in mountain grainfields. Their inner cheek pouches may hold as much as 350 grains of oats at one time. However, since their homeland is not in greatly developed agricultural country, they are not of much economic importance.

Although they do store food they hibernate when cold weather comes. They grow very fat just before entering their dens.

They probably do not have as large families as other Ground Squirrels. From four to six young to a litter and one litter a season are common.

There are several forms of these forest Ground Squirrels which differ slightly in different localities. Their genus name *Callospermophilus* means beautiful (Greek *kalos*) Spermophile.

Among Rocky Ledges

ROCK SQUIRREL   **Squirrel and Marmot Family**
(genus *Otospermophilus*)

The members of this genus of Ground Squirrels are known as Rock Squirrels in many parts of their range because they are often found on cliffs or among rocky ledges. Here they may be seen basking in the sun on top of boulders where they have a fine view of the surrounding country and can see enemies approach.

At a distance they look very much like Common Gray Tree Squirrels but their long tails are less bushy, their grayish-brown coats are mottled with wavy lines or faintly spotted. Sometimes they climb on logs or up bushes and a little distance up a tree but their home is on and under ground, like common Ground Squirrels.

There is but one species of these Rock Squirrels but several closely related geographic races or subspecies. They all live in the west from Mexico north through the Rocky Mountains to the Columbia River region. The genus name *Otospermophilus* is from the Greek *ous, otos* and Spermophile and refers to the formation of the inner ear.

California Ground Squirrel

Carrier of the Plague

CALIFORNIA GROUND SQUIRREL   **Squirrel and Marmot Family**
Rock Squirrel
(genus *Otospermophilus*)

The mottled grayish-brown California Ground Squirrel is an unpopular Rodent. He has been condemned by the Board of Health. This resulted from the fact that in the year 1900 he came in contact with Rats which landed from European ships on the wharfs in California. The Rats carried bubonic plague. The California Ground Squirrels became host to the fleas which transmit this dreaded plague to man. Ever since that time, periodic outbreaks of the scourge have occurred, the most recent being in the year 1941. When a case of the terrible disease appears, the Board of Health makes war on the Ground Squirrels as well as on Rats.

Besides being plague carriers the California Ground Squirrels like true Spermophiles are seed-loving Rodents. They enjoy cultivated crops as well as wild oats and weed seeds. They are especially fond of wheat and alfalfa. One land company in the San Joaquin Valley of California estimated that twenty of these little animals could eat as much as one cow during a year. They also eat nuts such as almonds and fruits such as grapes and peaches, as well as some insects and meat. In spring they like greens.

These Rodents have many enemies, among them Foxes, Badgers, and other animals of prey as well as Hawks and Golden Eagles. But their families are large, they become abundant. They have but one litter a year but there are from six to a dozen young in this litter. The Douglas Ground Squirrel, a close relative which is found from San Francisco north into Washington, has young which mature very slowly. They stay in their nests for two months.

In general, California Ground Squirrels have much the same habits as other members of the Rock Squirrel genus. Although they prefer to den in burrows under rock slides or stone walls they sometimes make holes in the open with piles of dirt at the entrance. They may be heard chippering or whistling to each other when danger threatens.

Like all Ground Squirrels they are about only during daylight. They hibernate in the cold parts of their range in the winter.

Antelope Ground Squirrel

Chipmunklike

ANTELOPE GROUND SQUIRREL
ANTELOPE CHIPMUNK
WHITE-TAILED CHIPMUNK
(genus *Ammospermophilus*)

Squirrel and Marmot Family

This Ground Squirrel is mistakenly called Chipmunk because of the stripes on his back. He is no Chipmunk but a true Spermophile, one of the little ground-dwelling "seed lovers." He is heavier than a Chipmunk, has fewer stripes, but a similar impudent manner. He chirps and trills and scurries around with nervous alert movements. He may be distinguished from true Chipmunks and from other Ground Squirrels by the manner of carrying his tail jauntily over his back, revealing its white under parts as an Antelope displays his rump patches. This gives the little Rodent his common name, Antelope Squirrel.

In color the bright little Squirrel is fawn gray on his back with whitish under parts; in winter more cinnamon brown on his back. The white stripe on his side, the showy white under the tail, and short ears are characteristic. One subspecies of Arizona has gray under his tail.

Antelope Ground Squirrels live on the dry plains and low mountainsides of the southwest, including true desert areas where the temperature reaches as high as 125 degrees in the shade. In the very arid parts of their range they climb cactus and desert shrubs to look for enemies and to gather food. They are also found up to 7000 feet in altitude among the juniper and piñons and sage of the plateau country. Restless and much more alert than most Ground Squirrels, they often wander far from their homes.

Like all of their kind they eat a variety of seeds, including cactus seeds, wild sunflower, greasewood seeds, saltbush seeds, mesquite beans, as well as cactus pulp and other fruit and insects and meat. When they enter cultivated land they are pests, eating quantities of newly planted grain, harvesting the ripe seeds to store for days of food shortage. They stuff their cheeks with corn and other grains. They also make nuisances of themselves by burrowing into ditches in irrigated country.

In the colder parts of their range they hibernate. They live in burrows which they dig for themselves or move into burrows deserted by other digging animals. In these holes they spend the hours of darkness, coming out only by day. They are active all winter in the southern part of their range.

Their home may be in the open or under clumps of desert shrub or under rocks. Here they have their large families of from four to eight young with perhaps two litters a season.

Like all Ground Squirrels they are easy prey to many enemies such as Weasels, Coyotes, Foxes, Badgers, and snakes and Hawks.

Genus *Ammospermophilus* means sand (Greek *ammos*) Spermophile.

A Rodent Which Lives in a "Town"

THE PRAIRIE DOG
MARMOT
(genus *Cynomys*)

Squirrel and Marmot Family

Few travelers through the west fail to see and be amused by the fat-bodied little Prairie Dogs, standing bolt upright at the entrance to their burrows. Since the "Dogs" are diurnal in habit, rising and retiring with the sun, they may be seen during daylight hours.

Their common name is misleading because they do not resemble Dogs. They received the name from the French Canadians who observed that their bark was like that of a *petit chien*. Actually these Rodents are first cousins to the Ground Squirrels.

They are very social, banding together in colonies or "towns," making their burrows close together and during their busy daylight hours showing a friendly attitude toward their neighbors. When undisturbed they often stretch out full length on their bellies and rest in the sun. They look at intruders with mingled curiosity and fear. When a stranger comes too close, they race toward their homes as rapidly as their short legs will carry them, their fat bellies sweeping the ground. There they stand on guard, scolding and chattering. Should the intruder approach nearer, they literally dive down their holes where they remain in a small side pocket a few feet underground, often barking and grumbling until they think danger is past.

Prairie Dogs

Several species and geographic races live in various parts of their range which includes all of the Great Plains from the northern border of the United States to southern Texas and into Mexico, as well as the semiarid plateau lands of the Rocky Mountain states. In the northern part of their range they hibernate during the winter months, venturing forth in the spring while snow is still upon the ground. All species have dull-white under parts, pale-tan backs. The color of their back fur is given a hoary look by a sprinkling of black and gray hairs. Some have white tips to their tails, but the tails of the commonest species are tipped with black.

With their long-toed feet, they dig deep burrows nearly straight down into the earth, often going over fourteen feet before they make a right-angle passage which terminates in a slight rise. Off the horizontal passage they dig a nest chamber and line it with dry grass. The species with black-tipped tails spend time shaping and maintaining the entrance to their home in the form of a crater. The mound of earth is at first but a few

inches high but grows with burrowing and serves as a water shed during the torrential downpours which occur at times in this arid country. Floods sometimes completely inundate the "towns," but few Prairie Dogs seem to be drowned. It has been suggested that the inrushing water traps air in passages off shallow burrows and there the little Rodents retire, breathing in these air pockets until the water subsides.

Like many true desert dwellers they are not dependent on water for drinking purposes. Their digestive system is adapted so that they absorb water from starches in their food. They also obtain liquid from the juicy fruits of cacti when they are in season. Grasshoppers are a part of their diet although their main food consists of fodder which grazing animals eat, the native grasses as well as cultivated plants such as alfalfa. Their voracious appetites make them unpopular with stockmen who state that seven Prairie Dogs may eat as much as a full-grown Sheep.

Prairie Dogs have but one family a year with from four to six young. The young and adults are prey to many enemies. Coyotes, Badgers, Foxes, Black-footed Ferrets, large birds, as well as the native American Indians, find the meat of the little animals good eating. It is a popular fallacy that Prairie Owls and rattlesnakes live in harmony in a single burrow with a family of Prairie Dogs. Burrowing Owls no doubt occupy abandoned "dog" holes but their presence and the presence of rattlesnakes means but one thing, the Owls and the reptiles are dining upon the unfortunate animals whose homes they invade.

Since these prairie Rodents have so many dangerous enemies and no effective weapon of defense save their alertness, it is surprising how abundant they are. In 1918 it was estimated that 90,000 square miles in the state of Texas were occupied by Prairie Dogs. In approximately one square mile of Arizona, 7200 burrows were counted. Aside from the quantity of fodder which these amusing animals consume, they often cause widespread soil erosion because it is their habit to strip the ground within their towns of vegetation. In these denuded areas which are riddled with "dog" holes, rain quickly eats away the soil, eroding deep gullies.

Thus this cunning little animal has unwittingly become a serious Rodent pest and as such has been exterminated with poison over parts of his former range. But where man leaves him alone, he multiplies in great numbers and the "dog towns" are very lively.

His genus name is based on his common name and his size. Genus *Cynomys* is derived from the Greek *kyon, kynos* (Dog) and *mys* (Mouse).

A Mammal with a Day on the Calendar

WOODCHUCK   Squirrel and Marmot Family
GROUND HOG
AMERICAN MARMOT
(genus *Marmota*)

Everyone is familiar with Ground Hog Day which falls on February 2. According to farmers' folklore, the Woodchuck will forecast the coming of spring on that date. If he sees his shadow he is said to return to his burrow for another nap, while by staying abroad he is supposed to show that an early spring is to be expected.

This folk story is based on the Woodchuck's real habits. It seems as if all summer he is merely preparing for his long winter sleep. He is a vegetarian and as summer advances he waxes fatter and fatter on the juicy clover and other plant delicacies which he devours along with as many of the farmers' cultivated vegetables as he can steal. A rather large Rodent, averaging ten pounds in weight, in early fall he is tremendously fat and retires below frost level in a burrow where he is lost in that curious long sleep known as hibernation. Before winter has really come, he lies in a state of torpor, his metabolism lessens, his body temperature drops, and he eats nothing. His heart beats slowly. His body is warmed and life is sustained by the layer of fat which he has been storing up all summer.

That he reappears on February 2 every year is, of course, a fallacy. A common animal all over the eastern seaboard, varieties occurring from Labrador to Georgia and west as far as North Dakota, his winter sleep is terminated much earlier in the southern part of his range than in the north where he does not appear until the severest winter is past, although he is abroad before the snow is gone.

Unlike his social little cousin, the Prairie Dog, he has no group instincts. The Woodchuck is of a very solitary disposition, each pair making their home rather far removed from their neighbors'. Frequently lone Woodchucks are seen sitting bolt upright at the entrance to their burrows, immobile, as if expressing their dignified aloofness to the herd instinct as they listen for sounds of enemies. This Rodent frequently clacks his sharp teeth together when he is angry or nervous.

During the summer the Woodchuck is a field

Woodchuck

and pasture dweller, although he often digs his home on the edge of woods, burrowing under stone walls or fallen logs. He may make his hole in the middle of a field, but one of his favorite habitats is a dry hillside where with his powerful legs and strong claws he tunnels a series of passages extending from twenty to forty feet underground and bearing upward, to prevent the rain from coming in. Off these passages one or more chambers are dug and lined with dry grasses and leaves. Here in the early spring the young are born, helpless and blind. The litters are usually small but sometimes contain as many as nine babies. After a few weeks the young ones may be seen playing at the entrance to the burrow which is always characterized by a fresh mound of earth.

The Woodchuck has no economic value. Only a few farmers praise the quality of his meat. His hair which varies in color from a light grizzly tan to a dark grizzly brown, sometimes even black, is coarse in texture and has no fur value. His burrows do little harm save when they are made in meadows where Horses dragging mowing machines may stumble into them. His love of good garden vegetables and flowers is mainly responsible for his unpopularity.

Marmots are clever and will not enter a garden when they think the owner is near. When they believe that the gardener is away they will burrow under or climb over many fences designed to keep them out. If discovered they run away on their short legs, their fat sides billowing like waves, their bellies sweeping the ground. When cornered, they will fight viciously, often inflicting damage to Dogs with their strong, chisel teeth.

Marmota, the genus name, is Latin for a Marmot, derived from *mus montanus*, meaning literally mountain Mouse.

Mountain Woodchuck

HOARY MARMOT
WHISTLER
ROCKCHUCK
WOODCHUCK
(genus *Marmota*)

Squirrel and Marmot Family

The Woodchuck of the high western mountains is quite a different beast from the Woodchuck of meadow and farmland. About twice as heavy as his lowland cousin, this great hoary Squirrel lives among the silent grandness of isolated peaks. He is wild and shy. He digs his den in a remote boulder field although he sometimes may den in the open. In the Rockies and the High Sierras from New Mexico and California northward he is usually seen only above timber line but he ventures down the mountains on barren and rocky slopes. Farther north he comes down glacial valleys and in Alaska he reaches sea level but here the low country is as remote and isolated as the mountain valleys where his southern relatives live.

Like an old man of the mountains he is grizzled and gray. Standing on the summit of a rock, propped up by his bushy black or dark-brown tail, he surveys the country for danger and utters a loud piercing whistle which may be heard a mile away. This serves to warn his neighbors that some visitor has appeared in his high homeland.

French Canadians gave the name Siffleur, the Whistler, to the Common Canadian Woodchuck but it should be rightly applied only to the Hoary Marmot of the mountains. The hearing of these Whistlers is acute and they are usually hiding before a hunter comes close. At most they are seen scuttering across a rock slide or over a snowbank.

Like his wood-lot cousin the mountain Marmot is a vegetarian. He lives on many kinds of greens, pink clover, yellow sedums. In the fall he waxes exceedingly fat on flowering alpine herbs. This means that he is preparing to go to bed for the winter. He is a true hibernator. In the mountains of New Mexico where he makes his home from 11,400 feet in altitude, a little below timber line, to the highest peaks, he goes into his grassy underground nest as early as October first if he is fat by that date. If still thin he stays out longer. When he goes below he curls up in a tight ball and sleeps soundly for perhaps six months but is out before the snow is gone in spring. Soon thereafter three or four young are born. They stay with the mother Marmot all summer and may hibernate the first winter in her den.

The Hoary Marmot is not often hunted by man. He is too high up to do harm to gardens and although European Marmot pelts are sold on the fur market, the American skins are used only by Indians. Among the worst enemies of the Mountain Woodchuck is the Big Brown Grizzly Bear

Hoary Marmot

which digs him out of his burrow. Mountain Lions, Wolves, Lynx, Wolverines, and Eagles also hunt the big Marmot.

There are several species and subspecies of this biggest member of the Squirrel Family. They differ only slightly in size and color of fur.

The Dam Builder

THE BEAVER
(genus *Castor*)

Beaver Family
(family *Castoridae*)

The Beaver is the Rodent genius. He is one of the few members of the gnawing group noted for very intelligent instincts. The industry and cleverness of this animal are known to everyone. According to records kept over the period of a year at the Allegheny State Park in New York, two adult Beavers:

"1—Cut 116 trees from 1 to 13 inches in diameter.
2—Built 2 dams, each over 200 feet long and
3—A total of 705 feet of dam.
4—Constructed a house with a volume of approximately 472 cu. feet."

Although Beavers usually fell trees under a foot in diameter, they do attack large trees up to thirty inches in thickness. If food is scarce near their pond they dig canals from the pond edge to the woods and float logs to their homes.

To accomplish this prodigious amount of work Beavers are heavily built and equipped with very strong chisel-shaped front teeth. They are the largest of the Rodents, averaging from thirty to forty pounds, and sometimes weighing as much as sixty. Short-legged and rather clumsy on land, they are well formed for an aquatic existence. Their hind feet are fully webbed, their tails are

Beaver

broad, scaly paddles; their silky brown under fur is covered with long outer hairs which keep them warm in severe climates.

Formerly several varieties were found in nearly all wooded parts of Alaska, Canada, and the United States where streams and lakes abound, from sea level to an altitude of over 9000 feet. They have been constantly trapped for their fine-quality fur. In colonial days Beaver territory was subject for many international disputes. Before the discovery of gold in America their skins were used instead of money.

Beaver is still one of our important fur animals but is no longer abundant. To prevent their extermination the government is giving them protection in many parts of the country, encouraging them to carry on their dam building which is now considered conservation work. In some sections the loss of Beaver population has seriously affected the level of the water table. Only in orchard country and in sections where irrigation ditches are used are they considered a nuisance.

Unlike his small cousin, the Muskrat, the Beaver resents the appearance of mankind within the area of his range. Towns and cities crowd him out. He is an extremely shy animal and in settled country he has become largely nocturnal. In the remote sections of the wilderness he may be seen swimming about by day, but at the slightest sound of man he dives to safety, slapping the surface of the water with his broad tail to warn his comrades of approaching danger.

If his habitat be a stream such as the Rio Grande which constantly changes water level, the Beaver digs a burrow into the high banks and tunnels up above reach of high water. In the shallow waters of the ponds he dams, he constructs a dome-shaped home from sticks and mud, making the base from eight to ten feet in width, the chamber above water level large enough to accommodate a mother and father and from four to five young. Beavers have but two young the first year, perhaps four the second, occasionally as many as eight. The young stay with the mother one winter, perhaps longer. It is not known just how much visiting is done between individual family lodges.

The entrance to a home is usually below water. The busy animals often drag branches and twigs to the bottom near their entrances and weight them down with stones so that when winter seals their ponds they have a fresh supply of their favorite food, green bark, at hand. They like to eat the bark of poplar and willow trees, and of cottonwood within its range, pin cherry, ironwood, shadbush, and many others. When farmers locate cornfields near their ponds, the Beavers sneak up and rob them of many succulent ears.

The scientific family name *Castoridae* and the genus *Castor* both are from the Latin word meaning a Beaver.

A Primitive Burrowing Animal

MOUNTAIN BEAVER
MOUNTAIN BURROWER
SEWELLEL (INDIAN NAME)
BOOMER
(genus *Aplodontia*)

Mountain Beaver Family
(family *Aplodontiidae*)

The range of this small "Beaver" of the hills is extremely limited, being confined to a narrow strip of the Pacific coast from southern British Columbia to mid-California. He is not a true Beaver but a rather primitive mammal with no close modern relatives. One of his cousins, a horned Rodent, lived in the lower Pliocene epoch some 9,000,000 years ago.

A secretive creature, he is rarely seen except when caught in a trap. Usually mild-tempered, he will turn on his captor, clacking his teeth and growling and biting but he becomes tame in cap-

Mountain Beaver

tivity, is usually silent, uttering only occasional plaintive cries. When caged he dies within a short time and little is known of his habits.

The largest of the species grow to the size of a big Muskrat. They have compact bodies, short legs and ears, vestigial tails, and small watery eyes with poor vision. However, the Mountain Beaver has little use for good eyesight as he spends most of his time in the burrows he digs, usually on hillsides where springs abound. He has long, strong claws and powerful feet for digging. He does not appear aboveground in the daytime but is said to swim out to secure water plants after dusk in neighboring ponds.

Primarily a ground animal, he spends his life within a colony among his own kind. The numerous burrows go straight down into the earth for a foot or two to main tunnels which extend far underground, some of which appear to be used by all members of the group. In springy places the tunnels carry small streams of water. The entrances are not plugged but are well hidden under dense vegetation.

In color the Mountain Beaver is a dark rusty brown above, with dusky nose and ears, and a small white spot at the front lower part of each ear. Under parts are pale brown. The fur is thick and short, being covered with short overhairs,

and has been valued by native Indians since pre-Columbian times; but, perhaps because this animal's range is so limited, the fur has practically no economic value today. The Mountain Beaver's appetite for all kinds of green fodder, coupled with his burrowing habits, makes him disliked by anyone who tries to farm in his land.

A vegetarian, with a liking for many kinds of green plants and barks, he cuts off willow and alder branches with his well-developed gnawing teeth and girdles maples and other trees. He is fond of azalea, lilies, lupine, and also eats ferns, dewberries, dogwood, hazel, and many other plants. During the summer he eats where he cuts his food. Then he drags more fodder to the entrance of his home where he stacks it neatly to dry. He uses part of the dried "hay" to line his nest and stores the rest for the winter. He does not hibernate, keeps active all winter, burrowing under the snow to get bark to supplement his diet of stored food. In the spring two or three young are born, blind and with little hair. Some authorities report five or six to a litter.

The form of their family name *Aplodontiidae* as well as their genus name is taken from Greek. *Apl(haploos)* means simple, *odon* means tooth, and refers to the simple structure of the grinding teeth.

Mammal with Spines

PORCUPINE
QUILL PIG
HEDGEHOG
(genus *Erethizon*)

Porcupine Family
(family *Erethizontidae*)

The Porcupine is a large, slow-moving, stupid-looking Rodent. Like the Skunk he has confidence in his weapon of defense, is afraid of few animals. The long quills which cover his back and tail are loosely attached to his thick hide, come out easily when touched. The Porcupine cannot, as commonly supposed, shoot his quills at will. However, when some of his quills are poked loose with a stick, he will sometimes shake himself like a wet Dog, the already detached spines may be thrown four or five feet but with little force. This probably accounts for the belief that the animal shoots his quills.

When he slaps a Dog or other animal with his strong tail, the spines are driven cruelly deep. They are difficult to pull out because they are barbed. Dogs soon learn to avoid this beast but some meat-eating mammals succeed in turning the Quill Pig on his back, then they attack his undefended under parts. It is difficult to make the spiny animal expose his underside. The Fisher is clever at this stunt. Fox, Lynx, Cougar, Coyote sometimes when very hungry attack a Porcupine but in general the animal leads a peaceful life and has few enemies. He is still found over most of his original range.

He is sometimes wrongly called Hedgehog. The true Hedgehog is a member of the Insect Eaters which include the Moles and Shrews. The Porcupine is a forest animal, a good climber, and is found in nearly all of the cool forest regions of North America from the Arctic Circle south to Pennsylvania in the east, south nearly to the Mexican border in the Rocky Mountains. He has a thick, warm fur coat, can stand the coldest weather with only a tree trunk for shelter. He may den in a hollow log but his favorite home is under a rock ledge or in a narrow crevice. Sometimes several individuals are found in one cave.

The Porcupine is a vegetarian with an appetite for the underbark of trees. In the summer he prefers to eat the leaves and twigs as well as the fruits and berries of shrubs. He likes among other things wild gooseberries, strawberries, currants, chokeberries, plums, and roses, the seeds and leaves of asters, dandelions, geraniums as well as the juicy roots and stems of pond plants such as arrowhead and pond-lily pads.

In winter when the snows are deep he removes the tough outer bark of trees with his strong gnawing teeth and enjoys the tender inner bark. In New Mexico a favorite winter food is the bark of yellow pine and piñon tree. He also gnaws Douglas, Engelmann, and blue spruce. In the northeast he eats mostly the bark of hemlock. The list of trees which he feeds upon in other parts of the country is long and includes oak, cottonwood, aspen, poplar, tamarack, basswood, jack pine, sugar pine, lodgepole pine, and others less frequently.

He moves from tree to tree, sampling a little here, a little there, but sometimes girdling whole limbs and stripping the branches, doing damage to the forest.

Where Porcupines are too numerous their numbers have to be reduced. However, in most parts of the country they do no harm. They do not multiply fast enough. They do not swarm over the country as most Rodents do. Unlike most Gnawers they have small families, usually but one baby a year.

The young one is born under a rock shelter. At birth he is extraordinarily well developed and very large. He is covered with fur, usually has spines and some teeth. He begins to nibble tender leaves a few days after birth and within a week is independent of the mother.

There are two species of Porcupine, the Canadian and the Yellow-haired Porcupine. The Canadian Porcupine and his cousin the Labrador Porcupine are the eastern Porcupines. They are large, weigh when fat from thirty-five to forty pounds, and reach over three feet in length. Their tails are short, their spines thick, their fur dark brown to blackish brown. Many hairs are white-tipped. They live from the mountains of Pennsylvania westward through the forests of the Great Lakes region, north through Nova Scotia and Labrador.

The Yellow-haired Porcupine is found in middle western and western forests from near the Mexican border to Alaska. In color he is yellowish and is paler and smaller than the Canadian and Labrador forms. Several subspecies exist. Albino Porcupines are sometimes found.

Yellow-haired Porcupines have several times been observed migrating. In the dry southwest they come down from the higher altitudes in the fall to winter in the sheltered forests. In spring they leave their winter grounds and seek the juicy new growth in the higher mountains.

This seasonal migration is not as noticeable in the parts of their range where rain is frequent. But when the weather is bad they tend to move to the shelter of rock dens while in spring they leave the cliffs and seek open meadows in the mountains where vegetation is fresh.

The genus and family name are both derived from the Greek *erethizon,* the present participle of *erethizein* which means to stir or rouse. They refer to the Porcupine's ability to arouse irritation with his quills.

POCKET GOPHER FAMILY
(family *Geomyidae*)

The members of this curious family of Rodents have little fur-lined external cheek pockets. This at once identifies them. The only other American Rodents which have these odd external cheek pockets are members of the Pocket Mouse Family which are very different in form. The two families need never be confused. Both families use their cheek pockets for food baskets.

Gophers are among our most abundant little mammals. They live over a wide range. Yet they are rarely seen. This is because they are among the few mammals which spend their entire lives molelike underground.

Gophers are well fitted for a subway digger's life. They have little use for eyes. Their eyes are small and weak but weep readily. The tear glands are well developed to wash away dirt. Large ears would be in the way for a tunneling animal. A Gopher's ears are very small. The incisor or gnawing teeth are large and strong. They make the Gopher look fierce because they stick out

completely in front of the animal's lips. The lips meet behind, keep the dirt out of his mouth while he gnaws.

The forelimbs of a Gopher are enormously developed, the big paws heavy with long claws. His head is broad and blunt. His scantily haired tail has a tactile tip, a tip sensitive with nerves which help guide the creature backward through the underworld. He moves backward almost as easily as he does forward.

There are nine genera, groups, of Pocket Gophers. They are found only in America. They live from sea level to slightly above timber line. They differ little in external appearance except in size. Three genera and many geographic races live on the continent north of the Mexican border. They are the Western Pocket Gopher, the Eastern Pocket Gopher, and the Chestnut Pocket Gopher.

The family name *Geomyidae* means earth Mouse. It is derived from the Greek *gaia, ge* (earth), and *mys* (Mouse).

Porcupines

Western Pocket Gopher

WESTERN POCKET GOPHER
(genus *Thomomys*)

Pocket Gopher Family

Under the ground over the far western plains into the mountains, under the desert and under plateaus from Saskatchewan and Alberta south into Mexico, lives this solitary Gopher. Like a Mole he chooses to live by himself except during mating season.

All year long, even in the coldest part of his range, the Gopher is active. With the energy of a Beaver he digs new holes, breasting the soil, pushing earth with his strong forelimbs ahead of him up to the surface where he leaves little piles. He closes all outlets soon after he makes them. He eats a great many roots but also ventures body length out of his hole to gather stems and leaves, scarcely letting the tip of his tail come out of his burrow. Quickly he locks himself in his underground home again.

Even in the northwest where there may be food to harvest at most seasons, the Gopher keeps working. He fills his little external cheek pouches with grain or with stems cut to fit his pockets, often stores more than he can eat. He puts his food in chambers prepared off his tunnels. In the winter he continues to seek fresh food, pushing along on the surface of the ground under the snow, piling loose earth into his snow tunnels. When spring comes and the snow is gone this discarded earth appears as queer, snakelike earth eruptions.

Unfortunately for Gophers their activity interferes with man's. They are vegetarians with a taste for cultivated crops. On the range these busy Rodents honeycomb the ground, eating grass roots, destroying fodder. When their burrows are on slopes rain gets in and starts erosion. The earth piles dull the knives of mowing machines. In irrigated country their burrows riddle levees. In fruit country the animals gnaw the roots of apple trees and cause the trees' death.

A Gopher is also fond of many wild tubers and bulbs. He likes the roots of wild parsnip which is poisonous to man, as well as the roots of burdock and thistle. He is so fond of wild onions that wherever he can get them he eats them until his flesh smells of onion. He also likes potatoes.

These harmful Rodents lead such solitary lives that they catch few diseases. They have few enemies. One of their worst natural enemies is the Badger who digs them out of their holes. Snakes and Hawks prey on them.

There are many geographic races of Western Gopher which differ little from each other. Abundant on the plains and plateau and arid valley country of the west they are also found in open forest of spruce and fir from 8300 feet in altitude to earthy slopes just above timber line in New Mexico.

In color Gophers vary from a rich rusty brown to pale buff yellow. A very pale Western Gopher lives in the southern deserts of New Mexico where he eats the roots of agave and cactus as well as the fruits of prickly pears which he takes aboveground.

Western Gophers probably have but one litter of young a year although it is thought that families living in country where the growing season is long and food is abundant may have two or three. From four to six young are born in each litter in a nest chamber in the mother's burrow. The babies live with their mother until the first cold, in the southern part of their range, then make burrows of their own. The adult Gophers keep neat tunnels, have special sanitary chambers.

The genus name *Thomomys* means heap Mouse (Greek *thomos,* heap, and *mys,* Mouse), and describes his custom of making little piles of earth.

EASTERN POCKET GOPHER
(genus *Geomys*)

Pocket Gopher Family

The Eastern Pocket Gopher is almost a twin for the Western Pocket Gopher except for the deep grooves on his gnawing teeth. He lives west of the Mississippi River to the foothills of the Rockies, and in the eastern Gulf states. In the southern part of his range where there are sugar-cane plantations he has developed a taste for the cane. He invades a field, cuts off the stalks below ground, draws them into his burrow. There safe in his hole he bites the stalk into lengths convenient to carry in his cheek pockets.

Genus *Geomys* has the same derivation as the scientific family name.

CHESTNUT POCKET GOPHER
(genus *Cratogeomys*)

Pocket Gopher Family

The members of this third genus of Pocket Gophers which live north of the Mexican border are similar in habits and appearance to the two described above, but they are yellowish brown in color, and are found from western Oklahoma and western Texas into eastern New Mexico and Colorado. Like all of their kind they are fond of roots and tubers. In the country where fruit trees and potatoes are planted they may do much damage.

Genus *Cratogeomys* is taken from *geomys* and the combining Greek form *krates* (member of).

POCKET MOUSE FAMILY
(family *Heteromyidae*)

The members of this family of desert Mice and Rats may be identified by their little fur-lined external cheek pockets. The only other American Rodents which have these convenient little food baskets in their outer cheeks are the Pocket Gophers which are so different that they could never be mistaken for a Pocket Mouse or Rat.

Most members of the Pocket Mouse Family live where there is no water to drink. They do not die of thirst because they are able to manufacture water within their bodies from the carbohydrates in their food.

Pocket Mice and Rats live in burrows as Gophers do but unlike Gophers they spend many hours aboveground. All have long hind legs, are good jumpers. Their forelegs and feet are tiny and delicate. Their tails are long and often tufted. In size they range from small Rats to tiny Mice which are among the very smallest mammals living today. Four genera are found north of Mexico. They are the Pocket Mouse, the Kangaroo Rat, the Dwarf Pocket Rat, and the Spiny Pocket Mouse.

The appropriate family name *Heteromyidae* comes from the Greek *heteros,* different, and *mys,* Mouse.

Pocket Mouse

In the Desert Night

POCKET MOUSE
(genus *Perognathus*)

Pocket Mouse Family

In the desert in the night the small Pocket Mouse is busy gathering seeds. He stuffs his pockets with frantic haste. His tiny forefeet work with deft ease of human hands to fill the fur-lined pockets in his outer cheeks. They hold about a half teaspoon of small seeds. With his pockets full the little desert Mouse runs to his burrow under the ground and hides the food for drier days.

During the brief harvest season in the desert this activity goes on all night. When the sun rises he goes down his hole. As he retires for the day he usually plugs the entrance behind him with earth to keep out heat and snakes. During the intense heat of day he remains hidden and does not venture out until dusk. Then he is rarely noticed because he is so small.

The smallest known Pocket Mouse lives in a shallow burrow a foot below the surface of the sand on the arid Pacific coast near the Mexican border. One authority claims that he is the smallest mammal living today, smaller even than the Pygmy Shrew. He is tiny and rare. There is little rainfall in his homeland but he may get plenty of water from the Pacific fogs. In captivity he will drink water.

Others taken from the true desert live in captivity with no water at all. When he is not given enough sand in which to make a burrow in his cage the Desert Pocket Mouse sleeps most of the day hunched up in a corner but occasionally arouses himself and whisks nervously around eating seeds, then stopping to kick sand vigorously behind him with the motions of a Dog digging.

Desert Pocket Mice are beautiful animals. One typical form is grayish white in color with pink ears and feet and long, almost hairless, pink-skinned, tufted tail. His body is tiny, his head big, his eyes enormous, luminous, and dark, his hair long and silky, his whiskers elegant.

Desert varieties live in country where the temperature may rise to over 125 degrees in the shade during the summer months. Then sun beats fiercely down on the arid wasteland. There is no water to be had for many miles. It rains perhaps three or four times a year. Yet Pocket Mice thrive in this climate, making their burrows under clumps of cactus and desert shrubs. They never have a drop of water to drink. Quite miraculously they never seem thirsty. Like many other species of desert mammals they are able to get the water they need from food within their bodies. When the desert is in brilliant flower for a short period they enjoy green leaves. They like cactus pulp. At certain seasons they live for long periods on dry grains which they harvest during the brief seeding season of the desert.

The tiny, delicate feet of Pocket Mice are not suited for heavy digging. Therefore, they are found only in loose or sandy soil where it is easy to burrow. The one species of these Mice is represented by many geographic races or varieties. They are found in the western United States wherever there is desert or semiarid country from the dry, short grass plains of the Dakotas south into Mexico, west over the arid plateaus of the Rocky Mountain region and the Great Basin to the dry sections of the Pacific coast. Their range includes Death Valley and the bleak desert area south of Yuma, Arizona.

Pocket Mice are nearly all light-colored, well camouflaged against their sandy homeland. Their coats vary from yellowish or buff to blue gray.

The young, from three to six in number, are born in nest chambers in the burrows. In some cases these nests are placed very deep. In eastern Washington nests have been uncovered six feet underground. The tunnels which lead to these nests spiral down, here and there circling to ease the grade. At the bottom are the small round nests of seed husks, weeds, and grass.

In the southern part of the range Pocket Mice may have more than one litter a year. But most of these little animals live in country where they are of no economic importance. In the semiarid land of the northwest they do some damage to ripening crops, cutting the stems, harvesting the seeds. They also dig up some planted grains.

One other curious thing about these little mammals is the ease with which they part with their tails. When an animal of prey grabs a tail of a Pocket Mouse, the tail comes off readily, the Mouse escapes. It has been suggested that these loosely attached tails act as a protective measure. This is true with lizards. Lizards part with their tails at the slightest tug, then grow new ones. However, Pocket Mice do not have the power to grow new tails. Once lost, they must live the rest of their lives with the stump lengthened only by growth of scant tail hairs.

The genus name *Perognathus* describes the unusual development of their cheeks. *Pera* is the Greek for pouch and *gnathos* means jaw.

KANGAROO RAT
(genus *Dipodomys*)

Jumping Rat

Pocket Mouse Family

In the dark of night over the desert and arid country of the western states, campers often see big cousins of Pocket Mice, the Kangaroo Rats, leaping on the sands. These handsome jumping Rats seem to dance as with timid but quick leaps they come close to a campfire, watching for an opportunity to carry off potato peelings or other refuse to their dens.

The Kangaroo Rat is different from common Rats. He is a very handsome Rodent with beautiful whiskers, large head, and big, almost black eyes. His hind feet are developed like those of a Kangaroo and furred underneath. His forefeet are so small that they look withered. They do not nearly reach the ground. When frightened the animal may make a speed of twelve miles an hour, leaping on his hind legs with the aid of his tail which is long and tufted and very useful. It acts like a rudder as he jumps through the air; it serves as an extra foot as he lands and takes off. When he sits, it is a prop.

The large ears have hooded tips to keep out dirt when the Rat is burrowing. Around the ear passages inside his big head are air chambers of thin bone which perhaps serve to detect sounds underground as a seismograph, the instrument for detecting earthquakes, catches earth rumbles. Another peculiarity of this creature is that it possesses a gland on the shoulder which produces a substance with a musky odor. This odor probably attracts his kind but also "waterproofs" his fur and keeps it glossy when he rolls in the sand. When he is kept without a sandbox in captivity his coat becomes dull.

The most prominent characteristic of this odd Rat as well as of all members of his family is the pair of external fur-lined cheek pockets. They lie flat against his face until he fills them. Then the muscles expand like elastics and permit him to carry off as much as a teaspoon of small seeds at one time. He empties his pockets with one quick motion of his forefeet.

There is but one species of Kangaroo Rat but many geographic races, some of which have five toes while others have four. They differ slightly in color and size. They may be pale buff above or pinkish cinnamon. They all have white under parts and characteristic black and white stripes on sides and on heads.

The large Arizona Banner Tail is dark buff above with a dark band across his nose, a white tip to his tail, and white stripes on tail sides. He lives on slopes of the foothills of the desert mountains and on dry mesa tops in a large mound which averages ten by twelve feet in area and about a foot and a half high. Mounds are usually far apart, but one or two to an acre. Several round holes enter the mound and are large enough to permit the owner to go home on the run. There may be as many as twelve holes. The ones which are occupied are generally plugged with earth during the day, to keep out heat and snakes.

Kangaroo Rats do not come out in daylight. They stay below ground where they have many tunnels and storerooms, some two or three feet beneath the surface. In the big mounds there usually lives but one solitary Rat or a mother with young. The mother chases the father away from the home. She keeps her nest neat and clean, takes good care of her three or four babies which are born helpless, hairless, and pink-skinned, with eyes and ears closed and no teeth. For the first few days the mother Kangaroo Rat sits on them as a mother hen sits on her chicks. The babies grow fast and at the end of a week have dark-gray coats with white under parts. At two weeks they have small teeth and their eyes are open. The mother carries them in her mouth if she cares to move them. When they get a little older they give her trouble. They squeak and cry and play, leaping and rolling in the sand. The adults are usually silent unless hurt or angry. The young spend a great deal of time brushing their beautiful whiskers and hair. In about two months or in mid-July they begin adult life by storing food for themselves.

Young Kangaroo Rats are found at several times of the year. It is not known whether in some sections there are several litters or whether the drought conditions in their range bring about an irregular breeding period and there is but one litter.

They are among the few animals which keep the play instinct when full grown. In captivity they enjoy running a revolving disk.

The adults appear timid and they do not bite when captured, but like many solitary animals they are quarrelsome with their own kind and fight viciously. During mating season males kick each other with the sharp toes of their hind feet and in captivity males may fight females. One female was known to kill its mate.

The big Banner Tails become very angry with their little cousins, a small race of Kangaroo Rats. The larger Rats store quantities of food which the smaller try to steal, rather than gather for themselves. The little Rats are extraordinarily quick. They rarely get caught but when they do the bigger Rats tear them to pieces.

These desert Rats are delicate feeders. They like juicy underground tubers, buds of small bushes, wild sunflower seeds, and the tiny seeds of purslane, pigweed, and tumbleweed as well as Mexican poppy seeds, desert plantain, primrose seeds, and mesquite beans. They shuck even the tiniest seeds and eat only the kernels. They also eat cactus pulp. At some seasons they enjoy greens but may go for months without green food or water. They live in a country where rainfall is scant and temperatures often high. Like all of their family they are able to take water from their food within their bodies.

The Tulare Kangaroo Rats which live in the San Joaquin Valley of California and near-by mountains up to 4000 feet above sea level do not make large mounds and the piles of dirt at the entrances are washed away by the rain except in the flats. They make about thirty-five feet of tunnel. Here they live, store food, rear the young. The babies are born in a nest of seed husks and grasses and roots from a foot to two and a half feet underground. These Rats breed from February to August. From two to five young are born helpless and do not open their eyes for fifteen or sixteen days. They do not leave the burrow for about a month and a half.

In Arizona the Rats store food in chambers underground both spring and fall, the biggest harvest taking place in September and October. In the arid country of the San Joaquin Valley, California, the Kangaroo Rats may be found harvesting in late winter and spring because food there is abundant at this season. These California Kangaroo Rats harvest seeds of pepper grass, evening primrose, and other plants in early spring and dry them in little surface pits around the mouth of the den. About two months later these stores are removed to underground chambers.

Kangaroo Rats are usually of little economic importance except in years of extreme drought. Then they hurt stock range by eating seeds and fodder. They also do some damage by burrowing into contour furrows where this kind of plowing is practiced to hold water in dry areas.

They have few enemies except the Badger and the Kit Fox and snakes. When they approach a clump of desert shrub they often kick sand into the clump. This is thought to be their way of finding out if a rattlesnake is hiding ready to strike.

The genus name *Dipodomys* is derived from the Greek *dipous, dipodos,* meaning two-footed, and *mys,* Mouse. A glance at the shrunken forelegs and feet of this Rat will show why he is called two-footed.

Kangaroo Rat

DWARF POCKET RAT
KANGAROO MOUSE
(genus *Microdipodops*)

Pocket Mouse Family

This big Mouse or little Rat is yellowish brown in color with light under parts and black end to tail and crescents on face. He lives in dry parts of the Great Basin. His habits are like his cousins'.

The genus name *Microdipodops* comes from the Greek *mikros*, small, and *dipous*, *dipodos*, two-footed.

SPINY POCKET RAT
SPINY MOUSE
(genus *Liomys*)

Pocket Mouse Family

This is another small Rat or large Mouse which is similar in habits to others of the family. His coat has spiny hairs or stiff bristles mixed with the silky hairs.

The genus name *Liomys* comes from the Greek *leios* (smooth) and *mys* (Mouse).

JUMPING MOUSE
KANGAROO MOUSE
(genus *Zapus*)

The Jumping Mouse Family
(family *Zapodidae*)

The Jumping Mouse looks like a Kangaroo but is no bigger than a Deer Mouse. He is handsome, has small ears, small eyes, very long hind legs, an extraordinarily long tail, and internal cheek pouches like those of a Chipmunk. He may be distinguished from the Pocket Mouse Family by absence of external cheek pockets and by his color. The Jumping Mouse has white under parts with blackish yellow or pale brownish buff band on back and brighter yellow sides. He makes wonderful broad jumps but is rarely seen unless accidentally disturbed because he does not come out in the daytime.

There are many species and subspecies of these little Mice and they are widely distributed from the Arctic Circle throughout most of Canada and the United States to North Carolina and California. In some places they are abundant but more frequently rare.

They have one habit which none of the other American Mice share. In the fall they get very fat. They fast for about a week, then retire to their burrows underground to sleep like other true hibernators. They curl up in tight balls like Dormice, usually on top of their coiled tails. Soon they are fast asleep in a deep torpor. Their hearts beat slowly, they seem almost to stop breathing, are cold to the touch. In the northern part of their range they sleep four or five months. Only when brought into a warm room will they arouse themselves.

These tiny mammals like meadow life, hunt beetles, moths, and also eat vegetables such as tender shoots of grasses as well as seeds and blackberries. In order to get at seed heads they cut down grasses, often leave little piles of short stalks cut up into pieces three or four inches long. Their enemies include the Canadian Lynx, Weasels, Foxes, snakes, and birds of prey.

One litter of from four to six young is born each season in round nests on the surface of the ground. Nests have one or two openings.

Jumping Mice are found on the borders of streams and marshes and in the tundra of the arctic as well as in meadows, and on plains which are not arid. They are known to be host to the tick which transmits Rocky Mountain spotted fever to man.

The genus name *Zapus* as well as the family name *Zapodidae* describes the development of his jumping feet. The names come from the Greek *za*, very, and *pous*, foot.

WOODLAND JUMPING MOUSE (genus *Napaeozapus*)

Jumping Mouse

Jumping Mouse Family

There is little difference between this Jumping Mouse and the common one. He has a white-tipped tail and less teeth. He lives from eastern Canada to North Carolina. His long winter sleep has been closely studied. One was observed for fifteen minutes without seeming to breathe. In the spring these Mice come out of hibernation weighing from thirty to thirty-five per cent less than they did when they went to sleep.

The genus name *Napaeozapus* is the common Jumping Mouse genus, *Zapus* plus *napaios*, meaning sylvan.

NATIVE RAT AND MOUSE FAMILY
(family *Cricetidae*)

The curious Pocket Mouse Family and the Jumping Mouse Family include none of the abundant and familiar species most frequently seen. These belong to a large family known as the Native American Rat and Mouse Family which includes the well-known Meadow Mouse and the Woods Mouse as well as many others.

The House Rat and the House Mouse do not as often supposed belong to this family, nor are they native to America but immigrants from Europe.

The family name *Cricetidae* is of Slavic origin.

It comes from *Cricetus*, which is possibly derived from *krecek* meaning a Hamster, a kind of European Rodent.

There are 16 genera in this family. They are the Field Mouse, Pine Mouse, Red-backed Mouse, Muskrat, Round-tailed Muskrat, Brown Lemming, Collared Lemming, Bog Lemming, Lemming Mouse and Red Tree Mouse, White-footed Mouse, Grasshopper Mouse, Harvest Mouse, Little Brown Mouse, Pack Rat, Cotton Rat, and Rice Rat.

Pretty Rodent Pest

COMMON FIELD MOUSE   Native Rat and Mouse Family
MEADOW MOUSE
MEADOW VOLE
(genus *Microtus*)

There are many species of this pretty Mouse which make their homes from the treeless barren grounds of the arctic to the southern border of the United States and on into Mexico. In the United States they are absent from very arid regions. Different species closely resemble each other in appearance. All have short legs and short tails, long coarse fur, rather thick bodies, round heads, and small eyes and ears. In winter their coats are grayish, in summer brownish, gray underneath. The shade of their fur and their size vary slightly. Albino individuals sometimes occur.

These pretty little wild creatures lack the creepy look of the true House Mouse. As their name implies they are meadow dwellers but are frequently found in marshes and on the edge of woods. The arctic species love the treeless tundra and valleys above timber line.

Shy and peace-loving little animals, they make grass homes in open meadows or under some protecting rock or log. In farming country they may move into corn shucks during husking season, using the shucks for shelter, the corn for food.

Their lives are full of danger. They scurry along well-beaten runways ever on the watch for their many enemies, Owls and Hawks in the air, Foxes, Weasels, and other animals of prey on the ground. Their largest enemy is the enormous Brown Bear of the north. The only weapon of these Mice is alertness. Their homes are weak but carefully constructed, keep them dry and warm even during heavy rainstorms or under snows. In the winter little melted areas show where the Mice have their snug houses. Warm air rises from the nests, forming chimneys. They tunnel under the snow, seeking food.

Field Mice are vegetarians. They like the green growth of clover and alfalfa and grains, as well as seeds and roots. In winter they add the bark of apple trees and shrubs to their diet.

They look too small to be of harm. But Field Mice are very prolific. They often have from four to six litters a season with about six young to a litter. At times they appear in incredible numbers. Then they do great injury to agriculture. From about every third to fifth year their numbers increase. During one of these periods they did $125,000 worth of damage to apple trees of the state of Massachusetts.

Sometimes mass outbreaks of these Rodents occur in the west. The most famous Field Mouse scourge was during the years 1906-08 in the Humboldt Valley of Nevada. The little animals increased so rapidly that small colonies merged into a great army. As many as 12,000 Mice were estimated to an acre. They completely destroyed 180,000 acres of alfalfa. They never have been reported as numerous as this in the east.

After one of these periods of abundance, the Field Mouse population suddenly decreases. They often become very scarce. The cause of these cycles of abundance and scarcity is disputed. Everything from sunspots to starvation has been offered as an explanation. Food shortage undoubtedly follows overpopulation. This and disease probably cause the decline of the hordes.

The genus name *Microtus* comes from two Greek words *mikros*, small, and *ous, otos*, ear.

Burrowing Meadow Mouse

PINE MOUSE   Native Rat and Mouse Family
(genus *Pitymys*)

This close relative of the common Field Mouse has finer, more glossy, short fur and much shorter tail. In color the several species vary from bright reddish yellow with tawny under parts to dark brown. Their eyes are very small, their ears hidden under the fur, and their front feet are strong. This is the form of a digger. In fact they look rather molelike and are burrowers which live a retiring life, tunneling under the earth in open forest or thick weedy places. They sometimes use Mole holes. The holes which they dig for themselves are small and have frequent openings. They find much of their food underground, eat grass roots, the roots of morning glories and other plants, and girdle the roots of trees.

When they stay in the woods they are of no economic importance but when they enter orchards in the Shenandoah Valley and elsewhere, they do as much harm as common Field Mice.

They also enter potato fields and eat that crop.

They breed several times a year but have small families, two or three to a litter. Active all year, they store food for winter.

They are found from southern New York and extreme southern Connecticut to Florida, west to the eastern border of the Great Plains, north to the Great Lakes, and south to the Gulf coast.

They are not confined to pine forests. One authority insists that they are found everywhere else but among evergreens. They frequent brushy areas, open woods, and farmland.

Their genus name *Pitymys* means pine-tree Mouse (Greek *pitys* plus *mys*).

Brightly Colored Forest Mouse

RED-BACKED MOUSE
RED-BACKED VOLE
(genus *Clethrionomys*)

Native Rat and Mouse Family

This short-tailed, brightly colored Mouse is closely related to the Field Mouse. About the same size, he may be distinguished from his cousin by his bright chestnut-colored back. Under parts are gray. Sometimes blackish phases may be found in the same litter with the reddish Mice and it is hard to tell them from their Field Mouse cousins. Black individuals are commoner in the north.

They are found in different country than are Meadow Mice. Red-backed Mice are forest animals. They range over most of the forested areas of the northern United States and Canada and even beyond the limits of trees in the arctic tundra. Further south they are found in high mountain forests.

They feed mostly on leaves and stems of plants, seeds and nuts such as chestnuts, acorns, hazelnuts, and beechnuts. They are also fond of snails and the leaves of the evergreen strawberry bush. They do not hibernate but store nuts and seeds for winter under old stumps.

They build bulky nests of dry grasses and moss and place them in burrows or in hollow logs or stumps or under roots. They have large families of from three to eight young and several litters a year.

Active both day and night the many species and subspecies of Red-backed Mice are frequently seen in the woods. Since they live in uncultivated country they are not harmful to crops.

An Important Fur Rat

MUSKRAT
MUSQUASH
(genus *Ondatra*)

Native Rat and Mouse Family

When at sunset you see a wide triangular ripple cut the surface of a pond or river pool with silvery streaks, look for the water-loving Muskrat. He makes his home along streams, in ponds, lakes, and marshes in nearly all parts of the United States and Canada. He is a timid animal but if you get close enough you will see that his body is heavily furred, his hind feet partially webbed,

Muskrat

his nearly hairless tail vertically flattened, serving as a rudder when he swims. There are several species or geographic races of Muskrats, but only minor differences in size, color of fur, distinguish one from another. Occasionally an albino individual is born.

These large Rodents do not build dams as Beavers do but they make beaverlike homes in the shallow water of lakes, ponds, or in marshes; or if they live where high banks border a stream, they frequently burrow deep into the banks and make homes similar to Woodchucks. The common dome-shaped homes are composed of reeds, grasses, and roots cemented together with mud. They rise three or four, sometimes even five, feet above the water's surface, and contain one chamber where from two to eight Muskrats live. Usually two or three doorways lead out beneath the surface of the water to the region where succulent water roots grow.

During winter in the northern part of the Muskrat's range, snow covers the houses, ice seals the surface of the water, but these animals have a high, dry chamber, their coats are thick, and they do not fear cold. The heat from their bodies penetrates the porous walls and melts the snow on the roofs. When they are hungry, they go boldly down through their submerged doorways into the dim-lit underice world where they swim about, searching for their favorite roots.

They eat only choice vegetables such as the roots and leaves of water lilies, the blanched tender basal stalks of grasses and sedges, cattails, and reeds. In the country where wild rice grows, they eat the young shoots. They vary their diet with shellfish, small turtles, and crawfish, and are fond of apples, alfalfa, and clover.

The young Muskrats, usually from three to six to a litter, are born hairless and helpless. The adults have many enemies, few defense weapons, and were they not so prolific they would no doubt have long ago become scarce. Naturally timid animals, they will fight viciously when cornered, defending themselves to the best of their ability with their sharp gnawing teeth.

The purpose of the musk glands for which they were named is not certainly known. They are said to attract the opposite sex, but whatever their purpose, they do not, as in the case of the skunk, repel enemies. Their musky flesh is enjoyed by

Foxes, Coyotes, Weasels, and Mink, as well as by large birds of prey. Human beings find their meat edible when the musk glands have been carefully removed. Muskrat meat is sold in the market under the name of Marsh Hare.

But by man Muskrats are chiefly valued as fur animals. They have been trapped since colonial times. The long overcoat of hair is plucked by the furrier, the soft rich brown under fur is often dyed and sold as "Hudson Seal." Large dark-brown skins such as those found on animals in the Chesapeake Bay marshes are used undyed.

In spite of the enormous number of skins sold yearly, the Muskrat is so prolific that he has lost little of his original range, and has been introduced into several parts of the United States where he did not formerly exist. Because of his value as a fur animal he was introduced from America to Europe. In the year 1905 four American Muskrats were taken to a nobleman's estate in Bohemia. The animals throve and spread rapidly. They were soon classed as undesirable aliens because they burrowed through canals and into the dams of fish ponds in the lowland countries, causing untold damage. So far they have survived the efforts of the German agriculturists to exterminate them.

Unlike their Beaver cousins, they do not let their native timidity rule their lives. The whir of the sawmill fails to drive them from their homes. These adaptable and courageous Rodents even continue to live in the marshes of Staten Island, New York City, within sight of the world's tallest skyscrapers.

The genus name *Ondatra* comes from Canadian French Huron.

In Florida Marshes

ROUND-TAILED MUSKRAT   **Native Rat and Mouse Family**
FLORIDA MUSKRAT
(genus *Neofiber*)

The small cousin to the common Muskrat has a round instead of flattened tail, very short ears, unwebbed feet, and a fine fur coat of soft under-fur with long shining guard hairs. His range is limited to Florida where he chooses to live only in peat bogs or in the Florida prairie land where there is good cover and marshy ground but not too much open water. He is little more than half the size of the common Muskrat.

He builds a lodge similar to his cousin's, globular in form and from about one to three feet across and from a foot to a foot and a half high. It is set on top of peat moss and anchored to marsh plants or a tree which happens to grow in the marsh. There are two entrances, one on each side, that lead into the nest which is so small that the animal can just turn around.

The Round-tailed Muskrat also makes a feeding station. He constructs a rough platform of moss and marsh herbs with a hole in the middle down which he can go into the bog. Trails and tunnels lead over and through the peat. Although the animal undoubtedly swims he is not as much of a water animal as his cousin. He is a vegetarian and lives on roots and bark and grasses.

Small animals of prey and large birds and snakes are his enemies. His genus name *Neofiber* is derived from the Greek *neos,* new or recent, and the Latin *fiber,* meaning Beaver.

Arctic Mouse

THE BROWN LEMMING   **Native Rat and Mouse Family**
(genus *Lemmus*)

This stout-bodied Rodent measures about half a foot from the top of his head to the tip of his extremely short tail. As in all arctic species there are few parts of the animal sticking out to freeze.

His ears are hidden under his very long, thick hair which is brownish gray in color. The soles of the feet are furred.

Unlike most arctic animals the Brown Lemming stays the same color all year and does not change in winter to the snow-white arctic coat.

The several species of the Brown Lemming all live in the far north from northern Canada to Alaska and the islands of the Bering Sea, and over the arctic tundra from the southern part of Hudson Bay to northernmost land. During blizzards of the dark northern winter they remain in this bleak land and do not hibernate. They come up from their summer tunnels under the peat moss and burrow along the surface of the ground under the snow. They are fierce and savage in temperament. Adults growl and bite when caught. Perhaps their fiery tempers help them survive in the cruel and frozen north.

In choice of food Lemmings are vegetarians. In the fall some move into storehouses to find food but in their sparsely settled, harsh homeland most of the little animals live all year on grasses and arctic plants, lichens, and mosses.

So well do they survive that frequently the tundra becomes overrun with Lemmings. They have large families of from two to eight young, and there are several litters a year born in a semi-circular nest underground or in hollows in grass clumps. During some summers families are even larger. So many Lemmings are raised that suddenly there are too many Lemmings for the tundra where they live. There is not enough food. They riddle the moss. Then one of the historic migrations of Brown Lemmings begins. They start out in hordes, blindly looking for a better land. These great migrations have been observed for many years in Europe and more recently in Alaska and other parts of North America. By the millions, so say witnesses, the little creatures move forward. Nothing stops them but death. They swim rivers, they swim lakes. Many drown. Large trout feast upon them. Disease walks with them and animals of prey eat nothing but the swarming little creatures. Bears gorge on them. Wolves stop hunting and feast along with birds of prey. In Norway Lemmings have been observed arriving at the edge of the sea, plunging in to swim to their deaths.

Finally the numbers of the Lemming population in the territory of overabundance are reduced. The migration is over and Lemmings are scarce until good seasons bring their numbers to a cycle of overpopulation once again.

The genus name *Lemmus* is a latinized form of the Norwegian Lemming.

The Only Mouse Brown in Summer, White in Winter

COLLARED LEMMING   **Native Rat and Mouse Family**
BANDED LEMMING
PIED LEMMING
SNOW LEMMING
(genus *Dicrostonyx*)

This is the one member of the Native Rat and Mouse Family which changes the color of his fur from summer brown to arctic white in winter. In spring this Mouse molts his white hairs and grows a summer coat of chestnut, reddish brown, or gray, banded about the throat and on top of head with darker hairs. In the fall these pretty little Mice shed their somber hues and all grow snow-white hairs. At the same time horny pads appear under the front feet between the middle toes and form extra "claws." These horny pads are molted in the spring with the winter hairs.

Banded Lemmings have stumps for tails, very short ears, are about the same size and form as their cousins, the Brown Lemmings. Their habits are similar. They do not hibernate. In winter they may be found in the same burrows along the surface of the ground as the Brown Lemmings.

Banded Lemmings eat mosses, lichens, and arctic grasses as their cousins do. At times they become very abundant on the barren grounds of northern Canada and Alaska. Then migrations of thousands are observed. However, they have never been reported in such hordes as the Brown Lemmings.

Their genus name *Dicrostonyx* comes from the two Greek words *dikroos* (forked) and *onyx* (claw) and is based on the odd development of their toes.

Collared Lemming

BOG LEMMING
(genus *Synaptomys*)   Native Rat and Mouse Family

This is another arctic Lemming which may be found as far south as North Carolina on the Atlantic coast and Iowa in the middle west. He is able to survive in this warmer climate by living in spring-fed peat bogs. In Canada and in the arctic this Lemming Mouse also prefers boggy places but may be found in dry grassy cover. Over his wide range he is rare.

It is difficult to distinguish the Bog Lemming from a Field Mouse. He is stout-bodied, a little smaller, and has a shorter tail. In color he is grizzly grayish brown. Close inspection will show that the incisors or gnawing teeth are yellow and the upper gnawers are grooved. The character of his teeth definitely sets him apart from a Field Mouse from which he also differs in skull formation.

The Bog Lemming Mouse eats grasses and roots and lives in the burrows of other little mammals. Since he is rare he is of special interest to collectors of small animals.

The genus name *Synaptomys* is derived from the Greek *synaptos*, meaning (literally fastened together) combined form of, and *mys*, Mouse.

LEMMING MOUSE
(genus *Phenacomys*)   Native Rat and Mouse Family

Most members of this genus of little Lemming Mice cannot be distinguished from small Field Mice except in the laboratory. They have shorter tails but otherwise differ only in skull characters and their teeth. Their molars, or grinding teeth, are rooted while those of a Field Mouse are not. These Lemming Mice are widely distributed over arctic America and northern Canada and south along the high mountains into New Hampshire in the east, New Mexico in the west, but they are very rare. Since they appear to be Field Mice but are not, they are called, in Greek, cheating Mice (from *phenax, phenakos*, cheat or imposter, and *mys*, Mouse).

Mouse Up a Tree

RED TREE MOUSE
(genus *Phenacomys*)

Native Rat and Mouse Family

Red Tree Mice are easily recognized by their long tails and their bright-red coats with whitish under parts, and their extraordinary habits. They live like Squirrels in the treetops.

Perhaps some enemy is responsible for making these Mice into climbers. In the Hawaiian Islands when the Mongoose was introduced many House Rats took up life in trees. Whatever the cause, the Tree Mice are so accustomed to life in their high homes that they would find it difficult, perhaps impossible, to live on the ground. They eat little else but the needles and the bark of twigs of evergreen trees. In captivity they eat a variety of other foods but if completely deprived of their favorite food they die.

They are dainty, even fussy, feeders. They eat only the fleshy parts of the fir needles, using the shreds to make nests. Their nests are often built thirty feet aboveground and have been reported as high as a hundred feet in one of the enormous western trees. These mice live in the forests of great evergreen trees on the Pacific coast in Oregon and northern California. One of their favorite haunts is the forests of Douglas fir but they are also found in Sitka fir and the great redwoods. In certain localities they are found in small trees which border the big forests.

Sometimes these little Mice move into nests deserted by Gray Squirrels but more often build their own homes of shreds of evergreen needles, small sticks, and lichens. Some nests are small, but a few inches in diameter and placed far out on limbs. Others may be as much as three feet thick and two or three feet high and contain several chambers.

Red Tree Mice are active all year. They come out by night more than by day. If disturbed they flee through the tops of trees from branch to branch or sometimes descend to the ground to reach neighboring tree trunks.

They have from one to four young.

A Common and Pretty Mouse

WHITE-FOOTED MOUSE
DEER MOUSE
WOOD MOUSE
(genus *Peromyscus*)

Native Rat and Mouse Family

These big-eared, large-eyed Wood Mice are among the prettiest little creatures of the woods. They are very abundant over a wide range, are found throughout a great deal of North America from the limit of trees in the arctic south over the Mexican border to the tropics of Yucatan, and from deserts below sea level to mountaintops.

There are many species and subspecies of White-footed Mice and in different localities they are variously known as Cliff Mice, Canyon Mice, Desert Mice, Cotton Mice, Plains Mice, Old-field Mice, Beach Mice, Golden Mice, and Parasitic Mice. The last name comes from the habit of this Mouse of associating closely with the Wood Rat in California. All may be recognized as White-footed Mice by the soft fawn-brownish or gray back color, white feet, and white under parts, long bicolored tail, and big thinly haired ears.

Common in open forests and in deserts they are also found about meadows where they move into barns and farmhouses in the fall and are caught in traps set for the disagreeable House Mouse. They do little harm except in grain bins. They are real woods animals and like to live on the edge of, rather than in, fields. Therefore, they do little damage to cultivated crops.

They collect a great variety of seeds and small nuts in their internal cheek pouches and store dry

White-footed Mouse

food and the cocoons of the Luna moth for the cold months. They do not hibernate. They are active all winter even in the coldest part of their range. Below-zero temperatures do not keep these tiny animals at home. After a severe night their tracks may be seen leading out from their dens over the snowdrifts. In the moonlight they make conspicuous spots on the white-covered ground. They come out only after dark and no doubt many are caught by Owls.

During the summer they add raspberries and other berries, fresh meat, some beetles and caterpillars and crickets to their diet. Their nests are made in a variety of places, sometimes on the surface, sometimes underground, sometimes in hollow logs or hollow trees, sometimes in deserted birds' nests which they cover with leaves and thistledown. They may drag grasses and plant fibers into deserted cabins and nest there. They line their nests with soft material such as plant down, feathers, or wool if they find it. There are no runways leading to their nests as in the case of Field Mice. They provide two openings. They keep their nests neat and clean.

Like most Rodents they are prolific, have several litters in succession all summer with from four to six in a litter. The mother takes good care of her many young. When frightened she may run away with her family clinging to her breasts but will return to pick up in her mouth any that may fall.

One species of White-footed Mouse, the Cliff Mouse, has the biggest ears of any native Mouse. Large and nearly naked ears have earned it the appropriate name of Big-eared Rock Mouse. This Mouse has long whiskers, long, well-haired, bi-colored tail. He lives like a Rock Squirrel among rocks and cliffs, is found in the mountains of the west from New Mexico and Colorado to the Pacific and south into Mexico. He likes the juniper-covered plateaus and yellow-pine forests and is found, among other places, in the rock crevices in the plateau region near Grand Canyon.

The smallest of the White-footed Mice is called

the Beach Mouse because he lives in the sand dunes of Florida. He is also found in the cotton fields of Alabama and Georgia.

Another species, the Desert White-footed Mouse, is a medium-sized, buff-gray little Rodent with the usual white feet and abdomen and nearly naked ears. The soles of his hind feet are naked. He lives in the desert country of the southwest from Utah and Nevada through Death Valley south into Mexico and west into western Texas.

From time to time some species of these abundant Mice have been heard "singing." Their voices are quite unlike common Mouse squeaks. They have been compared to canaries' voices.

Their genus name *Peromyscus* comes from the Greek *pera* (pouch) and *mys* (Mouse) and describes the development of pouches in their inner cheeks.

Wolf of the Mouse Family

GRASSHOPPER MOUSE
SCORPION MOUSE
CALLING MOUSE
(genus *Onychomys*)

Native Rat and Mouse Family

An appetite for grasshoppers gives this little Rodent his name. In season he feeds largely upon these insects and crickets. He is known as Calling Mouse because his faint squeak is more like a whistle or the voice of an insect. His taste for scorpions gives him his third common name. His habits have been compared to a Wolf or other large animal of prey.

Reaching nearly six and a half inches from the top of his head to the tip of his tail, he is sturdily built, and when he seizes a grasshopper by the shoulders no amount of kicking on the part of his victim will make the Mouse let go until he has bitten off its head.

While most of the Native Rat and Mouse Family feed largely upon seeds and vegetables, the Grasshopper Mouse is more fond of a meat diet. Besides grasshoppers he eats a variety of other insects including mole crickets, potato bugs, cutworms, dragonflies, caterpillars, and insect eggs. One captive Grasshopper Mouse is reported to have devoured fifty-three insects in a day. These Mice are also known to eat lizards as well as dead birds, other Mice caught in traps, and weed seeds.

Because of their fondness for harmful insects they are the farmers' friends. However, they are not usually abundant. They live on the western plains from Saskatchewan south into Mexico but are even more at home in the sandy soil of the Great Basin and the dry plateaus and real deserts of the western United States. Here they are associated with a growth of cactus and yucca, greasewood and mesquite. They live in burrows which they may dig for themselves but they prefer to move into deserted holes of other small mammals, Kangaroo Rats, Prairie Dogs, Ground Squirrels, Badgers, and other Mice. They are often found in the same territory with Pocket Mice and Deer Mice. They may be distinguished from Pocket Mice by the absence of external cheek pockets, from Deer Mice by their shorter and thick tapering tail, and by their very soft fur.

There are several species and subspecies of Grasshopper Mice which differ in color from dark brown to bright cinnamon buff. All have white under parts except the melanistic (black) phase which has only white blotches below. Several are under a half foot in length.

These Mice do not hibernate. In the northern part of their range they have one litter of from two to six young. In their southern range they may have more than one litter a year.

They are active by night. Their enemies include Owls, snakes, and animals of prey.

Their genus name *Onychomys* means claw Mouse (Greek *onyx*, *onychos*, claw, and *mys*, Mouse).

Looks Like a House Mouse

HARVEST MOUSE   Native Rat and Mouse Family
(genus *Reithrodontomys*)

The small Harvest Mice are widely distributed over the warmer parts of the United States but are not abundant. They live in grassy or bushy areas and build their nests on the ground or a little above. Some species burrow under weeds or trash piles.

These native Mice look much like small House Mice but they are very shy and rarely seen. In most cases they do not come near settlements. In some localities when they become numerous they may do harm to grain and grass fields but they are not wholesale pests like their cousins the Field Mice.

They may be distinguished from House Mice by their more hairy tails and browner colors. The coats of different species of Harvest Mice vary from rich brownish gray to brownish buff with grayish under parts. They have big ears. The surest means of identification in the field is to inspect their teeth. The upper incisors, gnawing teeth, of Harvest Mice have grooves running up and down the front.

Their range is wide but not continuous. In the east they are found locally in the southeastern states from Virginia south. The Golden Harvest Mouse which lives west of the Mississippi from southwestern Missouri south to Louisiana is frequently found in marshes where he makes a small round nest in the clumps of marsh grass above the ground. He uses marsh grass for building material. Other forms of Harvest Mice live in the salt marshes of coastal California and on Catalina Island. They are found as far north as Washington in the west, North Dakota on the plains.

They are most active by night but are also about in the daytime. They do not hibernate. They store grass seeds for the winter and in the summer also eat stems.

There are probably from four to six young in a family and probably several litters a season.

The genus name *Reithrodontomys* means channel-toothed Mouse (Greek *reithron,* channel, *odon,* tooth, and *mys,* Mouse) and describes their grooved gnawing teeth.

Little Brown Mouse

NO COMMON NAME   Native Rat and Mouse Family
(genus *Baiomys*)

These southern Mice are closely related to the Field Mice with which they were formerly classified. Tiny Mice, they reach but four inches in length. They are grayish or dark grayish brown above with buff under parts. They live in burrows

underground. They are found within our borders in the coastal region of southern Texas.

The genus name *Baiomys* comes from the Greek words *baios* (small) and *mys* (Mouse).

The Collectors

PACK RAT   Native Rat and Mouse Family
TRADE RAT
WOOD RAT
(genus *Neotoma*)

These big Rats resemble House Rats but are not as disagreeable looking. They have soft fur, big bright eyes, large ears, round, slightly hairy tails. One western species has a tail almost as

bushy as a Squirrel's. Pack Rats differ from the immigrant House Rats in skull structure, teeth, color, and particularly in habits.

The pretty native Rat may sometimes be found

Pack Rat

in houses but commonly lives in the open. He does not have the filthy habits of the old-world Rats. He is a wild Rodent, bold and noisy. When he moves into a mountain cabin he keeps everyone awake by dragging objects across the floor or thumping with his hind feet to signal to his friends.

There are many species and subspecies of these big native Rats which differ in color from ashy to dark gray, from buff to brown, with white or buff under parts. In the west they are found as far north as the headwaters of the Yukon River, as far south as Central America. Not as common or as widely distributed in the east, they are found from extreme western Connecticut south along the Appalachian highlands to Alabama, and along the Atlantic coast from Alabama to Florida, west to eastern Texas.

Pack Rats are of little economic importance. Sometimes they dig up pine seeds planted by the forest service or raid ranch grainfields but they do not invade cities in hordes as House Rats do. In fact, they often leave an area where settlements appear. They do small harm except to campers and people who own cabins in remote places.

When they find an empty cabin they pack piles of trash into it, gnaw the furniture, build nests of the owner's clothing in the cupboards. They are also camp thieves. Most active by night, they may also be seen by day carrying off any number of things which no Rat could possibly need. They like shiny objects, take knives, forks, and spoons and coins. They collect trash with equal enthusiasm. They pack off bits of cloth, pieces of broken china, empty cartridges, cow dung, and little sticks. This habit has earned them the name of Pack Rat in the west. When they live in little caves in cliffs they may collect as much as from twenty to fifty bushels of material.

In the west they live in a variety of homelands, are common in the desert, on the plains, in the high mountains up to timber line, and in forests such as the great redwoods of the Pacific coast.

In the desert they collect pieces of cactus and scatter them in front of entrances to their nests to keep out Foxes, Wild Cats, Coyotes, and other enemies. The Rats walk on the thorns but never cut their naked feet. They also climb cactus bushes without scratching their paws.

Western Pack Rats make their homes under

rock crevices, in trees, under tree roots, in thorny patches, or in burrows. They are good climbers. In Oregon large tree nests five feet high have been observed. In the desert they may build homes four or five feet wide at the base and as high, in cactus patches. These desert houses contain from about six to ten bushels of sticks, cactus cane, horse manure, stones and bones, and a variety of other things. There are several entrances and the house is used from generation to generation. Inside are rooms for storage and a neat clean nest made of soft bark shreds and plant fibers. Here from two to four young are born and there are probably several litters a season in the warmer parts of the range.

Desert Pack Rats eat cactus, mesquite beans, and mesquite bark, greens, seeds of juniper and wild gourds, bark of candle bush, acorns and other nuts, pine cones, and mushrooms. In one nest dried mushrooms were found stored, probably for winter use.

The Bushy-tailed Wood Rats are large, have big ears, long whiskers, almost Squirrel-like tails, and fur under their hind feet. Rock and forest animals of the mountains, they live from southern British Columbia over the Rocky Mountain region of the western United States. These Rats are credited with leaving stones, sticks, cactus cane, or some other object which they consider valuable in the place of what they steal. This habit has earned them the name of Trade Rat.

Some western Indians eat Pack Rats and they are sold by Mexican street vendors as "country Rats." Their meat is said to taste very good. Since they are not scavengers and eat clean food there is no reason why their meat should not have a good flavor. However, since the average person associates all Rats with unclean House Rats, the meat of Pack Rats will probably never be popular.

Wood Rats, eastern cousins of the Pack Rats, like to live on rock slides or cliffs, climb almost straight rock faces with ease and leap gaps a yard wide. Typical homelands of these Rats are the Palisades of the Hudson, the limestone caves of the south.

Among the things found in their trash piles are old nails, crow feathers, eggshells, horse dung, bits of paper, cloth, leather, tin and china, old bones, bits of old rubber tires, cedar bark, nuts, apple cores, chestnut burs, leaves, ferns, mushrooms.

These eastern Rats are known to eat puffballs, nuts, apples, twigs and seeds of hemlock and black birch, fruit and seeds of mountain ash, dogwood fruit, and rarely animal meat. The enormous trash piles include some of this foodstuff and are always near the large nests. The nests are made of fibers of hemlock and chestnut and other bark. The entrances to the nests are often barricaded with trash to keep out animals of prey.

The eastern Rats are most active in the night and their long whiskers seem to be sensitive and possibly help guide them along narrow ledges in the dark. After storms they are frequently seen hunting food by daylight.

They are known to be prolific, having two or three litters a year. Their first young are born around the middle of March. The babies, from two to four, are pink and naked at birth with eyes closed. By the fifth day a silky gray coat appears and at the end of two weeks they are all covered with silvery gray hairs except their tails. Their feet are white and there is a black spot about each eye.

For the first three weeks the young Rats spend most of their time clinging to their mother and feeding. Then their eyes open and within another week they are able to care for themselves. In two more weeks they are full grown and buff-colored, but not until the end of the second year do they have the rich buff coat of their parents.

Grown Pack Rats use their voices infrequently but squeal and chatter their teeth when angry and warn of approaching danger by thumping their hind feet on the ground.

Their genus name *Neotoma* means literally "new to cut" (Greek *neos* plus *temnein*) and refers to their activity in cutting sticks for their nests.

An Injurious Native Rat

COTTON RAT
(genus *Sigmodon*)

Native Rat and Mouse Family

While Pack Rats do little damage, their cousins, the Cotton Rats, are very harmful Rodents. They eat cotton plants and do enormous damage to that crop in Texas.

They are southern Rats, common from Peru over Mexico. In the United States they range over parts of the southeastern states, go as far north as Kansas and North Carolina, as far west as eastern Texas. They also locally invade the warm western river valleys such as the Gila River Valley, the lower Colorado, the Upper Santa Cruz.

They live in meadows and open or brushy places and are particularly at home in rich agricultural regions. They are called Cotton Rats because much of their range is cotton country.

Some years they are very abundant and often ruin fields of sweet potatoes, tomatoes, or other truck crops as well as cotton. In one acre of sweet potatoes as many as five hundred Rats have been poisoned. In the far south they are known to destroy as much as three fourths of a sugar-cane crop in one locality. In Florida they not only injure truck gardens at harvesttime but dig up squash seeds in the spring so that the squash beds have to be replanted. Great sums of money are spent annually to poison these pests which not only destroy crops but also are host to the tick which carries Rocky Mountain spotted fever.

In their native haunts the Cotton Rats eat greens, seeds, leaves, berries, and fruits and nuts of wild plants as well as sedges, small animals, the eggs and young of birds.

They have large families of six or more young and several litters a year. They make their nests in burrows, under rocks, or under logs.

In appearance a Cotton Rat looks somewhat like a Meadow Mouse but is larger. On the other hand they are but half the size of a House Rat. In color they are rich grizzled brown or buff gray, with whitish or buff-gray under parts. They have short ears, long coarse hair. Their size and grizzled appearance are distinguishing features.

The genus name comes from the Greek letter *sigma* plus *odon*, tooth (*Sigmodon*).

RICE RAT
(genus *Oryzomys*)

Native Rat and Mouse Family

Like the Cotton Rat the Rice Rat is a southerner. There are a great number of species and subspecies of these Rats but only a few range as far north as the United States. They enter the Gulf states, go as far north as central Kansas on the plains and southern New Jersey on the Atlantic coast.

Rice Rats live in open brushlands or swampy meadows and frequently use platforms erected by Round-tailed Muskrats in the Florida marshes.

They eat wild rye seeds, seeds of marsh grasses, and other seeds as well as sedges, berries, nuts, fruits, and insects, small animal life and mollusks which they find in the salt marshes at low tide.

In size they are between a Cotton Rat and a Meadow Mouse, have grizzled brown hair, coarse in texture, and rather short tails and short ears.

Their genus name *Oryzomys* means Rice Mouse (Greek *oryza*, rice, *mys*, Mouse).

Chapter V
Close Cousins to the Gnawers

HARE FORMS
(order *Lagomorpha*)

Hares and Rabbits were formerly classified under the Gnawers. Now they are generally grouped by themselves. They differ from the true Rodents in having four upper gnawing teeth instead of two. Only the center two are large enough to use and since the teeth in the upper and lower jaws do not meet squarely, Rabbits have to chew with a sidewise, grinding motion.

Because of their characteristic form, they are given the group name, order *Lagomorpha,* which comes from two Greek words, *lagos* meaning Hare and *morphe* meaning form.

There are two native American families in this group, the Rabbit and Hare Family and the Pika Family.

HARE AND RABBIT FAMILY
(family *Leporidae*)

All members of this family are at once recognized by their typical Hare or Rabbit form. They are long-eared and long-legged, built for running. Their tails are short. There are three genera in this family. They are the true Hares which include the Varying Hare, the Arctic Hare, and the Jacks; the Cottontails and the Pygmy Rabbit.

The scientific family name, *Leporidae,* is a form of the Latin word *lepus,* meaning Hare.

White in Winter, Brown in Summer

SNOWSHOE HARE
VARYING HARE
(genus *Lepus*)

Hare and Rabbit Family

The Snowshoe Hare is a Hare of cold climates. His long, broad, heavily furred feet serve as snowshoes in his frosty homeland. In summer he is brown but in winter he has an arctic coat of snowy white.

This change of color is not, as was formerly thought, a turning in the color of the hairs. The animals molt twice a year. The white winter hairs fall out in spring, new brown ones grow for summer. In the fall the animals shed the brown hairs and new white hairs grow.

This seasonal change in the color of the Snowshoe Hare's coat has given him the name of Varying Hare. In the more northern part of these

Hares' range the summer molting takes place early, while in their southern range they do not become pure white in winter except in very high mountains where the climate is severe. In the state of Minnesota Varying Hares are pure white during January and February. In March some individuals are still white, some are whitish brown, a few brown white, and a very few brown all over. By May all in this locality are in summer coat. They stay brown until October when they commence to change back to winter suits again.

Some authorities today suggest that since white radiates less heat than a dark color, the white winter coats of the Snowshoe Hares and other

Snowshoe Hare

northern animals serve to retain body heat. The older and more generally accepted theory explaining why these animals change their coats is camouflage. White is a fine protective coloring against snow. Occasionally a dark bluish or melanistic (black) individual occurs.

Foxes and Owls and Hawks and Lynx are always watching for these northern Hares. Even the smaller members of the ferocious Weasel tribe catch these almost defenseless creatures. Snowshoe Hares can deliver a powerful blow in the face of an enemy with their strong hind feet but their only weapon against large animals of prey is swift flight.

This Hare digs no burrows. His only home is what is known as a "form." A form is a protected spot under a log, in deep grass, or in a willow clump where the adult Hare rests during the day or seeks shelter during a storm. When the wind blows the animal sits facing the breeze in his hideaway and his fur is blown down to keep him warm. These "forms" appear to be the personal property of individual Hares. They are the only

homes the Varying Hares ever know unless, as some people report, they crawl into the deserted holes of other animals.

The young may be born in a "form" or they may be born wherever the mother happens to be. She makes no nests for her family which consists of three or four babies, sometimes six or seven, occasionally one or two. Like all American Hares the young are well developed at birth. They have their eyes open and a coat of brownish fur. They are able to move awkwardly around although if undisturbed they prefer to cuddle up in one spot. They grow rapidly. Within a month they are nine times their original weight. They soon can take care of themselves and run from their enemies.

These true Hares do not have as big families as Cottontail Rabbits but they have two, sometimes three, litters a year. Some years their families are large, they become abundant. From every eight to eleven years the country where they live may suddenly be overrun with the long-legged animals. Then the Canadian Lynx waxes fat, feeding almost entirely on Hares. Other animals of prey thrive. But suddenly the Hares become very scarce, the Lynx starves.

Several explanations have been offered for these cycles of abundance in Hares and Mice and other mammals. Some have tried to link the cycles with sunspots. However, this theory has not been supported by fact. Hares do not become scarce or abundant in all localities at the same time.

Disease seems to be an important cause of the sudden disappearance of the Hares. In the summer they are pestered by ticks, often use the same dusting places as Grouse in attempts to rid themselves of the parasites. When the population is dense, ticks and disease attack the animals like plague. At the same time there is not enough food for the millions of Hares to eat. Some migrate. During migrations their numbers are reduced by preying Hawks. The Hares are largely active by night. The Snowy Owls and Gray Owls and Great Horned Owls pursue them.

Thus disease and scarcity of food seem to be the most logical explanations of the sudden scarcity of Hares of the north after a period of abundance.

The Snowshoe Hare is halfway in size between a Cottontail and a common Jack. He is at home in the deep snows of Alaska, Canada, and Labrador but is also found southward along the high mountains into California and into New Mexico. In the eastern states he ranges along the Appalachian highlands to Virginia.

One of his favorite haunts is a willow thicket. In Ontario he lives in tamarack and cedar swamps, also frequents coniferous swamps and cut-over areas where poplar and birch grow.

Like all members of their family they are largely vegetarians although they have been known to take meat bait from traps. They eat herbs, grasses, and the new shoots of trees. In winter they eat the bark of such trees as willow, birch, and poplar, and the twigs and stems of bushes such as blueberry and wild rose. When spring comes, the depth of the winter's snow may be judged by the height of their gnawing.

The genus name *Lepus* is the root word of the family name *Leporidae,* and when translated from the Latin means Hare.

Arctic Hare

Hare of the Far North

ARCTIC HARE
(genus *Lepus*)

Hare and Rabbit Family

Close cousin to the Snowshoe Hare is the Arctic Hare. He lives in the far north, north of the limit of trees in the vast frozen arctic tundra. He is one of the few mammals which make their homes where winter means eternal night lit only by the weird display of northern lights, where snow comes early and stays late, where winter food is scarce.

These white Arctic Hares range from the open barren grounds of Newfoundland and coastal Labrador on the east, and from Alaska on the west, north along the shores of Hudson Bay to the near land's end of Ellesmere Land. In the southern part of their range they molt their winter coats and grow a coat of light gray or grayish brown. In the fall they shed this summer coat and grow a pure white coat all over save for black tips to the ears. In Ellesmere Land and the more northern part of their range they stay white all year.

These are large Hares, about the size of large Jack Rabbits and weighing more than ten pounds. Typical arctic animals, their body surface is re-duced to expose as little as possible to the bitter cold. The less body surface an animal has, the less there is to freeze. So while their cousins of the warmer climates, the common Jacks, have extraordinarily long ears and legs, the Arctic Hares have rather short ears and legs. Their coats are very thick, even the soles of their feet are heavily furred. Like the Varying Hares they have great, furry, snowshoe feet to carry them over the snow-fields. Their toes are fitted with stout black claws with which they dig away the snow to reach hidden crowberries, moss, willows, saxifrage, and grasses, in winter. Their front teeth protrude slightly forward so that they can use them for breaking crust.

They belong to the same genus of true Hares, *Lepus,* as the Snowshoe Hares and Jacks.

The Common Jack

BLACK-TAILED JACK RABBIT
(genus *Lepus*)

Hare and Rabbit Family

The common Jacks, although called Rabbits, are true Hares with very long legs and very long ears. These are the large Jacks frequently seen by transcontinental travelers. As they leap along the road in front of a car or speed beside a train, they may easily be recognized by their black tails.

They are abundant on the plains of the United States south of the Dakotas and westward through most of the Rocky Mountain region to the Pacific coastal states. Very swift, they can only be outdistanced by a Greyhound among Dogs. They run with a series of long leaps, with now and then an extra high bound, as if they were on springs. Like all Hares and Rabbits they run on their toes but frequently sit on the long ankles of their hind feet.

In the greater part of the Jack's range rainfall is scant, there are few large rivers. They seem never to be thirsty and like many other mammals of dry countries do not need to drink. They get water from food within their bodies.

In the very early spring they eat grasses and other green vegetation. They are especially fond of cultivated clover, alfalfa, grains, and vege-tables. They enjoy turnip tops, pea vines, cab-bages, melon vines, and the bark of young fruit trees. Since they are widely distributed and abun-dant, they often become serious pests. It has been estimated that approximately a dozen California Jacks will eat as much as a Sheep while sixty Jacks will eat as much as a Cow. Together with the western Cottontails they have been accused of de-stroying whole crops in sections of California.

They used to have many enemies such as Coyotes and Wolves but since these animals are being destroyed by man, man has to poison the Jacks to keep their numbers under control.

In the desert where no agriculture is practiced these animals are harmless and attractive. They eat juicy cactus, the bark of oily mesquite, a great deal of sage and other desert shrubs.

These Hares are most active in early morning, in the late afternoon, and at dusk. During the heat of day they sit in shady resting spots called "forms." A Jack's "form" may be any little hollow in the sand beneath a cactus plant or a similar spot under any western shrub. They do not live in burrows. Their home is the wide stretch of the plains or the arid uplands, and the dry open valleys where they hide among various shrubs known as Rabbit brush.

The young, usually from two to four, sometimes as many as six, are born right on the floor of the desert under a cactus plant, or on the plains under a clump of bushes. The mother Jack makes no nest for them. Their only shelter is such as provided by a "form," although some say that the mother Jack pulls out the soft hair of her breast and lines a hollow with it.

The little Jacks are born well developed, with a good coat of fur, and with their eyes open. They are soon able to care for themselves. There are several litters a year.

There is only one species of common Jack but several subspecies. The common Texas Jack is large, light gray in color with conspicuous black tips to his ears. The common Plains Jack is dark brownish buff in color, often washed with black. It has a conspicuous whitish rump patch. The Desert Jack follows the usual pattern of desert mammals. He is very light in color, an ashy gray with the middle of the belly white. There is very little black wash over his hairs. He has typical desert ears which means that they are very large and long. He lives in the arid regions of the west from below sea level in the Colorado Desert up to an elevation of from 7500 to 9000 feet on the edge of the pine-forest regions. The Arizona Jack is similar to the Desert Jack but is a little darker.

The common Jacks belong to the same genus as the Varying Hare and Arctic Hare.

Antelope Jack Rabbit

ANTELOPE JACK RABBIT
(genus *Lepus*)

Hare and Rabbit Family

This pretty Jack has the biggest ears. They reach a half foot in length and are broad. They are typical desert ears.

The Antelope Jack is strikingly colored. His back is fawn or buff, washed with black. His rump patch is light gray. He has no black tips to his ears, but even more characteristic are his sides and flanks which are white. The common Jack has grayish sides.

This desert Jack has an unusual method of signaling which reminds one of the American Antelope. The Antelope flashes a warning to his kind when he raises the white hairs on his rump. The Antelope Jack Rabbit pulls up the skin on one side of his body, forcing the darker back hairs over to the other side, and the white abdomen hairs with the white side hairs present a sudden flash. He does this when he is running, probably when frightened. It has been suggested that this is a signal to warn his friends of danger. It might also serve as a camouflage when the animal wants to disappear against the color scheme

of the desert background where he lives.

This Jack is more strictly a Mexican native. Two species range over our border into the arid plains of southwestern New Mexico and southern Arizona. They were formerly quite common as far north as Tucson but are now rare in that locality. They may still be seen in that Saharan-dry borderland of extreme southern Arizona where water holes are wide apart, rain is scant, heat in summer excessively high, the soil parched. Even where water is found these true desert Hares do not drink. They eat many juicy tubers, and the juicy prickly-pear cactus.

Closely related to the other Jacks, he belongs to the group of true Hares, genus *Lepus*.

The Giant Jack

WHITE-TAILED JACK RABBIT
(genus *Lepus*)

Hare and Rabbit Family

This largest of all Jacks reaches a weight of twelve pounds. Some of his range is the same as that of the common Black-tailed Jack from whom he may easily be distinguished by his tail which is white and gives him an antelopelike appearance.

White-tailed Jacks are plains and prairie Jacks but their range is more northerly than the common Jacks, and they also range up into the cold mountains. They seem to be closely related to the big Arctic Hare. They may be seen in the west from 1000 feet in altitude in Washington to 12,000 feet in Colorado, and on the Great Plains from northern Kansas through Alberta, Saskatchewan, and Manitoba.

In summer their fur is buff gray. In winter in the colder parts of their range they change to arctic colors. They shed their gray hairs, grow a pure white coat except sometimes for a black edge to the tips of their ears. Their ears and hind legs are not as long as those of the Black-tailed

Jacks, and in winter their feet become almost as furry as those of the Varying Hare and they serve as snowshoes when the snow is deep.

The White-tailed Jacks are very swift runners and have keen eyesight. Among the Dog Family only a Greyhound can overtake them. The Golden Eagle will send them to cover.

In summer they eat plants and grasses while in winter they are forced to nibble buds, twigs, and bark above the snow.

They do not have as many young as the Jacks of warmer climates where the season is longer. Four or five are born in May in highland New Mexico. There may be one other litter a year.

Where they are abundant they are shipped by the millions for meat to be sold in western and southern markets. Ten million Jacks are killed every year in North Dakota.

Like all others of the Jack Rabbit group, the White-tailed Jack belongs to the true genus of Hares, *Lepus*.

Rabbit of the Brier Patch

COTTONTAIL RABBIT   **Hare and Rabbit Family**
(genus *Sylvilagus*)

This is the pretty, soft-eyed little Rabbit familiar to everyone who has lived in the countryside of North America from Canada southward. The Cottontail is small when compared with the Jack. The color of its back fur is brownish. The belly is white. The ears are long but not as long as the Jack's.

Many different species and subspecies occur but nearly all are easily recognized by the puffy white hairs on the underside of their short tails. In two or three subspecies of the Cottontails the hairs on the tails are all brown. These brown-tailed Cottontails live in the far west, in the states of California, Oregon, and Washington, where they are frequently called Brush Rabbits.

Ranchmen sometimes call the New Mexico species Dog Rabbits or Prairie Dog Rabbits because of their habit of making their homes in the deserted holes of Prairie Dogs. They also live in deserted Badger holes, as well as the burrows of large Kangaroo Rats. These small, long-eared Cottontails live in the eastern plains country of New Mexico. They hide under clumps of bushes called Rabbit brush.

Cottontails usually feed in the early morning or late afternoon, and at dusk. In summer clover is a favorite food. They also eat many different kinds of grasses, alfalfa, weeds, flowers, and buds, and nibble twigs. When the snow is deep the northern Cottontails are dependent on bark and the small branches of shrubs and trees for food. They like the bark of apple trees, staghorn sumac, sugar maple, beech, ash, wild cherry, and the twigs of slippery elm, dogwood, basswood, oak, and raspberry and blackberry. When food is scarce they have been reported eating cocoons, snails, and insects.

They have many enemies, among them large birds such as Eagles, Hawks, and Owls. Coyotes, Foxes, and the gluttonous Badger are animals of prey which keep the numbers of Cottontails within limits in places where the enemies of Rabbits are not killed off by man. In some states Cottontails increase until they become serious pests. In California with the Jacks they have been accused of destroying whole crops.

To many people they mean food. More than a million Cottontails are killed every year in Wisconsin, an equal number in New York, for meat.

The eastern Cottontails are pasture and field animals. They do not wander far from the place where they live, the females ranging over about three acres, the males eight. They like brush lots, cut-over woodland where there is cover, and are particularly fond of brier patches. They frequently stay in open fields where the mother Rabbit builds a grassy nest in a shallow excavation. She lines it with the soft hair of her own coat. The young in the vicinity of New York state are born in late April, May, June, and July.

Frequently haymakers discover the nests and bring in a hatful of young. From three to seven are born in the average litter, and several litters are raised a season. Two litters are common in southern Michigan, while farther south it is possible that the mother Rabbit may have one family after another all year.

Unlike Hares the baby Cottontails are born helpless, with but a thin coat of downy hair and with their eyes closed. At the end of a week they can open their eyes but do not leave their snug nest for ten or twelve days. They are weaned early, however, and when still small they are seen nibbling clover. Suddenly surprised, the very young Rabbits will "freeze" in fright and may be picked up without a chase. In settled communities dogs often bring in the young. During spring, rains flood the nests, sometimes drowning the litter.

Young Cottontails are easily tamed. They soon learn confidence in a friendly house owner, sometimes take their noonday rest within a few feet of a porch. During the heat of day they retire to a "form." The Cottontail's form is any shady spot within a clump of bushes, under a log, or in a similar place where he may escape the sun and be hidden from enemies. Each form appears to be the personal property of one Rabbit.

Like all of their family, Cottontails are active all year. After a new-fallen snow the tracks of their feet making runways in the thickets or leading out into open pasture are familiar patterns to country dwellers. In summer they are unpopular because they raid gardens, are fond of parsley, lettuce, chard, beet tops, and almost all greens and herbs.

Usually shy animals, they will hide and sit perfectly still under a bush until they think they are seen. Then they run at full speed. A sharp whistle will stop them in their tracks. For a moment they will listen, then dash away to cover.

Tularemia, rabbit fever, sometimes attacks these Rodents. This disease may be fatal to man.

Cottontails are not members of the genus of true Hares but are classified as genus *Sylvilagus* meaning wood Hare (Latin *sylva*, forest, and Greek *lagos*, Hare).

Cottontail Rabbit

MARSH RABBIT
SWAMP RABBIT
(genus *Sylvilagus*)

Hare and Rabbit Family

Marsh Rabbits are Swamp Cottontails. They belong to the same genus or group. They live in swampy areas and in the summer build platforms of rushes on which they make their homes.

These Rabbits are darker in color than common Cottontails and their tails are not as conspicuously white underneath. Several species or subspecies live in the marsh areas of Florida and the coastal islands, north through the southeastern states in the lowland by rivers to the Dismal Swamp region of Virginia and west along the Gulf coast within the tidewater area to Matagorda Bay, Texas. They also range north in the middle west in swamp areas and river bottoms to southern Oklahoma and southern Illinois.

IDAHO PYGMY RABBIT
(genus *Brachylagus*)

Hare and Rabbit Family

This is the smallest American Rabbit, reaching but a foot in length. He looks very much like a small Cottontail but the under parts of his short tail are buff-colored, not white. He lives in the brush on the sagebush flats within the area where the states of California, Nevada, Oregon join, and also in southern Idaho. In summer his coat is grayish with buff or white underneath. His winter coat is more pinkish buff.

His habits are much like those of the common Cottontail. His genus name *Brachylagus* is taken from the Greek *brachys* (short) and *lagos* (Hare).

Rocky Mountain Pika

The Haymaker

ROCKY MOUNTAIN PIKA
Rock Cony, Little Chief Hare
(genus *Ochotona*)

Pika Family
(family *Ochotonidae*)

The Pika is a little, rabbitlike mountain animal. He is so small that he is of no importance as a game animal, nor is his fur of value. He makes his home high above farming country and is therefore not a garden pest like his Rabbit cousins. He is usually found at an altitude of from 5,000 to 13,000 feet although he is sometimes found in low altitudes. He lives in the western mountains of America from Alaska south to Mexico, making his home among masses of broken rock beneath cliffs or on steep slopes where he hides in deep caverns, running about by day over the rock piles on softly cushioned, fur-padded feet.

He does not look like his long-eared, long-legged cousins, the Hares and Rabbits. Small and stockily built, he looks more like a Guinea Pig. His legs are short, so are his ears short, and broad and round. His tail is so short that it is lost in his fur. He is easy to identify.

There are several species of Pika in America north of the Mexican line and several subspecies which vary slightly in size and color of fur. The shade of their hair differs with the locality in which they are found but is some shade of cinnamon brown or gray on the back, with cinnamon or buff under parts.

In habits the species are alike, wary, secretive, often successfully eluding animals which follow them into their retreats. Social little animals, they know how to give assistance to one of their own kind when danger threatens.

Martens as well as Weasels prey upon the little mountain animals, as doubtless do other meat eaters, but Pikas have relatively few enemies. They are abundant in their remote haunts.

The Pika is the one member of the Hare and Rabbit group which frequently uses its voice. Cottontails and Jacks are usually silent unless hurt. The Pikas communicate with each other in peculiar squeaky voices which have been compared to the bleat of lambs. They call to warn of approaching danger.

Although Pikas live in a climate which is very cold in winter they do not hibernate. When the snows are heavy they keep warm in deep rock caves and eat the food they have gathered during harvesttime. In late summer they store many kinds of plants and the leaves of some trees and shrubs. They stack them in haycocks in front of their homes to cure. This habit has won them the name of the "Little Haymaker." When the hay is dry they carry it to a sheltered crevice. In the mountains of New Mexico the haycock of one Pika was estimated to contain about a bushel. The hay was piled neatly under an overhanging rock, the fresh-cut plants on the very top, those half dried in the middle, and the very dry on the bottom.

Among the great variety of vegetation which they eat are nettles, goldenrod, chokeberry, elderberry, thistles, raspberry, rose, snowberry, syringa, lupine, various grasses, and aspen.

The young Pikas, from three to six in number, are born from late May to early September. The babies seem carefree, playing about the rocks and calling to each other. They occasionally help with the haymaking.

Not many people see the wary little Haymakers because they live so high above the world of man. Anyone walking quietly among the moss and lichened basalt rock slides on Mount Hood, Washington, or Crater Lake, Oregon, may see a cinnamon-brown Pika with black hairs sprinkled on his back and a buff-colored abdomen. The Pikas which live in the dark lava fields of southern Oregon and northeastern California are equally well camouflaged with deep gray fur, darkened by black-tipped hairs, the under parts cinnamon or buff. The Dusky Pika lives on the dark lava flows south of Mount Hood in the Cascade range. The climate here is humid and like most animals which live in wet localities, his fur is very dark.

The Pika which is common at 12,000 feet altitude to above timber line in New Mexico is brownish gray. He is found also as low as 11,000 feet on the cold northeast slopes of mountains. Another New Mexican species, the Dusky Pika, lives in the rock slides of broken lava from 9000 feet up. The Cascade or Brown Pika, which lives on the dark-gray rock slides of basalt which are covered with a growth of moss and lichens in the Cascades of Washington and British Columbia, has brown fur blended with black hairs and a buff-colored belly.

The Pika is frequently called a Cony but he does not belong to the same family as the European Cony. The American Pika's generic and family name are formed from *ochodona*, the Mongol Tartar name for a Pika.

Chapter VI
Primitive Animal Form

MARSUPIALS
(order *Marsupialia*)

The members of this curious group of mammals are very primitive in form. Their brains are primitive. Their young are born in an undeveloped state. Most of the Marsupials have skin pouches on their abdomens where they keep their helpless babies until they are able to care for themselves. The group name, order *Marsupialia*, comes from a Latin word meaning pouch or bag.

Marsupials abound in Australia, home of the Kangaroos. The one Marsupial which ranges north of the Mexican line into the United States is the Opossum.

A Primitive Mammal

COMMON OPOSSUM
VIRGINIA OPOSSUM
EASTERN OPOSSUM
(genus *Didelphis*)

Opossum Family
(family *Didelphidae*)

The Opossum is a survivor of an ancient group of mammals which flourished before modern mammals developed. One of the most curious characteristics of the Opossum is the birth and development of the young.

Opossums breed in January in the vicinity of Austin, Texas, probably several weeks later in the north. They have enormous families. As many as fourteen young have been reported although sometimes there are but six. There are two, occasionally three, litters a year.

After developing within the mother for a short period of eleven or twelve days, the babies are born. They are smaller than honey bees. Their hind legs are little more than stumpy buds. Their bodies and heads are likewise undeveloped but their front legs are strong and the front feet have sharp, hooked claws.

With these claws the tiny babies crawl up into the mother's pouch, a natural baby carriage on her abdomen. There the babies remain for about two months, clinging to the mother's breasts, feeding on milk. At the end of this time they are big enough to enjoy life in the open. They move about freely over the mother's back, sometimes clinging to her tail. When they get hungry or when they are frightened, they pop into the mother's pouch again. For thirty more days the mother Opossum carries her big heavy family about with her. Then they are ready to shift for themselves and leave their snug home.

Another curious characteristic of the Opossum is the scaly, monkeylike tail. It is developed for grasping, acts like a strong finger. The Opossum's toes are also like fingers and the fifth finger of the hind foot acts like a human thumb. Thus the animal is equipped for life in the trees where he spends much of his time. The mother is able to navigate among the treetops even with the wiggling load of her children on her back.

Opossums are equally at home on the ground. By day they den up under fallen trees, in hollow trunks or logs, in holes in stream banks, or curl up in the treetops. By night they prowl for food. The list of food which they like includes almost anything they can catch. They eat birds and their

Common Opossum

eggs, Mice, and now and then raid a hen yard. They skirt stream beds searching for frogs and their tadpoles, crayfish, and unwary box turtles. They are fond of wasps and grasshoppers, and even snakes. They root under leaves with their long snouts for centipedes and other insects. They also eat carrion, wild fruits, and mushrooms.

In the dark of night while these curious animals hunt for their food, many enemies hunt for them. Foxes, Coyotes, Bobcats, Great Horned Owls, and the larger animals of prey such as Mountain Lions find Opossum good eating. So do people, particularly the southern Negroes who talk of brother 'possum in their folk tales with great affection.

When cornered by one of his many enemies the animal "plays 'possum." He turns over on his side, his tongue lolls out, his eyes close, and he looks dead until an opportunity to escape occurs. Then he comes quickly to life.

The outer hairs of the Opossum's coat are black, mingled with white, making a grizzled gray color. The head is whitish or yellowish, black on top. The soft underfur is dark, the legs dark. About one out of ten specimens appears black because the underfur is so dark. Occasionally an albino (white) Opossum, is seen.

Opossum fur has recently brought a low price on the market but since the animal is abundant and easily caught its fur is important. Many pelts are exported to Europe where they are dyed to look like Skunk. Choice northern skins are made into coats but most Opossum is used for trimming inexpensive coats.

In spite of the popularity of Opossums as food and fur animals, they have such large families and are so hardy that they are not decreasing. Always abundant in the southeastern states, they are now extending their range northward. They are native from southern New York west to the Great Lakes and Texas, south to Florida. Recently they have been reported in Ontario and Vermont.

The Florida variety which lives in the lowland Gulf coast west to western Lousiana is smaller, darker, and has a longer tail than the Virginia Opossum. The Texas Opossum is large, frequently gray like the Virginia Opossum, but sometimes black with a dusky head and stripes from ear to nose.

Like the Skunk and the Raccoon the Opossum dens up during severe weather in the colder part of his range but comes out during mild spells.

The genus name *Didelphis* comes from the Greek *dis,* double, and *delphys,* uterus. The name describes the peculiar double womb of the Opossum.

Chapter VII

Browsers and Grazers

WITH HOOFS
(order *Ungulata*)

Members of this group of mammals have horny, rounded toes or hoofs and, in most cases, long legs adapted for swift flight. Most authorities divide the hoofed animals into two groups: the odd-toed or single-hoofed such as the Horse and the even-toed such as the Deer. The native American hoofed animals all belong to the second group, the cloven-hoofed, which includes many of the big-game animals of the continent.

The one small American member is the Peccary, a piglike animal which has many peculiarities. He is the only American hoofed animal which is not entirely a vegetarian. The others of the group are true ruminants, grazing or browsing animals which chew their cuds. This means that they swallow their food when they gather it, but later while at rest they regurgitate it, bring it up into their mouths, and chew it until it is ready for digestion when they swallow it again.

They have complicated stomachs divided in four parts. They have no teeth in the front part of their upper jaws. They chew with their back teeth, the grinders.

They belong to the scientific order *Ungulata* which is the Latin word meaning with hoofs.

There are four native American families of Hoofed Animals. They are the Cattle Family, the Deer Family, the Pronghorn Antelope Family, and the Peccary Family.

THE CATTLE FAMILY
(family *Bovidae*)

The milch Cow's wild cousins which are native to North America are quite different in appearance but all have true horns, hollow, unbranched, and permanent, and never grow but one pair.

So closely related to the barnyard Cow are these Hoofed Animals that the Cow and the American Bison can breed together and produce offspring. The calf is known as a Cattalo and a useless beast it has proved to be. The cross is unsuccessful either as a beef or a work animal.

All members of the Cattle Family are true ruminants, "cud-chewers." However, the lands where some of them graze are not, for the better part of the year, good grazing country and so with the exception of the plains Buffalo whose native range is an enormous meadow, American Cattle browse in strange places.

This family is divided into four groups, the Bison, the Mountain Sheep, the Mountain Goat, and the Musk Ox. The scientific family name *Bovidae* comes from a Latin word *bos* meaning Cow or Ox.

An Historic Animal

BISON   **Cattle Family**
AMERICAN BUFFALO
(genus *Bison*)

The Bison is one of our fiercest-looking native animals. His great humped shoulders and his low-slung head covered with a thick mat of bushy brown hair give him a strange appearance. Bulls grow very large, standing from five to six feet high at the shoulder, often weighing well over a ton. The females are smaller, weighing from 1300 to 1500 pounds and having smaller horns. The coats of the animals fade in the winter, are shed in the spring. At this time the herd looks moth-eaten. But when the new rich dark-brown coat comes in the fall, they are handsome.

Bison are herd animals. The herds which once inhabited North America were enormous. It is no exaggeration to say that the sound of their hoofs was like thunder. A Spanish explorer reported that these "humpbacked cows" were so numerous that he could compare them to nothing but the multitude of fish in the sea. Early travelers reported that Bison were so thick upon the plains that they blackened the landscape as far as the human eye could see. One traveler in the year 1859 said that he rode 200 miles with Buffalo always around him. Many herds were estimated to be ten miles wide, and a herd reported in 1871 on the Arkansas River was estimated to contain 4,000,000 animals, forming a mass fifty miles long, twenty-five wide. Early navigators of steamboats on the Missouri River complained of being stopped by Bison crossing the stream, and the first transcontinental trains were held up for hours by animals which crossed the rails. When they stampeded they formed a solid mass of creatures, but while grazing they split up into many small groups so that it was possible to pass among them. A conservative estimate of the total Bison population of America when the continent was discovered is sixty millions.

The Bison is a grazing animal which found food suitable to his tastes over an enormous stretch of the American wilds. He was at home from the Great Slave Lake in northern territory south into Mexico, from the plateaus of what are now the states of Idaho and Wyoming east to western New York, Pennsylvania, and the Carolinas.

Some authorities divide the Bison into three species, the Woods Bison, the Plains Bison, the Mountain Bison, but it is now more generally agreed that all three belong to the same species, their physical differences being only geographic variations. The Bison which lived in the mountains on the eastern slope of the Rockies from the present state of Montana to southern Colorado were smaller, darker in color, wilder in temperament than the Plains Bison and they lived in small herds of from ten to twenty. This Mountain Bison became extinct before the nineteenth century had ended. The Woods Bison was the largest of the three. His coat was thick and very dark, he lived in the woods of the far north eating herbs, mosses, pea vines, as well as the grass which was the main diet of the animals which roamed the plains.

Great masses of the plains animals migrated southward in the fall, seeking more favorable habitat from some 200 to 400 miles from their summer home. They moved generally northward in the spring. They were hardy creatures, the northern ones turning their faces to blizzards without fear. When the heat of summer brought a pest of insects, the Bison went to their wallows, natural bowls in the prairie which collected the scant rain water. They lay down and wallowed like Pigs in these holes, coming up plastered with mud. The mud dried, making the animals look filthy but serving as a protection against fly bites.

Early travelers reported the ground trampled deep beside every outcropping rock on the tree-less prairies. These rocks and the cottonwood trees in the swales were used as scratching posts. When the first telegraph poles were erected on the plains the Bison rubbed many of them down. The company put spikes into the poles to keep the

Bison

animals away but the Buffalo only rubbed the harder, finding spikes just the thing to scratch their tough hides. An irate settler in Pennsylvania reported that a herd of these big creatures had scratched his log house completely down.

The calves, usually one to a cow, were born between April and June. The little ones were a light yellow or tawny color, with almost red backs. They were very active but helpless against the attack of Wolves. The mother Buffalo was devoted to her young, keeping it with her for a year or until another calf took its place. The bulls stayed with the herd until the end of the breeding season, about the first of October, when they moved in groups by themselves.

All during the summer months the bulls were said to help protect the little ones. Early travelers reported seeing "fairy rings" trampled in the earth of the plains. The rings were made by the bulls circling around the cows when they were calving, keeping off roving Wolves. When a pack of Wolves or Coyotes approached, the cows formed a circle around the calves while the bulls ranged themselves around the cows, presenting a strong front to the raiders. The Wolves only captured strayed calves or old feeble animals.

But while Bison were clever in some respects, they were in other matters extraordinarily stupid. Usually rather sluggish in temperament the animals did not have frequent battles to the death among themselves in the wild state although terrible fights are sometimes reported between captive bulls. Angry bulls paw the ground, make rumbling noises in their throats, and fling their cowlike tails into the air, then charge. When two bulls meet they shove each other about, locking their great shaggy heads together. Because of the thick mats of hair on their heads and shoulders little damage is done to either unless one of the combatants slips. Then the other uses his sharp horns on the unprotected flanks and belly of his opponent. They are not cowards but instances of their mass stupidity have been reported.

When startled a whole herd would stampede madly over the plains, keeping so close together that when they reached a cliff the leaders would be pushed over by the crazy animals behind. An instance is reported of northern animals being caught in a blizzard. Having no fear of the storm, they drifted slowly into the wind, coming suddenly to a precipice. Fifty feet below lay another plain. The great herd kept moving, pushing row after row of the leaders over the brink. Later Bison bones were found piled from ten to fifteen feet high.

A similar instance is reported by an early trader. In late winter a large herd of Bison started to cross a river. In some places the ice broke, drowning the front line of Buffaloes but this did not deter the animals coming behind. So many were drowned that for three days after a thaw a continuous line of bodies of dead Buffalo drifted past the trading post. Allowing for some exaggeration, the disaster must have been enormous.

Yet with disasters such as these, coupled with loss by prairie fire, by thirst in periods of drought, and at the hands of Indians, the Bison were increasing when white men discovered America. By the year 1883 there were only a few scattered remnants of the big herds left! Gunpowder alone was responsible for the almost complete extermination of the American Bison. Although the thick mat of hair on their heads and the thick skulls made an armor which bullets of old-fashioned rifles could not penetrate, the hunters soon found a vulnerable spot behind the animals' shoulders. Buffaloes were shot for their robes and for their meat, often killed only for their tongues which were considered a delicacy; others were slaughtered just for the love of killing. The last big herd, some ten thousand strong, fled up into the mountains of North Dakota where they were trapped and butchered.

From the handful which remained scattered over the continent, two herds were built, one in Canada and one in the Yellowstone. Today the

Musk Ox

hardy but one-track-mind Bison is safe from extinction. There are now some 18,000 of the animals under government protection in Canada and nearly 5000 in the United States with 200 more in Alaska.

Through common use Buffalo has been ac-cepted as a name for our Bison although the American animal does not belong to the genus of true Buffalo which includes the Cape Buffalo of Africa. The American Buffalo is classified in the genus *Bison* which is also his correct common name.

MUSK OX
(genus *Ovibos*)

This funny-looking member of the Cattle Family lives all year round far in the north beyond the limit of trees. He is well formed for life in the arctic barren grounds where the short summers bring one endless day but where winter means intense cold, continual darkness, a vast midnight of ice and snow, northern lights weirdly replacing the light of the sun.

The Musk Ox is warmly clothed in a thick underfur overlaid by a great shaggy coat of hairs which are twenty inches long in places, and hang down like a skirt about the animal's knees. Like most arctic mammals he is built so that no extra surface is exposed to the cold. His legs are short, his ears almost hidden under his great coat; his tail is short and protected by hair. In color he is dark brown above, shading to white below. His horns are not the least curious thing about this curious animal. The horns of the young turn outward but in adults they are plastered over the head like wigs. Both sexes have horns.

Musk Oxen are herd animals, living in groups of from ten to a hundred. In May or June the one calf is born and during the summer the old bulls herd by themselves, leaving the mothers and calves to run together. The grown animals browse upon leaves of willows on the hillsides. During the harsh winter they come down into the more sheltered valleys where they paw up

Cattle Family

the snow and secure a meager fare of moss, some grasses, lichens, perhaps bark. In the bitter arctic cold they often crowd close together for warmth, standing so close that their breaths arise and form a warm area above them.

Their worst enemy is the Arctic Wolf. When attacked the Musk Oxen form a ring with the calves in the center, the grown animals facing the Wolves. These northern Cattle are not vicious but fight desperately when cornered. Bulls await a favorable moment to rush forward and gore the attackers with their horns, then return to the circle of defense.

If Musk Oxen see a chance to escape they are strangely agile considering their short legs. Often they run to the mountains, ascending rocky cliffs with the ease of Goats.

The herds which live today in Canada, north and northwest of Hudson Bay and east and northeast to Greenland's coast, are the last of a relic species which used to live in Alaska and all over bleak arctic America. A small herd has been introduced from Greenland to Nunivak Island, off the coast of Alaska. They are represented in Siberia and northern Europe today only by fossil forms.

Their genus name *Ovibos* comes from two Latin words, *ovis* meaning Sheep, *bos* meaning Ox. Their species name *moschatus* means musk.

MOUNTAIN SHEEP
Bighorn
(genus *Ovis*)

The wild Mountain Sheep of America are large handsome animals standing a little over

Cattle Family

three feet high at the shoulders and are about four and a half feet long. The rams have mag-

Mountain Sheep

nificent horns, the horns of the ewes are smaller.

These Sheep are acrobats, daring and nimble, and accustomed to life almost above the clouds. They like ledges and cliffs, not the mountaintops. Here they leap fearlessly from rock to rock, clamber down inclines where man and many animals of prey would not dare to follow, where a misstep would mean death. Proudly carrying their very large and heavy horns, the rams run and jump with ease and travel along ledges hundreds of feet above the valleys. Only the Mountain Goat is so sure-footed.

In the summer early in the morning these wild Sheep browse up steep inclines, nibbling on scrubby bushes and mountain plants, rarely grass. (In the Yellowstone during one month, July, they are reported to eat considerable grass.) At noon they rest on some rocky headland where they can scan the surrounding country. By midafternoon they wend their way down again to the cliff rim or the high slope where they will sleep. Here they can see enemies below and any coming from above would give warning by starting pebbles rolling. Each Sheep returns to the same bed every night, a spot he has scraped out for himself. The beds lie close together. The herds are small, perhaps a dozen or a dozen and a half in summer, larger in the winter, may be as many as fifty.

When the snows in the mountains are heavy the wild Sheep wander down into the lower hills, often enter the valleys in search of food. Then they may become easy prey to Wolves or Mountain Lions. However, the Bighorns' greatest enemy is man. The sportsman has always sought the handsome horns as trophies. Also their meat is good eating.

The one lamb is born in March or April and stays with the mother during the first summer and autumn.

Like the Mountain Lion the Mountain Sheep are at home in many climates. They are found from the icy mountains of coastal Alaska to the dry deserts of Arizona where the temperature often runs over 100 degrees and where water is scarce.

Within this long range there are several species and subspecies which differ slightly in size and color. The typical Bighorn of the Rocky Mountains is grayish brown with yellowish-white under parts in summer, a little lighter in winter. The Dall Mountain Sheep of Alaska and the Kenai Peninsula is nearly pure white. The Stone Bighorn of northern British Columbia and the Yukon is iron gray, sometimes almost black and is then known as the Black Sheep.

The Desert Bighorn is much paler than the typical Bighorn. He lives in a country where he must contend with heat and drought, not snow and cold. He can go without water longer than can domestic Sheep but he drinks, at least at certain seasons, and is often killed near the high natural rock tanks in the desert. In late summer and fall he feeds on the juicy fruits of cactus. Other feed consists of such desert plants as mountain mahogany, wild onions, yellow trumpet flower, Mexican tea plant. During the blazing heat of summer days he rests in a cool cave. Here the young Desert Bighorn is born.

Open season for Bighorns is now offered in few states. In spite of the fact that these handsome Sheep are given protection in many places, they seem to be decreasing. The cause cannot be animals of prey because they too are decreasing. Golden Eagles which carry off lambs are now scarce. The worst animal enemy of the Sheep, the Mountain Lion, is nearly exterminated. Overhunted in the past, the Bighorns are now finding it difficult to compete with domestic Sheep which drive them from some of their former range. However, the most important cause of the decline in numbers in the wild herds seems to be scabies, the disease which they apparently caught from the domestic animals.

The genus name of the wild Sheep is *Ovis,* Latin word for Sheep.

Rocky Mountain Goat

Mountaineer

ROCKY MOUNTAIN GOAT
WHITE GOAT
(genus *Oreamnos*)

Cattle Family

The wild Mountain Goat of America is not a true Goat but is more closely related to the Chamois of the old-world Antelopes. He looks so much like a Goat that it is easy to understand why he has no other common name. He is rather comical in appearance with his ample beard, his beautiful white hair which grows long all over the body down to the ankles where it is suddenly short above the smart black hoofs, making the alpine animal look as if he were dressed in a woolly ski suit. Males average under 300 pounds in weight.

These Goats have been extensively hunted by sportsmen but the black horns, common to both sexes, are small, give these animals less value as trophies than the Bighorns. Perhaps this is the reason that they have survived in greater numbers than their cousins.

Then too although they may range down almost to sea level, they prefer to live all year above timber line and are so hardy that they can stand the raging blizzards on fierce, windy heights. The snow does not drive them to the valleys and they have therefore been less preyed upon by Mountain Lions than have the wild Sheep.

When Lewis and Clark explored the northwest they reported that the fine wool of these wild Goats was used extensively by the native tribes. The Goats then probably ranged as far south as the region of California. They are not found today south of the Columbia River region in Oregon. They are quite scarce in Washington, Idaho, and Montana, more common in their range northward through Alberta and British Columbia to the mountains of coastal Alaska. Their native homeland is wild, bleak, and cold. Sure-footed, agile, they are wonderful climbers.

Oddly enough, they have recently become established in quite a different kind of home. They were never native east of the continental divide. Several which were brought from the Rocky Mountain National Park were exhibited at the Custer State Park Zoo in the Black Hills of South Dakota. One day two escaped, fled to the Harvey National Forest where they hid on Harvey Peak. Mount Harvey is a little over 7000 feet in altitude and the highest point in the United States east of the Rockies but it does not offer arctic mountain climate to which these Goats are accustomed. The summers there are very hot. But the peak has rocky bluffs, some caves, few Lions, no Bears or Wolves and here the two Goats thrived. In the heat of summer they stayed in the caves as the desert Mountain Sheep have learned to do. Luckily one was a ewe, one a ram. Soon there was one kid, perhaps two. One is the usual number of young in this family. Since then their numbers have increased to twenty-five. The herd seems to be thriving nicely on aspen and birch, some grass and lichens in the winter.

In Mount Rainier National Park they browse on huckleberry, rattlesnake plantains, brambles, and many other mountain plants.

Oreamnos, the genus name, comes from the Greek *oros* (mountain) and *amnos* (Lamb).

PRONGHORN ANTELOPE
AMERICAN ANTELOPE
PRONG BUCK
(genus *Antilocapra*)

Pronghorn Family
(family *Antilocapridae*)

The Pronghorn is one of our most beautiful animals. Dainty, fawn-colored, he is strikingly marked by white under his belly and chin and on sides of the face. Most conspicuous of all are

Pronghorned Antelope

the flashing white rosettes of hair on his rump. These rump patches are an Antelope's signal station. When the creature is alarmed the hairs on the rosettes stand up and make the spots visible at a great distance. He can signal to his friends one or even two miles away, then bound off over the plains on his slender legs at tremendous speed.

American Antelopes are intensely curious animals. Rather timid and shy, their curiosity often leads them into danger. They can be lured into gunshot by a red rag hung on a tree.

They also like to race, even with horsemen, and overtaking the rider may bound foolishly across in front. Man and his rifle have been the Pronghorn's worst enemy although Wolves preyed on the young in the days when Wolves were abundant. The fawns, usually twins, are born in the spring. The mother will fight bravely for the lives of her young, striking hard blows at her attackers with her sharp front hoofs.

Early reports say that Antelopes were once as numerous as the Buffalo on the plains but because of their protective coloring and their swift flight they never made as great a mass showing. They ranged over an enormous territory, making their home on the plains from what is now Edmonton, Alberta, south into Mexico, west among the mountains and over the plateaus to the Pacific coast. Like the Bison many were destroyed.

But unlike the Bison they seem able to adapt themselves to the range as they find it today. They are making a healthy comeback. Within the safety of park refuges they are rapidly increasing, there being about 165,000 on government and private land in the United States alone.

The name Antelope has become firmly established as the common name of the beautiful Pronghorn of America, although the animal does not belong to the same family as the old-world Antelopes. No true Antelope ever has branching or pronged horns. These pronged horns curve backward like a Goat's and are formed like all cattle horns of a horny sheath over a permanent bony core. Yet unlike any Goat or other member of the Cattle Family this Pronghorn sheds the horny sheaths in October or November and grows new ones in the spring much as members of the Deer Family shed their antlers and grow new ones. Neither Antelope, Goat, nor Deer, he is scientifically classified by himself in genus *Antilocapra* of family *Antilocapridae*. These words come from the Greek *antilo* (Antelope) and Latin *capra* (Goat) which places him in an intermediate position between the old-world Antelopes and the Goats.

Border Animal

PECCARY
JAVELINA
MUSK HOG
WILD PIG
(genus *Tagassu*)

Peccary Family
(family *Tagassuidae*)

This small Hoofed Animal is quite different from other American animals with hoofs. He is frequently called a Wild Pig and he looks most like a member of the Pig Family. But true Pigs are not native to North or South America. They all come from the old world. It is probable that the Peccary and the true Pig had a common ancestor and when Asia and North America were joined by a land bridge, this remote ancestor came to the new world. But the American Peccary of today is not closely enough related to the common Pig to be included in his family. He is formed so differently that he is put in a family by himself.

He has a complicated stomach like other American Hoofed Animals but he is not a ruminant, a "cud chewer." He has a full set of teeth in both jaws and his canine teeth are tusklike and look like the teeth of a meat eater, one of the carnivorous group, rather than a member of the browsers. His strong piglike snout is used to root out the variety of food that he enjoys.

The Peccary is a southern animal, common south of the Mexican border and in South America. Two subspecies come over the border into extreme southern Texas, Arizona, and New Mexico. Both are grizzled gray and black in color, have long coarse hair and a mane of stiff hairs which stand up all along the back from head to rump. They weigh from forty-five to fifty pounds. They travel in small bands through the dense cover of chaparral, hunt among sand dunes, in caves, along canyons for insects and reptiles, for

acorns and juniper berries, for worms and snakes, for roots and cactus fruit and wild potatoes and many other foods which they like. They are desert animals but farther south are found in the mountains.

Once abundant, they have been killed in large numbers for their hides which are used as pigskin for gloves. They are also killed for their meat which is good if the musk gland over the hips is immediately removed. So strong is the scent from this gland that herds of Peccaries may often be smelled at quite a distance.

The family name *Tagassuidae* comes from the Amazon Indian *tupi tagasú*, a Peccary, plus *suidae* from the Latin *sus*, a Pig.

Peccary

DEER FAMILY
(family *Cervidae*)

The members of this family have handsome branching antlers which in all American species are shed once a year. This process is remarkable when one considers the great length and sweep of some antlers.

The growth which takes place within a few months happens as follows. Buck Deer have two solid bony bumps or pedicles which appear on the front of their skulls shortly after birth. These bumps are covered with knobs of velvety skin.

When the antlers begin to grow, this skin becomes sensitive. A hard bony substance is deposited forming a burr or a coronet around the pedicle. As the antler grows it is soft and covered with velvetlike, hairy skin which is full of blood vessels. The antler reaches full growth in the late summer or early fall when the bucks rub them against tree trunks, scraping away the dried blood vessels and skin, polishing the exposed bony structure which shows clearly the path of the blood vessels.

One cannot, as commonly supposed, tell the age of a Deer by the size of his antlers. The animal has but a single spike the first year. The Black-tailed Deer usually has branched spikes the second year, three points the third year, but thereafter no regular increase in number of tines, as the points are called. The eastern White-tailed Deer may have three or four points the third year. With very old age the bucks may have fewer tines, smaller antlers than younger animals.

The growth of antlers is generally considered a secondary sexual characteristic, like the beard of a man. With the exception of the Caribou, they grow only on bucks. They are of no use to the males during spring and summer because they are soft, and since in many species they are shed soon after the mating season, they are not present when they might be of great use in fighting off hungry winter animals of prey. For many months the buck's only weapons of defense are his sharp front hoofs with which he can strike a vicious blow.

The antlers are primarily used during the rutting or breeding season for combat between bucks. Sometimes during a struggle the great branching antlers of two males become entwined, the animals are locked together and suffer a slow death.

The scientific family name *Cervidae* comes from the Latin word *cervus* meaning a Deer.

The Deer Family is divided into four genera or groups, the Deer, the Moose, the Elk, and the Caribou. Teeth are lacking in the front part of their upper jaws but some Deer have more teeth than do members of the Cattle Family.

The Broad Jumpers

MULE DEER   **Deer Family**
BLACK-TAILED DEER
(genus *Odocoileus*)

This western Deer gets his common name from his large ears. His is not mulelike in form although he is heavier-set than the White-tailed Deer from which he is easily distinguished by the size of his ears, by the black tip to the end of his tail, and by the shape of his antlers which have branching prongs. In color the hair on the back is yellowish or tawny brown, the under parts darker, the rump patches white. In winter his coat is gray.

When in action the Mule Deer do not raise their tails like flags as the White-tailed Deer do. They may also be recognized by their peculiar gait. Instead of running, they spring off the ground with all four feet at once, landing again on all fours, progressing by jerky, stiff-legged bounds. Not as swift on level ground as the white-tailed forms, in their own country, open badlands or open forest, they are superior to running animals because their gait is suited for broad jumping over broken terrain.

The Rocky Mountain or typical Mule Deer is the largest of the small Deer. His ears and eyes are very large. Bucks average from 200 to 300 pounds in weight, sometimes weighing as much as 500 pounds. These animals live in open country or open forest, being most often at home where rough, steep slopes may be found. There with their peculiar bounding gait they flee swiftly up or down hill. They prefer to escape enemies by flight rather than by hiding in thickets.

In summer the bucks particularly enjoy the

Mule Deer

heights of rocky ridges where, with their sensitive growing antlers, they are free from the pest of flies. By day they may frequently be seen resting near the top of a ridge where they have a clear view of the surrounding country where they may see an approaching enemy.

In winter Mule Deer move to the foothills.

In the Rocky Mountain region the antlers of the bucks commence to grow in April. They peel the velvet in September just before the mating season which usually occurs in November. Antlers are shed again from January to March.

The sexes herd together only part of the winter. When the fawns are born, the does are alone.

Twins are usual with Mule Deer, rarely one fawn and rarely three. The young Deer are very pretty with white-spotted, tawny coats and whitish bellies. In August or September they molt their baby hair and lose their spots.

The fawns are prey to Coyotes, Bobcats, and Golden Eagles. Old Deer and wounded animals fall prey to Mountain Lions and Wolves.

Like their cousins the White-tailed Deer, the Mule Deer are dainty feeders. They browse for leaves, buds, seed capsules, and the flowers of a great variety of bushes and plants. Among their favorite foods are mountain mahogany, raspberry, and rosebushes. They usually do not eat grass except in the spring.

There are several species of Mule Deer, all like the typical form except for slight variation in size of body and antlers and in color. The Desert Mule Deer or Burro Deer which lives in the western desert regions of the United States is large with heavy antlers, but like most desert animals pale in color. The Mexican Mule Deer is also pale but smaller. He is found near the Mexican border in western Texas, New Mexico, and Arizona. The California Mule Deer is another southern species, small, cinnamon brown in color with a dark stripe running down his back and onto the upper part of his tail. Others are found from British Columbia to California and east to Oklahoma and Kansas.

The genus *Odocoileus* includes all of the small American Deer. The name is derived from two Greek words, *odon* (tooth) and *koilos* (hollow).

COLUMBIAN BLACK-TAILED DEER
COAST DEER
MULE DEER
(genus *Odocoileus*)

Deer Family

This Black-tailed Deer has the same stocky body as the typical Mule Deer, the same branching antler tines, the same way of running with stiff-legged bounds, but is slightly smaller, the ears while broad and mulelike are slightly shorter; the tail is wider and instead of being black-tipped is black on all the upper surface, white beneath. The white rump patches are absent although there is white between the hind legs. The main coat of the Columbian Black-tailed Deer is tawny to reddish yellow with whitish under parts in summer, grayer in winter. Bucks weigh up to 200 pounds. They range from British Columbia south to northern California.

In habits they differ from the closely related common Mule Deer. They are wary and cautious, preferring to hide rather than to depend on flight to save them from enemies. They make their home in dense, leafy forests of the humid coast both in the mountains and in the lowlands. Here they hide in the chaparral or among the thick foliage of the trees from the Mountain Lions which will attack full-grown Deer, and smaller animals which prey upon the fawns. They have survived better than any other species, perhaps because they are so wary. They are abundant in Oregon.

The Columbian Black-tailed Deer breed in October or November. The pretty spotted fawns are born in May or June, sometimes as early as March. The young ones lose their spots in the autumn.

The bucks shed their antlers in January or February and by the first of September the velvet is usually gone from the new growth of bone.

Like the common Mule Deer they browse for leaves, seed capsules, the tip end of branches, the berries and buds of a variety of trees, plants, and shrubs. They are fond of buckbrush, barberries, mountain mahogany, willows, ferns, raspberries, and in the fall they eat acorns. They also like fruit and fungi.

There are several varieties of these Deer. A southern one has larger ears than the typical species and its color is paler. He lives in the coastal region of California south of San Francisco Bay. The Sitka Black-tailed Deer of south-eastern Alaska and the islands of the Alaskan Archipelago is smaller, with shorter ears, and black on the tip half of his tail.

The Flag-tailed Deer

WHITE-TAILED DEER
VIRGINIA DEER
FLAG-TAIL, FAN-TAIL
(genus *Odocoileus*)

Deer Family

Few country dwellers but are familiar with the Deer which raises a white flag when he is alarmed. The brilliant white underhairs of the tail flash when this Deer runs or high-jumps cleanly over fence or fallen log, giving away his identity as clearly as if he shouted his name. The color of the coat is reddish rust in summer, brownish gray in winter, white under parts. The fawns, usually two in number, are pretty, tawny brown, spotted with white. They lose their spotty baby coat in the molt of fall. Now and then an albino baby is born.

The Flag-tail has figured as one of the most important American animals since colonial days. Not only did the settlers of the eastern seaboard shoot him for his fine-quality venison but they made their clothes out of buckskin. Today this animal is considered one of the best game animals.

Native hardiness coupled with wise conservation has saved these pretty animals. They are probably as plentiful now as they were when the new world was discovered. Forest Deer, they do not like dense woods but prefer open glades, thickets, and brushland such as is common over much of our deforested country. They are shy but thrive in the brush near populated communities.

Like other Deer the White-tails are browsing animals, eating a great variety of twigs and leaves, berries and buds and seed capsules of plants, trees, and shrubs. In their northern range during winter they make yards or runways through the deep snow which they keep open by trampling. In this restricted area the needles of balsam fir form a large part of their diet. They also eat the needles of pine, spruce, white cedar, the tips of willow and birch branches and a little grass.

The favorite food of the Minnesota White-tail in fall and winter is balsam fir and species of pine and willow and birch family. In central Wisconsin they eat among other things the leaves and twigs of oaks, sweet fern, wintergreen, willows, red maple, dock, soybeans, witch hazel, acorns, sumac, low-bush blueberry, aspen.

In summer they like to browse on the suckers growing from old stumps. They also like dogwood, honeysuckle, heath, laurel, nettle, pond lilies, deer grass, wild raspberry and blackberry, and a great variety of other plants, some fungi, mosses, and algae, and eat beechnuts as well as acorns when they appear in the fall.

The bucks shed their antlers a few weeks after mating season or during the winter up to March. The new antlers begin to grow a few weeks later and are full branched in late summer. In early September the bucks rub off the velvet against trees. Mating takes place from late October to early December. Like all Deer they are polygamous, the bucks battle for the does and are bold and cross at this season.

The Virginia Deer is distributed from the Atlantic seaboard west to the Pacific coast, and from Ontario and Alberta south to the Gulf of Mexico, and in the east to Florida. Several species and subspecies live in different parts of the country and differ from each other only in size of body and antlers and slight color variation. The Northern White-tailed Deer is large, has a wide antler spread, a redder coat in summer, and is found in northern New England, northern New York, west to Wisconsin and Minnesota, and in Ontario. The Western White-tail, Plains White-tail or Bannertail is paler in color. The Texan White-tail is also pale, smaller than the typical species, shorter of leg, smaller of antler. The Louisiana White-tail of the Gulf states is also pale but with heavier antlers, while the Florida White-tail is small and dark. The Arizona White-tail is small and like most desert animals pale. The Columbia or Oregon White-tail is very similar to the Plains White-tail. The Keys Deer which lives on the Keys off

Florida is the smallest of the group and pale.

The Cougar is enemy of all small Deer but is no longer abundant. In the deep snows Wolves and Dogs and Coyotes can pull down full-grown White-tails. Other enemies include the Lynx and Wolverine.

American Stag

WAPITI
ELK
(genus *Cervus*)

Deer Family

These large handsome Deer are among the most important game animals in America. A buck may weigh from 700 to 1000 pounds. His great branching rack of antlers may have from five to seven tines or points on each side and in record cases a spread of five feet.

Elk antlers and the mounted heads are trophies which all sportsmen prize. Elks were also sought for their canine teeth, absent in some Deer but rather large in bull Elk. These teeth were formerly used as a symbol of a fraternal order, the Elks.

In colonial times Wapiti were distributed over the greater part of the United States and southern Canada. They were exterminated in the east and for a time their existence was threatened in the west. They were given protection and have made a remarkable recovery. Their range has been reduced to the Rocky Mountain area and local sections of British Columbia, Manitoba, and Saskatchewan but today there are open seasons in many of the western states. During 1939 it was estimated by the Wildlife Survey that there were well over 200,000 of these big Deer in the states on government and private land. They became so numerous in Yellowstone that there was a shortage of their winter browse and several thousand had to be killed. Recently some have been introduced to an island off the coast of Alaska where they will do well if they do not increase to such an extent that they rob the Caribou and Sheep of food.

Like all of their family, Elk browse on leaves and twigs of a variety of plants, trees, and shrubs. In the spring they turn to the high mountains going slowly up into the forests, even up to timber line. In the early fall the snows crowd them out, and they go slowly back to the valleys in small bands. Soon the bugle call of the bulls is heard challenging other bulls to combat over the cows. Their antlers are now free of velvet and polished ready to do terrible battle. Occasionally the great racks interlock, then both combatants are doomed.

The spotted young are born in May or early July, usually one calf to a cow, but sometimes twins, rarely three. Their baby coats are molted in the autumn, replaced with a tawny-brown hair.

The name Wapiti is an Indian name and is the only one that should be used for this Deer. The settlers misnamed the animal Elk. Close cousin to the Stag of Europe, the Wapiti does not look like the old-world Elk. But the name Elk is now firmly established for this American Deer.

The genus name *Cervus* means Deer.

Largest Deer

MOOSE
(genus *Alces*)

Deer Family

This largest member of the American Deer Family is also found in the deep forest of northern Scandinavia and Russia where he is known as the Elk. The Moose looks like a beast which has sur-

White-tailed Deer

vived from prehistoric days. The animal is stately but grotesque. Bulls average from 900 to 1400 pounds. Their magnificent, widespread, scooped antlers are trophies prized by sportsmen and may reach a width of six feet. A hairy tuft of skin and hair hanging under the neck and called a bell is characteristic. It becomes heavier and short in old males. Another characteristic is the oddly shaped nose which hangs well over the underlip. The high-shouldered, heavy body is carried upon long, rather slender legs. Females are much smaller and without antlers.

During the summer and winter months the bull Moose is very shy, will stalk through the forest scarcely making a sound. When running the Moose does not gallop or jump but has a sort of shifty gait, shaking his head as he moves. It is remarkable how the male animal with such an antler spread can travel easily through the thick forest. When he comes to a fallen log he steps over the obstacle with his long-legged stride without slacking his pace.

In the fall during mating season he is bold, will crash through the underbrush in response to the call of a cow or of another challenging bull. In battle the bull Moose fights not only with his enormous antlers but strikes out savagely with his front feet.

In the summer, Moose feed mostly upon water plants. They can be seen standing belly-deep, with their heads entirely underwater, searching for pond-lily roots. At times they go completely under the surface.

In the winter when food is scarce they live on green wood and particularly the pitchy foliage of evergreens. During this period of the year Moose stay well concealed in the forests. In the northern part of their range where the snows become too deep to walk about they tramp many paths in the snow, forming a labyrinth sometimes covering several acres. These places are called Moose yards and here several families stay until the early spring when they wander down through the meadows and browse upon the tender branches of willow, birch, and maple. They also eat mushrooms, some grasses and sedges, asters, the leaves and twigs of mountain ash, alder, poplar, and other trees.

In the fall of the year Moose hunting is a favorite sport among big-game hunters. The bull Moose is often lured into gunshot range by sounds from the hunter's birch-bark horn which imitates the call of a cow Moose.

The young are not spotted like the fawns of most other members of the American Deer Family. They are reddish brown. There is usually but one calf the first year, two the next, rarely three. The adults are very dark brown in color.

Moose today are found in northern North America from the arctic forests south to Maine and Minnesota and in a narrow belt down the Rockies in the United States. The Wildlife survey of 1939 estimated that there were over 14,000 of these biggest Deer on government and private lands within their rather restricted range in the United States.

There are several forms of Moose. Their antlers differ greatly in shape. The largest species, the Alaska Moose, weighs as much as 1800 pounds.

The genus name for the Moose, *Alces*, is Latin for Elk.

Deer of the Far North

CARIBOU
REINDEER
(genus *Rangifer*)

Deer Family

This is the only member of the Deer Family in which both males and females bear antlers. Does' antlers are smaller than the bucks', the fawns have one straight spike the first year. The full rack of antlers looks quite unlike those of other Deer. They vary greatly among individuals but one or both brow tines (points) are usually flattened like shovels. They are not used for shoveling snow as

Moose

Caribou

is sometimes supposed. The animal digs away snow to find food with his hoofs.

The hoofs of a Caribou are sharp, round, and wide and cup-shaped, formed for traveling over ice and snow in winter, and over the swampy tundra of the north during the arctic summer.

These are medium-sized Deer. The mountain bucks weigh a little over 350 pounds average, the females less. The different species closely resemble each other, although they are generally divided into three groups, the Mountain Caribou, the Woodland Caribou, and the Barren Ground Caribou. They have their greatest abundance in the land where few kinds of animals can survive the winter, where the arctic night is long, bitterly cold, and where food is scarce. Arctic Wolves prey on these Deer of the north but their worst enemy is the hunter with a gun.

Alaska-Yukon Caribou are essentially mountain animals. They are frequently found on the swampy tundra of the arctic coast, but real Caribou land in this territory is above timber line. In the Mount McKinley Park area they are nearly always found in open country. They do enter the woods seeking mushrooms and lichens but they more often seek open ridges where the wind sweeps away the snow in winter.

They are herd animals and during some years immense migrations have been reported. Formerly abundant at different seasons, over the whole Alaskan-Yukon Territory, they are now gone from the Kenai Peninsula and are being driven from range where European Reindeer have been introduced, but herds in the interior are thriving, there being an estimated population of one or two millions. During 1921 a herd of probably a half million was observed on the march. The animals were scattered over an area about sixty miles wide and took twenty days to pass a certain point, although on some days as few as a hundred animals went by. Other days as many as 1500 were counted.

Many reasons for these occasional migrations have been offered. They have no relation to shelter because the animals move to the same type of territory they have left. There is a seasonal movement in the Mount McKinley district from the southern slopes where they summer to the north where the slopes are blown free of snow in winter. But when enormous herds make a mass migration it is thought to be associated with the slow growth of lichens. Lichens take from fifteen to twenty years to reach a height of four or five inches in the north. The instinct which leads the animals to migrate now and then is fortunate because it is estimated that every animal would need from forty to sixty acres of browsing land if they did not move.

They are good swimmers and cross streams during migrations. A doe generally leads the herd.

In the winter they eat grasses and mosses as well as lichens but in spring they like to browse the willow and birch tips; also they may root out stores of arctic Mice when they are very hungry, and herders report that they even eat the Mice when food is scarce. The European Reindeer gnaw their discarded antlers, probably for the minerals they contain. Perhaps the American Caribou also have this habit.

When these arctic Deer run they move with a swinging trot, their ankle tendons make a clicking sound. Fawns and does grunt to each other, the bucks are more silent.

In September the bucks get fat. A layer of tallow two or three inches thick at the rump lies on their backs. This was formerly thought to be a reserve food supply for winter but is now known to be used during the rutting season when the bucks fight strenuously over the does. Bucks are thin at the end of the breeding season. The does and the fawns do not get particularly fat in the fall.

During the cold months the does and bucks sometimes herd separately, the yearlings herd together in the spring. The fawns are born from mid-May to mid-June. They are able to trot after their mothers soon after birth.

The large antlers of the old bucks begin to grow in late April. They carry the tender new growths carefully, try not to bruise them. They

Wapiti

shed the velvet in early September, the antlers themselves are shed in November and December. The does may keep their antlers until late spring, even June, or until the fawns are born.

The fawns may have a faint suggestion of spots but they have the same general color pattern as the adults, lacking the white neck. Bucks are cinnamon brown with white necks and whitish and grizzled sides and under parts and fine long white beards. Does are often paler. They all fade during the winter to a dirty white and in June shed their coats, grow new ones by July or August. Individuals vary greatly in color.

The Barren Ground Caribou are rather smaller with lighter antlers. They are closely related to the Reindeer of Europe and they make their home on the great stretches of tundra in the north. The Woodland Caribou is more southerly in range in the east, was formerly abundant in Maine, but is now gone from that territory. He is heavier and with stockier antlers. The southern range of the Mountain Caribou is now just over the Canadian border into Minnesota in the United States where only fifteen of these animals were recorded during the last Biological Survey.

The coat of the typical Caribou is gray brown on upper parts, whitish on under parts, lighter in winter. The Peary Caribou of Ellesmere Land is very light in summer and white in winter save for a few grayish-brown hairs on the back.

The genus name *Rangifer* is medieval Latin for Reindeer.

Chapter VIII
With Claw and Fang

THE FLESH EATERS
(order *Carnivora*)

The Flesh Eaters form a large group of native American mammals which include many game and fur animals. They vary enormously in size from the tiny Least Weasel which is but half a foot long to the giant Kadiak Bear which may weigh three quarters of a ton and whose footprint may be fourteen inches long.

The members differ greatly in appearance but all have claws and are well furred. Their jaws are formed for seizing prey and eating meat. Sometimes the canine teeth are tusklike.

All are four-legged animals adapted for living on the ground, but some spend part of their lives in trees, some have their homes under the earth, and a few spend much of their time in the water, although none are specialized for life in the sea as are the Walrus and Seal Group. The feet of a few are webbed and these swim well.

Some eat a quantity of vegetables and fruits but most of the carnivores live on a meat diet. Their group name, order *Carnivora*, comes from two Latin words, *caro* (flesh) and *vorare* (to devour).

THE WEASEL FAMILY
(family *Mustelidae*)

The Weasel Family is large and diverse. All members are small or medium-sized. Some are long and slender, others broad and squat. Some live on the ground, others live in trees, one spends nearly his entire life in the sea.

The Weasels which live in North America north of the Mexican border are divided into nine genera, or groups. They are the true Weasels which include the Minks and Ferrets; the Striped Skunks, the Spotted Skunks, the Hog-nosed Skunks, the Martens and Fishers, the Wolverines, the Badgers, the Land Otters, and the Sea Otters.

The family name *Mustelidae* comes from the Latin *mustela*, a Weasel.

A Small But Savage Mammal

WEASEL
ERMINE
STOAT
(genus *Mustela*)

Weasel Family

The Weasel has a long, slender, sinuous body and a ferocious temper quite out of keeping with his small size. This little animal seems to kill just for the love of killing. His natural food is the blood of his victims, sucked from a wound in the neck or head. There are records of one Weasel killing thirty or forty chickens in a night, and when one of his kind dens up near a chicken pen he has to be caught. However, the harm done by a few is more than balanced by the number of

Weasel

Rats and Mice killed by other Weasels. A lone Rat is credited with killing 190 baby chickens in a night and his kind also destroy many young birds on game farms.

In their native haunts Weasels hunt by night but are also about by day. They ferret out Chipmunks, rob birds' nests, eat insects such as grasshoppers and beetles and earthworms. In the West they prey upon Striped Ground Squirrels. Large Weasels catch Rabbits many times their size. All Weasels are the terror of Rodents. Small, narrow-bodied, they slip into crevices, follow frightened little animals into their holes. When on a hunt they often stop, rise up on their hind legs, and sway their heads from side to side, then hearing or smelling prey, they scurry over the ground, following like a dog by scent. Although they are ground animals, they often follow their prey up trees and are good climbers. When put in a cage with a large Rat they are said to make the Rat cringe and give up without a struggle.

Fearless, they do not even seem afraid of man. They do not leave settled areas. Boldly they follow stone walls and often enter buildings. Great wanderers, they may cover more than a hundred acres in a night. Very curious, confident in their strength, they are easily trapped. Although never numerous, they hold their range in spite of their value as fur bearers.

Ferocious and relentless foes, they are among the few mammals which seem to stay mated for any length of time. They breed in midsummer. The young Weasels, from four to six, sometimes twelve in number, are born in early spring in the southern part of their range but not until June in the arctic. Their home is a burrow under a rock ledge, stone wall, barn, or in a hollow log or the burrow of another animal. The father Weasel helps the female bring Mice and other food to the babies and even after the young are gone from the nest, a pair of Weasels may be found in one den.

There are some thirty-six species or subspecies of these small creatures which live in a variety of habitats all over the North American continent from the southern lowlands to the arctic barren grounds. They may at once be recognized by their form, by the strong musky odor common to members of the Weasel Family, and by the color of their fur which in summer is brown above, white below with black-tipped tail. In winter they are pure white save for the black-tipped tail. A slight variation in size, shade of fur, separates the several kinds of Weasels from each other. Only the Least Weasel lacks the typical black tail tip. All the males are larger than the females.

A Weasel does not, as was formerly thought, suddenly change the color of his brown hairs to white when the first snow falls. He molts his brown hairs slowly in the fall, taking up to a month to grow a new, pure-white coat. In the spring he sheds the white hairs and grows his summer fur of brown and white. The time of change depends upon the climate. In the northern part of the range he gets his white coat early. In the south he may stay brown all winter. However, a species that changes from brown to pure white molts this same way even if he is taken from his cold home to a steam-heated apartment. The color change is one of the inherited traits of certain geographic species.

The large Tundra or Arctic Weasel is a close relative of the old-world Stoat or Ermine. All of the northern Weasels which turn white in winter are known in the market as ermine. Ermine was formerly worn only by royalty. For the coronation of King George VI 50,000 Canadian Ermine were said to have been used for trimming clothes.

Today the brown summer fur is as valuable as the white, but the coats of those changing color are worth but a few pennies.

The Least Weasel and his close relatives are the smallest of the carnivorous mammals. They are the dwarfs of the Weasel Family. In Alaska, the land of the largest Carnivores, the Big Brown Bears, these midget Weasels, scarcely as big as a Squirrel, feed upon Mice, Shrews, Lemmings. The Eskimos admire these little hunters. They often trim the belts of their sons with the fur. They believe that the fighting spirit of the little Weasel will in this way be transferred to the bodies of the boys.

Farther south the Least Weasels live about farms, or in woods, or under stone walls. Their main diet is Field Mice.

Bonaparte's Weasel is a common Weasel in New York state, New England, west among the woods of the Great Lakes region into British Columbia. He also lives in Labrador and southeastern coastal Alaska.

The New York Weasel is common from central New England south to North Carolina, west to Illinois. In the southern part of his range he does not change from brown to white coat in winter.

The Bridled Weasel is a large southern Weasel with a long tail and with white markings on his head. He lives in rich bottom lands of stream valleys and in fields, although he has been found high in the hills of Kansas, and apparently wanders far. He makes war on Pocket Gophers and Mice.

Other species and subspecies of Weasels are found from Florida to California and north to Alaska and to the arctic. Their genus name *Mustela* is Latin for a Weasel.

A Giant Weasel

THE BLACK-FOOTED FERRET
(genus *Mustela*)

Weasel Family

This is a large Weasel, big cousin of the Least Weasel, Bonaparte's Weasel, the Arctic Weasel, and the other smaller Weasels. His closest relative is the Siberian Ferret. Males reach twenty-three inches in length.

In color this husky Weasel is buff yellow and brownish on the back, cream yellow underneath. His paws, a band across his eyes, and the tip of his tail are black.

The home of the Black-footed Ferret is the Great Plains where the Prairie Dogs live, from northern Montana and western North Dakota to Texas, east of the main range of the Rockies.

Great wanderers, they are sometimes found high in the mountains. Prairie Dogs are their main food. With the character of their kind, they stand up in Dog towns, sway their heads back and forth, look nervously around. Then, spying a little Dog, they pursue him into his hole.

They are curious, and great fighters, killing Rabbits, birds, and eating bird eggs. When disturbed by a hunter, they duck into a doghole, but soon boldly thrust up their heads to look at their enemy and are easily shot. When cornered, they hiss and fight, but can be tamed.

Black-footed Ferret

The Water Weasel

MINK
(genus *Mustela*)

This member of the true Weasels has webbed hind feet, spends much of his life along stream banks. Not as specialized a water animal as the Otter, the Mink is a swift swimmer and catches trout. In the winter he does not hibernate. When streams are frozen, the tracks of the restless Mink may often be seen coming up from the icy river water and leading over the snow to another air-

Mink

hole. This animal like his Weasel cousins is a wanderer, may cover as much as a hundred acres in a single night. He is also active by day.

The Mink is about the size of the Ferret, has rich dark-brown fur. This fur is one of the most expensive in the market, is used for high-priced women's coats. These animals are one of the two important fur bearers which have been raised with commercial success in captivity. Carefully selected stock are bred for rich, dark fur, and bring a better price than many of the trapped animals. Southern stock have lighter furs and are less valuable.

This member of the Weasel Family weighs about two pounds, averages two feet in length. Females are much smaller. The animals are solitary, except during the breeding season. The mother Mink usually makes her den in the banks of a stream and lines it with grass, feathers, leaves. She may also den up under a rock or tree root. The young, five or six to a litter, are born in April or May. There is but one litter a season.

The adults live on frogs and crayfish as well as fish. They also catch Muskrat. Restless and inquisitive, they do not always stay close to water but pursue Rabbits away from riverbanks, sometimes visit hen yards where they display a true Weasel's lust for killing more than they can eat.

In spite of their popularity as fur bearers, Mink are holding most of their original range which includes wooded stream areas from Florida and the Gulf of Mexico north to the arctic barren grounds. The Alaska Mink is very large.

There is but one species of Mink with several closely related subspecies.

Common Skunk

Unpopular But Valuable Mammal

COMMON SKUNK
Large Striped Skunk
(genus *Mephitis*)

Weasel Family

The Common Skunk dares to face another mammal many times his size. Slow-moving, deliberate, he keeps on his way down the center of a path and has but to raise his large bushy tail to scare much larger animals. The Skunk's weapon is stronger than claw or fang. The odor of the yellow liquid in his two scent glands is so strong that few care to brave it. Since the Skunk can throw this liquid twelve feet, and the scent is carried far on the wind, the animal is more often smelled than seen. The common belief that the Skunk shakes the scent from the hairs of his bushy tail is not true. He looks as though he did, but actually he ejects the scent directly from the glands.

Dogs will kill Skunks and a few of the larger Flesh Eaters as well as Owls and Eagles take the young and perhaps also larger Skunks when the big animals and birds are driven by hunger. Most animals let the Skunks alone. The liquid from the glands is not only disagreeable but if it hits the eye it may cause temporary, even permanent blindness. The odor clings fast to cloth. The only way to rid clothes of the scent is to bury them underground.

Although their offensive weapon makes Skunks unpopular, they are very valuable animals. Insects are among their favorite foods. They devour great numbers of grubs and larvae. They like cutworms, grasshoppers, and beetles, the potato beetle included. The ground in their home territory soon becomes peppered with little holes, showing where they have been digging for ground insects.

During a survey in Manitoba, Canada, it was estimated that Skunks destroyed nearly 15,000 grubs to the acre in an eight-acre tract. In New York state they ate so many hop grubs that, at the request of the hop growers, a bill was passed, protecting Skunks. In New Mexico these animals were found to be enemy to the range caterpillar.

The Common Skunk varies his insect diet with Mice, Gophers, Spermophiles, and other small Rodent pests. He also likes carrion, honeybees, ripe cactus fruit, and, when opportunity offers, he will enter a hen yard, eat eggs or a chicken.

The large dark Northern Plains Skunk is common around the lakes where wild fowl breed. There he digs for insects and probably also eats many eggs as well as the young of ground nesting birds. On the other hand, he is fond of turtle eggs and turtles and will also eat young ducks.

In one marshy section of New York state, Skunks were blamed for raiding the wild duck nests. Then Skunk fur became high-priced, Skunks were killed in great numbers. Whereupon the snapping turtles flourished, became very numerous, and ate so many young ducks that they nearly drove the adult ducks from the marsh. About that time Skunk fur dropped in price, the Skunks came back. With the help of commercial turtle hunters they kept the turtle population under control, and the ducks came back.

This is only one example of the delicate balance of nature. Sometimes when man destroys an animal he thinks is harmful, he is protecting a worse animal of prey, as in the case of Skunk versus turtle. The looting of hen yards and the nests of ground birds is more than offset by the number of Rodent and insect pests destroyed by Skunks, and by their value as fur animals.

Skunks of the cold climates are usually large and black with little white fur. Their pelts are the most valuable. The Arizona Common Skunk, found also in New Mexico, is smaller, shorter of tail, has a great deal of white in his coat. Skins with much white on them bring a low price in the fur market. The white is cut away, the black fur is used for trimming coats. Albino Skunks sometimes occur. Since the market value on all Skunk skins is usually low and since these animals are costly to raise in captivity, Skunk farming has not been successful.

In spite of the great number of Common Striped Skunks trapped, they continue to thrive over their wide range. Several different species are found from Hudson Bay south into Mexico.

One species is strikingly different. This is the northern Hooded Skunk. He usually has a hood of white hairs on the top of his head. Sometimes an individual is white all over his back and the top of his tail. The Hooded Skunk is smaller, more slender, more active than his striped cousin.

In the northern part of their range Skunks hibernate. When the temperature falls to twenty-five degrees or a little lower, they den up, but they do not go into as deep a sleep as do the true hibernators. Their temperature does not drop greatly as it does in the long sleepers such as Woodchucks and Bats. They may stay underground for several weeks but if a thaw comes they awaken and come out of their holes.

They make their homes in burrows which they dig or in holes deserted by Woodchucks or Badgers. A favorite spot is under a stone wall or under the porch of a house or the floor of a cabin. Skunks have from four to seven young, sometimes ten in a litter. When the babies are strong enough the mother takes them with her while she hunts for insects. On a moonlit night the little black and white babies may be seen trailing after her, sometimes in single file.

Skunks are easily tamed and make cunning pets. Their scent glands may be removed by a slight operation. Without these glands a Skunk is unable to live up to his genus name *Mephitis* which is Latin for a bad odor.

Spotted Skunk

The Smallest Skunk

SPOTTED SKUNK
POLECAT, LITTLE STRIPED SKUNK
HYDROPHOBIA SKUNK, PHOBY CAT
(genus *Spilogale*)

Weasel Family

This is the smallest of the Skunks. Much more active than his big cousins, he sometimes climbs trees or runs across the roof of a cabin. Several species or subspecies are found in southern and western United States. In some localities they live in the woods but prefer rocky canyons and cliffs where they dig holes under rocks for burrows. Often they live in holes deserted by other animals.

Unlike Common Striped Skunks they are at home in the real desert. Since the Spotted Skunks travel at early dawn or twilight or at night, campers in the hot desert country are sometimes frightened by them. Not only do they have powerful scent glands common to their kind but they sometimes go "mad." There are authentic cases on record of "mad" Skunks biting people and causing their death. These cases are rare. A Common Skunk will also become infected with hydrophobia if he is bitten by a mad Dog or a mad Coyote.

In color the Spotted Skunk is black with white lines and spots. The small pelt usually brings a very low price but many skins are sold in the fur market each year and used for short coats or trimmings.

The little Skunk's taste for food is much like that of his large cousin. He eats many insects and probably Rodents, birds, and some chickens.

Spotted Skunks have from two to six little ones. Their range is the southern United States from the Atlantic coast to the Pacific. In the east they are found as far north as Virginia. In the west they enter British Columbia.

Their genus name *Spilogale* comes from two Greek words, *spilos* (spot) and *gale* (Weasel).

Hog-nosed Skunk

A Mexican Border Skunk

THE HOG-NOSED SKUNK
WHITE-BACKED SKUNK
(genus *Conepatus*)

Weasel Family

This is a southern Skunk which ranges over the Mexican border into the United States in Texas, Arizona, and New Mexico. A large Skunk, he is well equipped for digging, has very long claws and a long, bare, hoglike nose. His fur is brownish black with white back and white tail and is of no value on the fur market.

Like his cousin, the Common Striped Skunk, he eats grasshoppers, beetles, larvae, the fruits of prickly pears, fresh meat and carrion, and takes some chickens and small game. But since he lives in little-settled country he is not important to farmers, either as a pest or an insect destroyer. His home is the arid country although he does not live in the real desert, as the Spotted Skunk does.

In habits he is much like the Common Striped Skunk.

His genus name *Conepatus* comes from a Nahuatl (Aztec) word meaning small Fox.

Pine Marten

The Weasel of the Treetops

PINE MARTEN
AMERICAN SABLE
HUDSON BAY SABLE
(genus *Martes*)

Weasel Family

The beautiful Marten is small cousin to the Fisher and closely related to the Russian Sable, one of the most valuable fur animals. The Marten's dark golden-brown fur is also valuable.

This animal looks like a very large Weasel. The male weighs five or six pounds and reaches a length of well over two feet. Nervous in temperament, he moves with weasel-like quickness, darting over the ground, searching under the leaves for small prey. He spends much of his life among the trees of the deep forests, leaping so swiftly from branch to branch that he can catch Red Squirrels.

Because he is a real tree animal, the Marten is not found beyond the limit of woods. These animals' toes are fingerlike, have long strong claws for grasping rough bark. Shy and wary, they retreat from settled country, are rarely seen except by fur trappers. They are easy to trap. In lodgepole pine and spruce forests of Colorado they are sometimes pursued by hunters on skis, an exciting sport.

Like all of the Weasel Family they have strong scent glands and in temper are ferocious. Caught in a trap, captive Martens hiss and growl and may shriek. Yet they tame easily and make cunning pets.

Efforts to raise Martens in captivity were until recently unsuccessful. Their breeding habits were not understood, and they were found to be difficult to handle in groups. When caged together, they fight among themselves. A male may kill a female by biting through her skull. Given separate feeding pens and sleeping quarters they may be allowed a common runway and experiments to farm them are now being successful.

In his native habitat the Marten catches Squirrels, Rabbits, Chipmunks, Mice, Shrews, as well as small birds and Partridges. He also preys upon birds' eggs. Like his cousins he eats many other foods including frogs and fish, insects, carrion, nuts, berries, and honey.

Adult Martens mate in June, July, or as late as the third week in August. From eight and a half to nine months later the young Martens are born in a grass- or moss-lined nest in a hollow tree. Sometimes their home is a hole in the ground. From one to five are born in a litter, sometimes more. At birth they are naked and helpless. When large enough they go about with their mother until they are able to care for themselves. Then they take up the solitary way of their kind.

These valuable fur animals are still caught in numbers by trappers. Over 16,000 pelts were taken in Alaska in the year 1937, but only a few over 1000 in 1939.

Their original range covered most of the forested area of North America from the limit of trees south across Canada into the mountain forests of Pennsylvania, New Mexico, and California. The Marten is now protected in several states.

The genus name *Martes* is Latin for Marten.

Fisher

Big Marten

FISHER   **Weasel Family**
PEKAN, PENNANT MARTEN
BLACK CAT, BLACK FOX
(genus *Martes*)

This brown-furred member of the Weasel Family looks like a large Pine Marten. The males reach a little over three feet in length, weigh from eight to twelve pounds and may weigh as much as eighteen. Females are much smaller, weigh about five pounds.

Large and powerful, the Fisher is equally at home on the ground or in the treetops. He is very quick and catches Tree Squirrels, leaping nimbly from tree limb to tree limb. So swift is this big Marten that he can capture his speedy and crafty small cousin, the Pine Marten.

On the ground the Fisher is not as agile but with the persistence characteristic of the Weasels he pursues Snowshoe Hares and catches them. He also conquers Porcupines. He turns these spiny animals over on their backs, attacks their unspined bellies. He frequently gets the barbed quills in his head but this does not stop him.

His fondness for fish gave him his name. The Fisher also enjoys frogs. Like many animals of prey he has a regular route which he follows through the forest. Sometimes he may take several days to make the rounds. He often follows trap lines, stealing bait or the trapped animals, as his cousin the Wolverine does. Not as mischievous as the latter, he will attack a Dog ferociously, kill Fox, Raccoon, and has been known to overcome a Deer.

In the latter part of April or the first of May two or three little Fishers are born. Sometimes there is but one, sometimes five in a litter. Their home is a hollow tree, or sometimes a rock crevice or a den under a fallen log. The young follow their mother when quite small, stay with her until full grown.

The soft fur of the Fisher is very valuable. It is frequently worn as a neckpiece. Extensively trapped for many years, the range of this animal has shrunk. The Fisher used to range over the forested parts of North America from Hudson Bay and the Great Slave Lake south along the Alleghenies to Tennessee; and in the West along the Rockies to Wyoming and California. He is now protected in many parts of the United States and Canada.

But one species of Fisher exists with but one subspecies, and they belong to the same genus as the Pine Marten, genus *Martes*, Latin for a Marten.

The Glutton

WOLVERINE   Weasel Family
Carcajou, Skunk Bear
Indian Devil (to trappers)
Quiquihatch (in French Canadian)
(genus *Gulo*)

The Wolverine is one of the most hated animals. Among the largest of the Weasel Family, he has big curved claws, a long dark-brown coat with yellowish bands on the side, a grizzled head. He weighs about thirty pounds, reaches three feet in length. Not slender like the little Weasels, his heavy body looks like a small Bear's.

In his native habitat which is from the arctic to northern United States, formerly as far south as Maryland, he is not frequently seen by any except trappers and woodsmen who hate him for his mischief. The clever animal stalks trap lines, stealing the catch before the trapper arrives. Not swift but wary he sneaks into camps, carries away even things he cannot eat.

He has great courage and an enormous appetite. He devours many Mice, Lemmings, Woodchucks, Ground Squirrels, Hares, Beaver, baby Foxes, Grouse, also berries, frogs, reptiles, grasshoppers. So great is the bravery of this rather small animal that he can fell a Caribou or Deer and has been reported to bring down a Moose.

The Alaskan Eskimos believe that by wearing a Wolverine's skin, the animal's courage will enter the body of the wearer. Hunters therefore make their belts and hunting bags of fur from the head and legs. They trim the hoods of their parkas with the fur in order to acquire added courage.

This truly fierce animal has extraordinarily strong jaws. A captive in a zoo was reported to have ripped his way out of a cage that would have held a medium-sized Bear. Another was reported to have gnawed through a log "as thick as a man's thigh."

The Wolverine is now too rare to be of economic value. Formerly the long, rather coarse fur

Wolverine

was prized for arctic coats because it does not collect moisture. Today the animal is scarce in Canada, gone from the United States save for a few in Yellowstone Park and a few more among the sequoias of California.

The northern trappers still trap the animal whenever they can, more to keep him away from the trap line than for his fur. Five or six hundred skins are still sold by Canadian trappers yearly.

The Wolverine lives in a burrow, the mother has five or six young which she defends fiercely.

The adults all kill more than they can eat and bury the remains under the snow. No other animal cares to eat food the Wolverines have touched because it becomes tainted with the musk smell common to Weasels.

Known everywhere for his gluttonous appetite, this unpopular and now rare beast is classified in genus *Gulo* which appropriately is Latin for a glutton.

The Digger

BADGER
BLAIREAU (French Canadian)
(genus *Taxidea*)

Weasel Family

The Badger does not look like a common Weasel. His short-legged, flat, wide body reminds one of a turtle, but his coarse fur, long at the sides, is that of a very hairy animal. In color he is grizzly gray with yellowish white on the under parts and striking black and white markings on face and head.

The Badger is among the larger members of the Weasel Family. He is powerful. His forelimbs are strong and his forefeet have claws an inch long, well developed for digging. His homeland is the prairie and open woodland in central and western North America from Saskatchewan to Mexico. He spends much of his time hunting the multitude of small Rodents which live in his country, and stockmen complain of the numerous holes he makes where saddle horses may stumble.

His favorite diet is animal and insect pests. When he finds a Rodent hole he digs out the little animal with amazing speed. Among the

Badger

Rodents which he digs are the Ground Squirrels. Although the Badger also enjoys the eggs and young of ground nesting birds such as Pheasant, the Ground Squirrels which he pursues are one of the worst enemies of Grouse and other game birds. He kills so many destructive little Rodents that he does more good than harm. He feeds upon Field and Deer Mice, Kangaroo Rats, Pocket Mice, and turtle eggs. He eats a variety of other small mammals such as Wood Rats, and insects such as beetles, grasshoppers, and scorpions as well as lizards.

A fast digger, he walks slowly. Like other members of the Weasel Family he is ferocious and fearless. When cornered or caught in a trap he snarls and fights. His thick hair protects him from blows and he has few enemies but man. Stockmen and trappers have killed them until today they are gone from much of their former range.

The fur of the Badgers used to be considered too coarse but recently the pelts rose in price The coarse hair is used for lining women's coats and for pointing up furs of cheap grade. Long Badger hairs are carefully glued to the hide where needed.

The Badger hibernates but is not usually a deep sleeper. In the climate of southern Michigan and Iowa he generally dens up for a week or less at a time. In the cold high altitudes of the mountain slopes of Idaho Badgers den up by the first of the new year and are not usually seen again above ground until the middle of March. In colder climates they may den up two months earlier and not come out until April.

The young Badgers are born in May or June. There is but one litter a season, from one to seven in a litter. The average number is four.

Taxidea, the genus classification, comes from the Latin *taxus,* a Badger.

An Animal Which Likes to Play

OTTER   **Weasel Family**
RIVER OTTER
LAND OTTER
(genus *Lutra*)

The River Otter is a very large member of the Weasel Family. Some specimens reach a little over four feet in length. Active all year, this water-loving animal has a rich brown fur and a layer of fat beneath the skin which keep him warm when rivers are frozen. His feet are

Common Otter

webbed, he is a swift swimmer and catches water animals in the streams and lakes where he makes his home. Otters feed largely upon cold-blooded prey, fish, crayfish, frogs but sometimes kill warm-blooded creatures.

One of the most interesting characteristics of the River Otter is his play. He is one of the few wild animals which spends much time in sport after attaining full growth. Groups of Otter go tobogganing together. In summer they seek a bank of oozy mud. In winter they choose a snow bank with an icy pool of water at the bottom. With their short legs turned backwards they slide down these slippery places. They toboggan for the joy it gives them to whizz downhill as children enjoy coasting. The several Otters which use one slide seem to enter into friendly rivalry in their play which has no connection with the rough play of mammals in the breeding season. As many as fourteen Otters have been seen using one slide in the ricefields of Georgia.

Otter slides are frequently so steep and slippery that the animals have to return to the top by a roundabout path. As they run, they hump their bodies in true Weasel fashion.

They are great travelers. They wander many miles, often crossing from one stream to another. In the winter when the rivers are frozen they wander until they find rapids where the water is open. In the far north their tracks may be seen going for miles over the snow always ending in some ice hole where the animals find their way back into a river.

They make their dens under the banks of streams or lakes with entrances above or below water, or under shelving rocks. They have from one to three, sometimes five, young.

Their call is a shrill whistle. They also growl and sniff.

Otter fur is valuable. It is used for sports coats for women and is exported for trimming cloth coats, particularly collars for men's coats. In Asia the width of the trim of Otter fur on a garment shows the social standing of the wearer. The best American skins come from northeastern United States and Labrador.

In spite of their fur value, Land Otters have not been nearly exterminated as have their big cousins, the Sea Otters. Never abundant, shy and wary, they are not often seen. They are native over an immense territory, are found from within the Arctic Circle to our southern border.

The genus name *Lutra* is Latin for an Otter.

Southern Sea Otter

A Very Rare Animal

SOUTHERN SEA OTTER
Sea Beaver
(genus *Enhydra*)

Weasel Family

Few people of today have seen this beautiful sea mammal. Since the year 1876 he was thought to be practically extinct. Occasionally fishermen would report seeing one. Then suddenly in the year 1937 a herd of nearly a hundred was reported off the coast of California. Scientists scoffed until they verified the fact. The Otters had apparently been hiding in the waters off the coast of Monterey where sheer cliffs rise several hundred feet from the Pacific. The Monterey fishermen shunned this dangerous area and if they sighted the animals they no doubt thought they were Seals or Sea Lions.

The Otters were scared out of hiding by a school of the ruthless Killer Whales. Since then as many as one hundred and fifty have been seen. The state of California immediately assigned a warden to guard the members of this lost race to see that they were not captured for their fur.

Adaptation to life in the water is often accompanied by a tendency to hairlessness. The awkward Sea Elephants and Walrus which can only crawl on land are scantily haired; the Whales and the Manatees are practically hairless. But the coat of the Sea Otter is magnificent. It is soft, thick, rich tawny brown in color and so valuable that it nearly brought about his extinction; so fine in quality that several thousand dollars have been paid for a single first-class skin. It is considered the most valuable fur in the world. The bearer of this fur has been relentlessly taken by Americans, Russians, and the English.

Now the Sea Otters have learned to shun land. Peaceful, shy animals they rarely leave the water, eating and even sleeping in the sea. It is said that they used to follow the habits of Seals, haul out on rocks to rest and sun themselves, but to save their hunted lives they have adapted themselves to an almost completely aquatic existence.

Largest of the Weasel Family, the males sometimes reach six feet in length. Their long, low-slung, short-legged bodies resemble those of their cousins, the small Weasels and Mink, but the Sea Otters are stouter, their tails are thick and flattened slightly, and their hind feet are broadly, fully webbed and shaped like paddles.

They seek all of their food in the sea. Their favorite meal is red abalone and sea urchin. They dive and find an abalone, then rise to the surface and lie on their backs to eat, using their chests for tables. They lay a piece of abalone shell on their chests until they have finished eating what is already in their mouths. One authority reports that they often bring up a rock, crack open shells with it, and rest it on the "table."

When tired they rest in the kelp beds. They have learned to catch hold of kelp, wrap it around their bodies so that they won't drift away from the herd. While asleep they lie on their backs with their heads on their chests and their tails sometimes waving lazily back and forth. They may be suddenly awakened by the bite of some parasite, then they roll over and lose their hold on the kelp. They are frequently heard yawning, growling, or making other sounds like "awk."

When not hurried they swim in spirals and are as playful as Sea Lions or their river cousins, sometimes leaping clear out of water.

The young, usually a single baby, does not seem to be born at any one time of year. And since no one has ever seen the young born on land, it is thought that they are born in the kelp beds. The pups have golden-brown hair and are well over a foot long at birth. The mother takes good care of them, the father takes no interest. When the mother is hunting food the baby floats. He rests and sleeps on his back until he is able to swim and dive from the kelp beds.

The Northern or Alaska Sea Otter is smaller than the southern form, reaches but four feet. He too has been nearly exterminated but individuals and small herds are occasionally reported in the chain of Aleutian Islands off Alaska. Here they still have the habit of hauling out on rocks but in other ways they are much like their southern cousins. Since there are no red abalones in Alaskan waters they feed mostly on large purple sea urchins.

The report of the Biological Survey is that with continued protection these interesting animals should increase.

Their genus name *Enhydra* comes from the Greek *en*, meaning in, and *hydor* meaning water.

RACCOON
Coon
(genus *Procyon*)

Raccoon Family
(family *Procyonidae*)

This stout-bodied animal is closely related to the Bear. His form and gait remind one of his large cousins. The Raccoon moves rather slowly and clumsily on the ground but when he runs he treads in unbearlike fashion on his toes. He sits on the soles of his feet.

He is a good climber, usually makes his home in a hollow tree trunk. The Mexican Raccoon is frequently found among cliffs in New Mexico where he prefers to den up under rocks along the side of a canyon.

Raccoons are nimble-toed, their feet grasp like the hands of a Monkey. But their tails are bushy, clublike, not formed for hanging from the limbs of trees as are the tails of true tree animals such as Monkeys and Opossums.

The cunning little face of the animal with its characteristic black mask across the eyes is often seen in zoos. Raccoons are intelligent, make amusing pets. They have an odd habit of vigorously washing their food whenever they are near water. In Sweden this has earned them the name of "Wash Bear."

Although these animals do find part of their

Raccoon

food away from water, their favorite haunts are the borders of streams, the shores of ponds and lakes where they can wash what they eat.

Raccoons are rarely seen in their native haunts because they usually come out only at night. Through the hours of darkness they prowl about, seeking to satisfy their appetites. In late summer and fall they raid cornfields. When the young juicy ears are ripening, corn is a favorite food. Crayfish are second choice. They also follow streams and pond shores to catch frogs. Little piles of mussel shells on logs show where a Raccoon has been enjoying a meal of shellfish. When streams are low the clever animals scoop out fish with their nimble fingers.

In the fall Raccoons like nuts and hackberries. They eat many fruits in season, wild plums, grapes, cherries, watermelons. In the arid parts of the west they eat cactus berries, the beans of mesquite. They also feed on Mice, insects, earthworms, turtle eggs, grain, and birds, sometimes raid a hen yard killing many hens and fearlessly returning the next night to the same coop. Like Bears they are fond of honey, raid beehives. Their heavy coats protect them from stings. They are very curious, will examine shiny objects, and can be lured into a trap by the glitter of metal.

Raccoons hibernate during the coldest weather but they do not fall into a deep torpor. The temperature of a Raccoon does not drop greatly when he dens up, as does the temperature of true hibernators such as Bats. Even when the temperature in their den falls below freezing, the body of the Raccoon keeps warm. In the southern part of their range they hibernate but a short time. Even in the north they do not usually sleep more than a month at a time.

From four to six young occupy the family

home until they are well grown which accounts for several large Raccoons being found in one hollow tree at the same time. When the babies are young their mother carries them by the nape of the neck in her mouth as a Cat carries her kittens.

In pioneer days the ringed tails of Raccoons ornamented hunters' caps. The pelts were used as barter. More recently the grizzly and yellow-ish-gray fur has become familiar in the bulky, bearlike Coon coats of college boys. Very dark, almost black (melanistic) pelts are not uncommon.

Coon are game animals as well as fur bearers. Coon hunting at night with especially trained dogs is an exciting sport. The sport is usually followed in November when snow is on the ground.

Wary old Raccoons are hard to catch.

About a million Raccoons are taken by hunters each year in the United States. Over 20,000 were taken in Canada in the season 1934-35.

In spite of the numbers caught, the Raccoon is still rather common in most of his original range which is from southern Canada over most of the wooded areas of the United States except very high altitudes. There are two species of Raccoon. The typical species has several geographic races or subspecies. The second species is the Desert Raccoon, pale in color as are most desert mammals.

The family and genus name are both derived from the Latin *Procyon,* a constellation which rises before the dog star, and from the Greek *prokyon* (*pro,* before, and *kyon,* Dog).

Coatimundi

Southern Cousin to the Raccoon

COATIMUNDI
COATIMONDI
(genus *Nasua*)

Raccoon Family

The Coati is really a Mexican mammal. This slender member of the Raccoon Family was formerly very rare north of the Rio Grande. He is a tropical animal but today is quite common in southwestern New Mexico and southern Arizona. Two or three have been reported in Texas but there is some doubt as to whether these came in by themselves or were brought in as pets.

This southern animal looks like an elongated Coon. His tail is long and comes to a point, his snout is long, slender, and slightly turned up at the end. The color of a Coati's fur is rich brown with a little gray about the head. Sometimes the tail fur is faintly ringed, Coon fashion.

The tail of this funny-looking mammal is partly adapted for grasping. The feet are long-fingered and clawed, suited for clutching rough bark or limbs of trees.

Coatis hunt for food in troops. They like to eat iguanas. They hunt these reptiles in the treetops. Some Coatis stay on the ground to catch the lizards as they fall.

Like the common Raccoon they are also fond of insects and their larvae, small Rodents, birds, various fruits, and almost anything they can swallow.

The genus name *Nasua* is derived from the Latin *nasus*, a nose.

Coonlike Animal

RING-TAILED CAT
COON CAT, CIVET CAT
CACOMISTLE
CACOMIXTLE
(genus *Bassariscus*)

Ring-Tailed Cat Family
(family *Bassariscidae*)

This animal is closely related to the Raccoon Family but his teeth are different. His handsome bushy tail, marked with alternate dark and white bands, reminds one of a Raccoon but is longer. So is his body, longer, more slender, and his face reminds one of a Fox. He has catlike feet.

Being of an inquisitive disposition he frequently prowls through small western towns in the dark of night, leaving behind little catlike tracks. But he is no Cat, and the name Civet Cat is not correct because the true Civet Cats of Europe belong to another family.

This beautiful little animal is rarely seen since he never goes abroad by day and his range is limited. He is a southerner, a native of warm Mexico where he lives from sea level to an altitude of ten thousand feet. He is also native to southwestern United States where he ranges north through Arizona and New Mexico even to

Nevada and Colorado, and on the west coast into Oregon.

Sometimes these Coon Cats are found in the woods. On the plains of southern Texas they live among the clumps of chaparral but their favorite home is the country of cliffs and canyons where they hunt for Cliff Mice and Wood Rats and den up in small caves or haunt the deserted houses of the ancient cliff dwellers.

Their three or four young are born in May or June, sometimes in a cliff dwelling. In Mexico they are found among the Aztec ruins and are known by the Aztec name Cacomistle.

Sometimes they den in hollow trees or under houses convenient to hen roosts. Often in the warm country where they live, chickens roost in trees and are easy prey. However, Ring-tailed Cats are not very common, are of little economic importance. Unimportant in the fur market, a few

Ring-tailed Cat

of the buff-brown pelts are dyed and used for trimming cloth coats.

They do not live entirely on meat. They are very fond of fruit. They eat cactus fruit and ears of corn. On the west coast they visit fig and date-palm orchards where they pick up fallen fruit.

They also eat centipedes and their larvae.

Intelligent animals, they are said to make cunning pets.

The family and genus names come from the Greek *bassaris*, Thracian for a Fox.

DOG FAMILY
(family *Canidae*)

The domestic Dogs belong to this family. The members which are native to America are all very much like Dogs in form. They are medium-sized Carnivores and all have long, bushy tails.

The family name *Canidae* comes from the Latin *canis* which means a Dog. In America the following four genera, groups, of *Canidae* are found: the Wolves and Coyotes, the Red and Kit Foxes, the Gray Foxes, the Arctic Foxes.

Timber Wolf

Outlaw

TIMBER WOLF
LOBO, GRAY WOLF
(genus *Canis*)

Dog Family

The large, yellow-eyed, cruel-looking gray Timber Wolf and closely related species used to be common over most of North America from the arctic all over the temperate zone except the hot desert areas. The last Wolf in the Adirondacks was killed in 1893. Early in the nineteenth century they were gone from New Jersey. With settlement of the east and scarcity of game, the Wolf departed. In the Rockies of Canada and the United States as well as on the Great Plains and in forested country around the Great Lakes, Wolves survive although man makes continual war on the destructive beasts.

Clever, resourceful, showing all the intelligence of their cousins, the domestic Dogs, these big Lobos range over the western plains and mountains and in northern forests preying on Cattle and Sheep where once they brought down Buffaloes. In Colorado some years ago one outlaw Wolf was credited with destroying $3000 worth of stock before he was killed. In Wyoming two Wolves destroyed one hundred and fifty head of Cattle and seven colts in a month. Governments have paid millions in bounty for the destruction of these animals. Men have shot them and poisoned them. The eerie hunting howl of the Wolf is still heard. They are now wary, gone over much of their wide range, but in some places they are increasing. Very prolific, they have from eight to twelve pups. The young are born in a den under a rock, in a hollow log, or in a hole in the ground. They are blind and helpless at birth. The large, fierce father Wolf has a strange instinct for family life, quite unlike most other wild beasts. He guards the pups as anxiously as the mother Wolf and when they are big enough to eat meat he kills and brings home the food. Some say Wolves mate for life.

They are known to hunt in pairs and when the young grow large, several families may join, forming a small pack. Packs are usually small but may number as many as thirty in the winter.

Members are clever, helping each other until they bring down a Deer, even a Moose. They always follow a set route, year after year, covering a chosen area in a wide, irregular circle.

They do not always chase big prey. When Rodents are abundant they eat the smaller animals including many Mice.

In Michigan it has been suggested that Wolves are good for the Deer population. Without these beasts of prey, crippled and diseased Deer survive. Wolves keep the fittest on the jump, kill the unfit. The balance of nature in forest reserves is found to be very delicate and when interfered with by man is sometimes overbalanced on the harmful side rather than on the good.

Closely related to the Siberian and European Wolves, American Wolves have always been rather afraid of man. Perhaps because in the early days of their abundance there was plenty of game in America, they never became as bold, were not pressed by hunger to the point of attacking people as their European cousins have been.

So closely related to domestic Dogs are Wolves that they belong not only to the same family, *Canidae,* but also to the same genus.

There are several species of American Wolves. The species which lives in the Mount McKinley region of Alaska is often black, sometimes grizzled gray. A reddish-brown Wolf lives in the Puget Sound region. In the far north lives the White Wolf.

In the Far North

WHITE WOLF   Dog Family
ARCTIC WOLF
TUNDRA WOLF
(genus *Canis*)

In the barren grounds of America beyond the limit of trees lives the White Wolf. Large, weighing as much as a hundred pounds, he is the most dreaded enemy of the White Caribou and the Musk Ox which share with him the long endless night of winter in the tundra. These big shaggy creatures slip through the arctic night over the immense wastes like ghosts. Here few men hear their hunting cry.

In the summer they get fat on the wild fowl which migrate to the arctic to breed. During a season when arctic Mice are abundant the howl of these fierce northern Wolves stops. They no longer stalk big prey, the Caribou and wild fowl are left in peace, and the Wolves as well as other northern Carnivores wax fat on the Mice millions.

When Mice become scarce, the Wolves start hunting game. Their howl is heard again. They pursue the Arctic Hare, catch an occasional White Fox, harass the Caribou and the Musk Ox. Packs of the Wolves range over an immense amount of ground, following the same route in a wide, irregular circle, traveling even thirty or forty miles a day. Some authorities say that they may be gone two or three weeks and cover several hundred miles before they come back to the starting point on their chosen trail. Each pack has a set path which it travels year after year.

The White Wolf is so closely related to the Timber Wolf that he belongs to the same genus, *Canis,* meaning Dog. He is not always white. Individuals may vary to nearly black.

Small Wolf

COYOTE   Dog Family
PRAIRIE WOLF
(genus *Canis*)

The dismal howl of a Coyote under the western moon might well be compared to a lost soul. So weird, so lonely, so wild but human-sounding is the call that it scarcely seems to be real. Yet it is the voice of the mean, slinking but extremely clever little Wolf of the plains.

Occasionally a Coyote gets rabies, goes mad like a domestic Dog. Then he bites any beast or man which comes in his path. Otherwise he is shy and avoids people. This small cousin of the Timber Wolf has none of the bold daring of the larger animal, often follows his cousins to pick the bones of prey killed by the bigger Wolves.

Coyotes eat a great deal of carrion and a great many Mice, Ground Squirrels, Prairie Dogs, and other harmful Rodents, as well as Rabbits. If they confined their tastes to food on this list they would be welcome on the range. However, they are also very fond of mutton and veal. It has been estimated that each Coyote in ranching country may do $50 worth of damage a year. Ranchers make continuous war against them to protect the calves and lambs.

In South Dakota game wardens taught the farm boys to trap Coyotes. This helped reduce their number and at the same time gave the boys an income. The rather coarse grizzled fur is extensively used in the fur market. In color it is some shade of gray or tawny, shot with red and yellow.

But Coyotes are wary of traps. Their numbers do not greatly decrease when trapped or hunted. They even learn to avoid poisoned meat. They become suspicious, other harmless animals take the bait. Even though destroyed by the thousands, Coyotes do not become scarce. They have very big families with from three to ten pups, sometimes fourteen. The young are born in a burrow in the ground and like the bigger Wolves the father and the mother both care for them. The pups are born with darker coats than the adults and are limp-eared, pug-nosed. At four weeks their ears stand up, their noses are longer, more foxlike. At five weeks they eat meat, are nearly grown by February.

In the region of Michigan, Coyotes mate in midwinter. Often seen in pairs it is thought that perhaps they mate for life.

They generally hunt in pairs or threes, rarely in large packs. They are extremely clever hunters. They seem to understand the habits of Jack Rabbits. A pair will pursue a Jack in relays, one resting while the other gives chase. They know that the Jack will run in a wide circle, return soon to the spot where the first Coyote is waiting to relieve his companion.

Usually satisfied with small game they sometimes attack Antelopes. A pack of Coyotes will run around and around one of these fleet animals, finally tire him out. They are also among the few animals who care to roll a porcupine and kill him. Even in Indian mythology they figure as the clever and mischievous ones.

The range of these Prairie Wolves is wide. They may be seen trotting through the sagebush plains. When frightened they run with great speed. They are at home from sea level to high mountaintops. They generally like open country, grassy plains, brushy areas, open wooded spots. They are found from western Iowa, south to the Gulf, west to the Pacific, north through Alberta and British Columbia.

Over this great territory several species and geographic races of Coyote have developed. They differ slightly in size and shade of fur. They shed their winter coats in the spring, new coats grow by autumn and are kept through the winter.

The smallest and one of the prettiest of the Coyotes is the Mearn's or Arizona Coyote. This is the desert Coyote of southern Arizona and the lower Colorado River region, one of the starkest, hottest, dryest areas in the United States. Here the rainfall is but a few inches a year, water holes are far apart. The bright tawny-colored desert Coyote finds Kangaroo Rats, Pocket Gophers, Desert Jack Rabbits. He also eats mesquite beans, the juicy fruit of cactus, and raids the small desert communities for corn and watery melons. He often raids hen yards. Desert campers come to know his clever thieving ways when in the night the bacon disappears.

In quite different country such as Michigan,

Coyotes

the Coyotes eat apples, dandelions, grasses, besides meat such as mutton, Rabbit, Muskrat, venison, Mice, Squirrels, sparrows, chickens and their eggs.

The Coyote is the third member of the genus which contains the domestic Dog, genus *Canis*. This is the Latin word for Dog.

Red Fox

Very Valuable Fox

RED FOX
AND ITS COLOR PHASES
BLACK FOX, SILVER FOX
CROSS FOX
(genus *Vulpes*)

Dog Family

Golden reddish yellow in color, with a fine bushy tail, this common northern Fox is the animal of Fox-hunting fame, the game of hunter on horseback as well as hunter afoot and trapper. His brush or tail is the Fox hunter's pride.

He is one of the most valuable of our fur animals because in some litters the rare melanistic, Black, or the Silver pups are born. More common are the Cross Fox pups. The Cross Fox is halfway between the Black and Red. He has a reddish-yellow coat with a dark band over the shoulders and a dark back band forming a cross. He also has a band of black from throat over abdomen.

These Foxes have been farmed more than any other wild animals. The animals are bred for a true strain of Silver. In the early days as much as $2500 has been paid for a fine Silver Fox pelt in London. Today the ranch skin of a Silver Fox will

bring about $45. Many of these Foxes are raised on the biggest fur farm in the world. This is the Fromm Fur Farm of Hamburg, Wisconsin. Here 12,000 or more Silver Fox pelts are produced a year. It is the biggest fur farm in the world and covers over 12,000 acres. Each year the Foxes on this farm are fed a carload of cod-liver oil besides their regular diet of nearly 10,000 Cattle, over 2000 tons of bread and cereal, 600,000 pounds of liver, 100 tons of lettuce, 800,000 pounds of carrots as well as other vegetables.

In spite of their value, Red Foxes survive over a greater part of their former range. Wise, wary, keen-eared, keen-sighted, and with keen noses, these Foxes do not disappear with the cutting of forests but are able to live by their wits in cleared pasture land where there is cover. They generally range over about a square mile of territory unless hunted very hard when they may run over new land.

That they survive at all is remarkable. Every farmer is their foe because they raid hen yards. They have also been accused of killing great numbers of Grouse, Quail, and other ground birds. Recent experiments prove that game birds form a very small percentage of their diet. In Minnesota, Red Foxes were found to prefer Mice. Second choice was Rabbits. These two animals made up the greater part of their meals. Only about four per cent of their food was found to be Pheasant, a little more poultry, probably some of this carrion.

This was also found to be true of Red Foxes in New York and New England. In Virginia Red Foxes were found to eat more Rabbits than Mice and a small percentage of game birds.

Among the Mice they take are Meadow Mice, White-footed Mice, House Mice. Other prey are Squirrels, Woodchucks, Chipmunks, Spermophiles, Muskrats, eaten now and then. Small birds, carrion, some vegetable matter, fruits in season form a small part of their diet. As stated in Aesop's fable they like grapes. They also like persimmons, blueberries, apples, and strawberries, beechnuts, peanuts, corn. They eat some insects, rarely a frog. In winter they bury what they can't eat, under the snow.

The voice of the Red Fox is a sharp bark or a long, dismal, high-pitched yowl which may often be heard on moonlight nights. They are most active by night but are also found abroad in daytime. They den in hollow logs, under rocks, or dig burrows in hillsides. From four to nine young are born in early spring and like the Wolves the father helps the mother bring food to the young when they are big enough to eat meat. Some authorities think Foxes mate for life. If true this is extraordinary among mammals which are nearly all polygamous.

The Red Fox is a northern animal widely distributed over the colder parts of the United States and over Canada into Alaska and Labrador. In the west they follow the mountain ranges into New Mexico. In the east they were formerly found only in the northeastern states but have been introduced southward and are found today as far south as middle Alabama and Georgia. The biggest species is the Alaska Red Fox. He is very large with a long, bushy tail and short ears.

Commonly found in the woods, Red Foxes also invade the plains. The Northern Plains Red Fox is large and beautiful golden yellow in color. He is found on the northern plains from Alberta to the Dakotas and east to Minnesota and Manitoba.

Vulpes, the genus name, is the Latin for a Fox.

In the Desert and on the Plains

KIT FOX
SWIFT
(genus *Vulpes*)

Dog Family

Close cousin to the Red Fox is the Kit Fox. He is rarely seen because he hunts food mainly at night and is very shy. By day he may be seen resting on a prominent rock ledge, watching for enemies. If he thinks he is seen he lopes swiftly away. He runs with great speed and ease, is commonly known as the Swift.

A beautiful Fox, the Swift is slender-bodied, the smallest Fox in America. Unlike his cousin he always lives in open country, is found over the

Great Plains from Saskatchewan and southeastern British Columbia into southwestern Texas and Wyoming; also in the blistering dry Colorado and Mojave Deserts as well as arid plateau and valley country of other parts of the southwest.

The common Kit Fox is buff yellow in color. The Prairie Kit Fox is reddish gray in summer, dark gray in winter. The Desert Kit Fox is small and pale grizzled gray.

The Desert Fox is at home in the country of

cactus and mesquite where in summer the sandy, waterless wastes blaze with heat. He lives largely upon Kangaroo Rats, Ground Squirrels, Pocket Mice, and other small desert mammals which come out only at night.

The fur of the Kit Fox is of little value and the animal is of no economic interest but he is some-times poisoned by meat set for Coyotes.

His home is in a burrow which he digs with several entrances on the flats or in a little mound. Four or five young are born each year.

He belongs to the same genus as the Red Fox, genus *Vulpes*.

Kit Fox

Fox Which Climbs

GRAY FOX
Tree Fox
(genus *Urocyon*)

Dog Family

The Gray Fox has shorter ears, coarser fur, than the Red Fox, longer legs, longer body and tail. His coat is gray fringed with red and black. In the west when chased by dogs he frequently climbs juniper trees. He also climbs to get juniper berries and piñon nuts and sometimes just to look around the country.

In other habits the Gray Fox is much like the Red Fox but he is not considered so clever. His range is more southerly. He does not go north of New Hampshire in the east. Here he is an animal of the woods, like his red cousin. Different geographic races are found south into Florida. In the west the Gray Fox lives from Oregon south into Mexico and Central America, and unlike the Red Fox he ranges over the arid plains and pla-teaus where he dens up under rocks and in hollow trees more often than digging a burrow.

The mother Gray Fox has smaller families than the Red Fox. From three to five young are common and they are born black. Like other members of this family the father helps care for the young which are blind and helpless at birth. When they are large enough to eat meat he brings food to them.

Their taste for food is similar to the Red Fox's. In Minnesota the food habits of the Gray Fox were carefully studied by the Bureau of Biological Survey. They were found to prefer Rabbits. Mice were second choice. A small percentage caught Pheasants. They ate quite a little more vegetable matter than the Red Fox in this area.

They ate grass and fruits in season. Pocket Gophers, Muskrats, Squirrels, Shrews, and some carrion and poultry made up the rest of their diet.

In the southwest they visit date gardens and watch for falling fruit at night. They are more active after dark than by day.

Their fur brings about half the price of common Red Fox, is frequently dyed and used for coat trimmings.

The genus name *Urocyon* comes from the Greek *oura*, a tail, and the Greek *kyon*, a Dog.

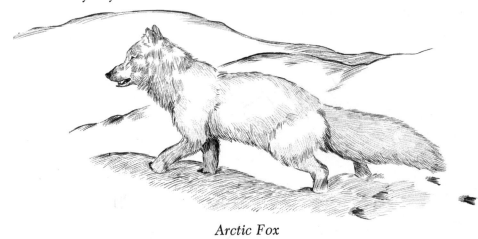

Arctic Fox

Valuable Arctic Fox

ARCTIC FOX   Dog Family
WHITE FOX AND A COLOR PHASE
THE BLUE FOX
(genus *Alopex*)

The White Fox is brown from June or mid-July to late fall or early winter. When the sun is gone and the long continuous winter night of the arctic comes, the White Fox turns the color of snow. To make this color change he sheds his hair as do many other animals of the north. He sheds again in spring and grows a new coat of brown.

In the spring from five to eleven young Arctic Foxes are born, usually aboveground, and are carried by their mother to a den under a rock or down a burrow she has dug. Sometimes in a litter there is a Blue Fox born. This Blue Fox is a color phase of the White Fox, just as the Silver Fox is a color phase of the Red Fox. The fur is very valuable.

In the days when the Fur Seals were slaughtered on their breeding grounds, the Pribilof Islands, off the coast of Alaska, the Arctic Fox fed on the carcasses. With the help of artificial selec-

tion by man the Blue Fox became the common type on these islands. White individuals which drifted from the mainland were killed, a strain of Blues was developed and became the common type on the Pribilofs.

Blue Fox are now farmed on several Alaskan Islands where they are fed Hair Seals, sharks and other fish, and allowed to run free which improves the quality of their fur. They do not turn white in winter.

The white phase is trapped in his native haunts, brings less than the blue but is valuable, is easily dyed. These fur bearers are one of the most valued animals of arctic economy.

The Arctic Fox is a beautiful, delicately built animal, much smaller than the Red Fox. He looks large because his fine hair is soft, very fluffy, and long, his tail very bushy. His ears and nose are rather short, do not stick far enough above the fur to freeze. His feet are thickly padded with fur.

The homeland of this northern Fox is from the limit of trees northward over the arctic tundra as far north as mammals go. They eat whatever meat their harsh land harbors. In summer they feed upon the many wild fowl which come to the arctic to breed. They also prey upon the pups of the Seals. One of their important foods is the Lemming. Foxes store Lemmings under rock crevices to be eaten when food is scarce. During the bleak northern winter they do not hibernate. They catch Lemmings, may also catch an Arctic Hare or a Ptarmigan, or follow the Polar Bear out over the polar ice and feed on the remnants of Seal or other prey the large animal has killed.

When a Whale carcass happens to be washed ashore, the Foxes have enough food for a year.

Unlike their southern cousins these Foxes are quite tame. Arctic explorers have reported that they often come near a campfire, sit in the snow near by, and watch the fire and bark like Dogs. Cases have been reported of their following close behind the heels of explorers on the arctic islands.

They are easy to trap. Polar Bears and Wolves are their enemies, and the Snowy Owl may also take their young. But man is their worst enemy.

The genus name *Alopex* is the Greek word meaning a Fox.

CAT FAMILY
(family *Felidae*)

This is the family which includes the domestic Cat. The members which are native to America vary from about the size of a Red Fox to big Cats weighing up to two hundred pounds. Like members of the Dog Family, all American Cats are wild. They are mostly of slender build, all have sharp claws which they can sheathe.

Their original range is over the greater part of the continent from the arctic to the Mexican border. The family name *Felidae* comes from the Latin word *felis* which means Cat.

King of the American Beasts

COUGAR
MOUNTAIN LION
PUMA, PANTHER
(genus *Felis*)

Cat Family

The American Mountain Lion is a beautiful, sinuous Cat. He was king of the new world before America was settled by Europeans. Large and powerful, he feared no other native animal. His one enemy has been man.

These big Cats measure from seven to nine feet in length from the tip of their noses to the tip of their very long tails. They average from 150 to 200 pounds in weight, the males may weigh over 200. Females are much smaller, rarely reaching 120 pounds.

Formerly the Cougars ranged over North America from the east to the west coast, from as far north as British Columbia and Alberta south over the South American continent to Patagonia. They were found in the forest and in the arid deserts. Their range was largely determined by the range of animals they preyed upon.

Today these big beasts have been exterminated in the east, except for a few in the wilds of Florida and Louisiana. In the west they are still found from British Columbia and Alberta south over the Mexican border but are rarely seen. Secretive, wary, harassed by stockmen, they have gone into the remote mountains or hide out among the canyons and cliffs of the desert. Campers are

Cougar

now and then startled by a weird, womanlike scream which tells that one of these big Cats is somewhere near.

They hunt mostly at night and then they go cautiously, stalking big game without the slightest sound. They leap upon their victims with great force, breaking the backs of their prey and causing instant death. When finished with a meal they cover the remains with leaves and sticks to save the food for another day.

They used to live mainly on Elk. Today their favorite prey is Deer. They are most abundant near the haunts of Mule and other western Deer. They hunt over a chosen path, following a wide circle, sometimes taking several days and walking as many as fifty miles in their rounds. They also catch small animals, Rodents, Mountain Beaver, Porcupine, and unfortunately for the Lions, they like beef and particularly the meat of colts. When Deer are scarce they prey on Cattle and Horses. Every stockman is now naturally their enemy.

Men also hunt Lions for sport. Dogs are trained especially for this exciting chase. Men follow on foot or often on horseback.

Many of the big Cats have been destroyed to save Elk and Deer. Of late there has been some question as to whether extermination of Cougars would help or do harm. Observers say that Deer which fall prey to stalking Lions are often the feeble, the slow, the old, and the diseased. When these animals are allowed to live they weaken the herds.

Limited Lion control is of course necessary.

But trying to keep a balance in modern times is very difficult. In Canada Deer became so numerous that they raided the gardens and trampled lawns in the city of Banff. Predatory animals were allowed to increase to control the Deer. After three years a Cougar appeared on the city streets. He was after Deer and Sheep.

Mountain Lions have always been feared by people. Many terrible tales are told about Cougars leaping on unsuspecting campers. These stories seem to be mostly fiction. One authority states that there is no authentic case on record of a North American Cougar attacking a man, unprovoked. Others say that in a few cases they have been known to kill people. These cases are certainly rare. Men spend years in Cougar country and never catch so much as a glimpse of even his long tail. The Mountain Lion is an exceedingly shy beast.

Several species and geographic races of Cougar exist. They all have beautiful, lustrous, soft hair. The color of their coats may be tawny tan, fading to lighter under the abdomen and pure white under the chin and on whiskers. Another species is dark reddish brown.

They do not hibernate, but are active all year. The cubs are born in a cave or sometimes in a clump of dense vegetation. Twins are common although sometimes there is but one. Litters of five have been reported. The young are marked with darkish spots on the body and bars on their tails. They are very playful like house kittens.

The genus name *Felis* is the root of the Family name *Felidae* and means Cat.

Biggest Cat

JAGUAR
TIGER
AMERICAN LEOPARD
(genus *Felis*)

Cat Family

The Jaguar is a jungle Cat, big, powerfully built, biggest of the American Cats. He is a little heavier than the Mountain Lion. He is a very handsome spotted Cat. The ground color of the

coat of the American beast is yellow tinged with orange, the tail is broadly banded with black, and the spots and rosettes which mark the body are mostly large. The rosettes often have small

Jaguar

black spots in the center, and in this the marking differs from that of the Old World Leopard. The American Jaguar also has a shorter tail and is of heavier build.

Very few people in North America have seen a Jaguar outside of a zoo. Not only is the beast wary and secretive, like the Mountain Lion, but he is a southern animal now rarely seen north of the Mexican border. Formerly he ranged into the southern states up the Mississippi Valley and up the Rio Grande Valley and into warmer parts of the eastern and western states. Occasionally one is reported today in the jungles of Florida or in parts of the southwest but most Jaguars are gone except to the south over the border in their real homeland, the jungles of Mexico and southward.

Like the Cougars they have developed a taste for Cattle and Horses. Stockmen exterminate them whenever they are reported near their ranches. South of the border the animal is greatly feared. His coughing roar strikes terror into the hearts of natives and certainly the Jaguar is powerful enough to justify these fears. However, as in the case of the Mountain Lion, no authentic case of these Cats attacking a man, unprovoked, has been reported, at least on the northern continent. These Cats are not known to become man-eaters as some of the old-world Tigers have been.

The Jaguar spends much of his time stalking herds of the Peccaries which belong to his jungle homeland. He covers an immense amount of territory on his hunting expeditions which are mostly in the night. When he creeps up on his prey only his yellow Cat eyes gleaming in the dark betray his presence.

From two to four cubs are usual in this big Cat's family.

Although very differently marked, this spotted Cat belongs to genus *Felis,* which includes the Mountain Lion.

Ocelot

Mexican Visitor

OCELOT
TIGER CAT
LEOPARD CAT
(genus *Felis*)

Cat Family

The pretty little Tiger Cat resembles a Jaguar but his markings are varied and he weighs no more than twenty-five, perhaps thirty-five pounds. On a background of tawny yellow or yellow buff an intricate pattern is formed with oblongs, spots, rosettes. The tail is banded.

A southern Cat, he comes over our borders only into southern Texas where he is rarely seen. He hunts at night among the chaparral and the thorny mesquite for Mice and Rats, Rabbits and birds. He eats some reptiles, an occasional snake, and raids hen roosts.

Only one species enters the United States. He is most frequently found in the lower Rio Grande Valley in the haunts of his cousin the Jaguarundi.

Farther south in Central and South America he is common.

Two young are the usual number in a family.

This medium-sized wild Cat belongs to the same genus as the big Jaguar and the Mountain Lion, genus *Felis,* meaning a Cat.

Jaguarundi

JAGUARUNDI
Yagouaroundi
Cacomitl, Eyra
(genus *Felis*)

Cat Family

This Cat with the clumsy names is the smallest Cat to come into the United States. Like the Ocelot he is a southerner. He comes over the Mexican border into the Lower Rio Grande Valley where with the Ocelot he lives in the dense chaparral, the almost jungle thickets of cat's-claw and other underbrush around clumps of mesquite.

Formerly it was thought that the Eyra was a different species from the Jaguarundi. Then it was discovered that both are born in the same litter. They are color phases of the same Cat, just as the Cinnamon Bear is but a color phase of the Black Bear. The name Eyra is generally applied to the red phase. The dark smoky-gray phase

is more frequently called Jaguarundi.

The form of this southern Cat is quite uncat-like. He has a long, minklike body, short legs, small flat head, and ten-inch tail. His total length is about forty inches.

Like most Cats he hunts at night for birds and small animals but may be seen abroad in the day. He is a shy animal, secretive, and avoids people. He is much wilder than the Ocelot. When captive he stays in the back of his cage uttering little wild Cat cries.

Close cousin to the Ocelot and the big Jaguar and Mountain Lion, he belongs to the same genus, *Felis.*

Northern Bobtail

CANADIAN LYNX   Cat Family
WILDCAT
(genus *Lynx*)

The Canadian Lynx is one of the handsomest of our native animals. Stylish is the word best to describe his tufted ears, his smart cheek fur, his black-tipped little tail, and there is something modish about his whole appearance although he changes but slightly the color of his grizzled hair from season to season. He is browner in summer, grayer in winter. He is a northern animal but like all Cats he stays active throughout the coldest parts of the year. He has a fine, rather long-haired fur coat and his enormous feet are furred below in winter. They help hold him on the top of the snow. His legs are heavy and long, his body short. He may weigh as much as thirty pounds.

His former range was from the Arctic Circle south over forested Canada and along the colder parts of the mountains into Pennsylvania in the east and to Colorado and Mount Whitney, California, in the west. Secretive and very shy, this forest Cat dislikes settlements, disappears when people move into his homeland unless there is dense cover near by.

Lynx may den in hollow logs but prefer rocky ledges where they may find small caves. Here the spotty kittens are born, from two to five in number.

The Canadian Lynx hunts Mice, Squirrels, Foxes, and birds but in the more northern part of his range he is largely dependent for food upon the Snowshoe Hare. When these Hares have a period of abundance, Lynx wax fat. When these Hares are very scarce the Lynx are found gaunt and starving in the woods. Then driven by hunger they may attack Deer and Mountain Sheep. Many of them perish before the Hares increase.

The relation between the life of the Lynx and these northern Hares has been shown by returns in the fur market. The best Lynx pelts come from Hudson Bay and Alaska. The fur is used largely for trimmings and coat collars. During periods when the northern Hares are reported to be scarce, fewer Lynx skins appear in the trade.

Although this northern Bobtail has a reputation for being fierce he will not attack man unless cornered and forced to fight.

His common name is the same as the name of the scientific genus to which he belongs, *Lynx*. This is a Greek word.

Small Lynx

BOBCAT   Cat Family
BAY LYNX
WILDCAT
(genus *Lynx*)

The Bobcat is small cousin to the Canadian Lynx, and is about two thirds of the size of the bigger Cat. The Bay Lynx has less tufted ears, a more slender build. The bars on his tail are characteristic of the smaller animal.

The range of the Bobcat is more southerly. He is found from southern British Columbia and Nova Scotia over most of the wooded areas of the United States and into Mexico.

The habits of the Bobcat are quite similar to the habits of the Canadian Lynx. He likes rocky country where he may den under ledges but also may den in hollow logs. Not as shy as his big cousin, this short-tailed Cat continues to live near settled regions, his Cat cry is familiar to many, and the animal himself is sometimes seen in daylight although he usually hunts at night. He lives on small mammals such as Wood Rats, Mice and Rabbits, Muskrats, Squirrels and is one of the few animals which cares to attack a Porcupine.

Canadian Lynx

When driven by hunger the Bobcat will prey upon animals many times his own size, has been known to fell both Deer and Sheep. He also eats some carrion, a little grass, a few insects.

From two to four kittens are born early in the spring, usually under a rock ledge or in a cave.

Very closely related to the Canadian Lynx, the Bobcat has similar grizzly-gray-brown fur. He belongs to the same genus, *Lynx*.

Bobcat

THE BEAR FAMILY
(family *Ursidae*)

To this family belong some of the largest of our game animals. All are heavy in form and big. One is the biggest of the *Carnivora,* the Flesh Eaters. Characteristic of the family are short tails, heavy legs, and the manner of walking on the soles of the feet rather than on the toes. All except the Polar Bear are land animals.

The Bear Family in America contains three genera, groups. They are the Black Bear (including the Cinnamon, the White, and the Glacier), the Grizzly Bear (including the giants of Alaska), and the Polar Bear.

The family name *Ursidae* comes from the Latin word *ursus* which means Bear.

The Common Bear

Bear Family

BLACK BEAR and a color phase
CINNAMON BEAR
ALSO GLACIER BEAR AND
KERMODE BEAR
(genus *Euarctos*)

Some form of the Black Bear is found in most of forested North America from the northern limit of trees in Alaska and Canada to Florida and northern Mexico. Today he is a familiar and tame animal in parks. The Cinnamon Bear was formerly thought to be a different species, but Black and Cinnamon cubs appear in the same litters. The Cinnamon Bear is now known to be

Black Bear

just a color phase of the Black Bear. Sometimes Cinnamon cubs turn black when they are grown.

In Alaska a bluish Black Bear lives in the icy mountains between Copper River and Lynn Canal. His coat is frosty-looking. He is known as the Glacier Bear, is classified as a distinct species but is thought to be but a rare color phase of the common Black Bear.

In the coast region of British Columbia the Black Bear is white. This very small Bear is known as the Kermode Bear, is also classified as a separate species but by some is thought to be an albino form of the common Black type.

None of these bears is ferocious and they generally avoid people. On the other hand they are very inquisitive and while hiding unseen in the bushes they often watch fishermen or men working in their gardens.

They have been driven from some of their former range by settlers. They are abundant in most National Parks where they are fed and become very tame, and sometimes rough. They are so fond of sweets that they have been known to rip the top off a car to get a bar of chocolate.

One of their favorite foods is honey. When a Black Bear finds a beehive in a hollow tree he does not hesitate to dig out the honeycombs, even enduring painful stings on his nose. He is also very fond of berries, is frequently disturbed in berry patches where he seeks blackberries, raspberries, and blueberries. He also eats buttercups, the leaves and fruiting capsules of mountain laurel and wintergreen, sweet fern buds, grapes, the seeds and buds of various shrubs and hemlock and pine needles. In the fall he enjoys acorns.

He is not entirely a vegetarian. He is very fond of ants and grubworms, eats an occasional bird, Mouse, or Squirrel. Another favorite food is pork. One of these Bears will boldly approach a pigpen in the night and carry off a young Pig for his supper. They also like smoked pork, will steal bacon from camps.

In the fall they get very fat. Then they look for large hollow trees or shallow caves in which they may go to sleep. Sometimes they crawl under a large root, or even bed down in deep moss with only the thick foliage of evergreen branches growing on the surrounding trees to cover them. While the snows are deep and the temperatures low, the Bears sleep. Their breathing is very slow. They take only three or four breaths a minute. They do not eat nor drink. Yet they are not considered true hibernators because their body temperature does not drop as it does in Bats. They do not become as torpid, they do not sleep as long. In the more northern part of their range they may sleep for three months. During this time the cubs are born. They weigh less than a pound at birth, they are not well developed, their eyes do not open for six weeks. For nearly two months the mother Bear keeps them warm and feeds them milk. Then they are big enough to follow her about. There are usually twins, sometimes one, occasionally three cubs.

The genus name *Euarctos* comes from the Greek *eu* meaning true and *arktos,* a Bear.

A Fierce Bear

GRIZZLY BEAR   Bear Family
SILVERTIP
(genus *Ursus*)

The Grizzly Bear is very large and the most ferocious Bear in the world. When he rears up on his hind feet he is often taller than a six-foot man, sometimes will weigh as much as a good-sized Horse, about 1000 pounds. This tawny-colored Bear frequently has a sprinkling of white-tipped hairs in his coat. This gives him the name of Silvertip.

He is so powerful that he can easily carry away a full-grown Deer under his arm. But for all the Grizzly's strength, he senses the power of people and prefers not to come too close to man, his

Grizzly Bear

worst enemy.

As a rule Grizzlies will not attack a man unless they are cornered or wounded. But if driven by hunger there is no doubt that these Bears would charge a man and break him in two with a blow from their powerful paws, or rip their prey open with their long, curved claws.

It is well known that a Grizzly will attack a full-grown Cow or even a Moose. But generally this large, ferocious Bear is satisfied with small game, such as Mice, Moles, and insects. He loves to turn rocks over, looking for ants and grubworms. He likes berries and acorns. When he kills big prey he may bury the leftovers under leaves and sticks to save the food for another day.

Through the mountains of the west the deep scratches made by this Bear high up on the trunks of yellow pine may be frequently seen. Woodsmen say that this mark is a challenge to other Bears who cannot reach as high to keep away from that territory. However, small females are known to have this same habit. It is doubtful whether it is for the purpose of showing strength.

The Silvertip is becoming very rare. It was estimated that there were not many over a thousand left in the United States during the last big game census. Many of these are in parks where the big creature is protected and often fed. He does not become as friendly as the smaller Black Bear and is often cross.

A few wild ones may still be found in the high Rockies from Arizona to Alaska. In the wintertime they seek a cave or other shelter and like the Black Bears they den up. The tiny cubs are born about midwinter. They are very undeveloped. The young Bears stay close to the she-Bear during the spring and summer and go back with the mother into her den the following winter.

The Grizzly belongs to the genus *Ursus* which means a Bear and is the root for the Latin *Ursidae,* the family name.

Giant Bear

ALASKAN BROWN BEAR
Big Brownie
Kadiak Bear
(genus *Ursus*)

Bear Family

These northern Bears are the largest Bears in the world. The Kadiak Bear which lives only on Kadiak Island off the coast of Alaska is the biggest of them all, sometimes weighing nearly three quarters of a ton. The size of this Bear reminds one of the giant prehistoric Bears.

Other Big Brownies are found on the coast of Alaska, the Kenai Peninsula, and near-by islands. There are a dozen species known, none of which differs greatly. It is very hard to tell the difference between the Alaskan Brown Bears and the Grizzlies. They are very closely related. There is a slight difference in the shape of the skulls, but the color of the hide is sometimes the same. The coats of the Big Brownies vary from almost black to blond yellow, almost white, but they are commonly light brown, not often as grizzly as their cousins. If you get close enough you will see that the front claws of the Brownies are shorter, thicker, more curved than on a true Silvertip. However, none of the differences are certain to be found in every individual.

The Giant Bears live in little-populated areas in the deep underbrush of dwarf pines and alder and other shrubs. They leave their winter quarters in early April or a little later. When snow is still on the ground they go down to the shore and eat seaweed and perhaps dead fish. During early spring they also consume quantities of willow catkins but as soon as the fresh greens appear in the meadows among the thickets they graze like Cows, living mainly upon sedge grass and other plants, but adding small animals to their diet. They go about looking for the burrows of

Alaskan Brown Bear

Mice, and Ground Squirrels, and when they locate one they quickly dig out the little Rodent. That is the way they live until the salmon come up the rivers to spawn. Then the big Bears move down to the river edges and feast upon the fish. They wade out into the shallow streams, scoop up the surprised salmon, or, if the streams be deep, they sometimes wade out until they are almost submerged and catch the delicious prey. They are fond of water, are good swimmers.

During the salmon season they live beside the streams, resting when they have had their fill. They hide in the dense thickets on the banks. In August they leave the streams for a time to feast upon the numerous wild berries which abound in the north, the cloudberries, crowberries, and others. In the autumn they eat quantities of the berries of the mountain ash and the seeds of dwarf pine.

If they have had a good summer and have laid up a store of fat they hunt for winter quarters sometimes as early as October. If they are thin they stay abroad longer. The northern guides say that just before hibernation they eat quantities of cranberries which act as a purge. Then they eat fibers of tough roots. Thus when they are ready for the long sleep their stomachs and intestines are probably empty, save only for a plug of bark.

They seek inaccessible places under the mountain underbrush. Here they dig dens in the dry hillsides and sleep during the bitterest parts of winter. During the cold months the cubs are born, usually twins, sometimes one, sometimes three.

In general this great Bear is rather timid, will flee at the sight of man. Even the faint odor of man will set this giant in flight unless he is cornered or the females are with cubs. Then they will fight fiercely. They also may attack if suddenly disturbed. The natives are careful to shout when they follow the Bear paths through the thickets, knowing that they would be killed or maimed if they came suddenly upon one of the big brutes.

In the spring their temper is particularly fierce. They are lean and hungry. At this season they seek big game, sometimes steal Horses or Cows. However, they prefer to eat salmon, small Rodents, and grasses and berries and lead a peaceful life.

They were formerly numerous in sections where the salmon streams are located. Like most big-game animals they have been overhunted. Sportsmen seek their hides as trophies. The natives use the skins for beds and for making thongs. They eat the Bear meat and consider the fat of the pads of the paws a particular delicacy.

The Alaskan Brown Bears belong to the same genus as their close cousins the Grizzlies, genus *Ursus* which means a Bear.

The Swimmer

POLAR BEAR   Bear Family
WATER BEAR
ICE BEAR
(genus *Thalarctos*)

In the arctic regions where the summer nights are lighted by the midnight sun and the winter days are long and dark, lit only by the strange northern lights and stars, this is the home of the Polar Bear, a Bear which differs in shape from all of the other Bears known.

The hair of the Polar Bear is white and thick.

Even the soles of his feet are furred. He has a long neck and slender, pointed head. He is very large, ferocious, and brave.

In summer the Polar Bears rarely visit land. They live on the ice floes and can often be seen splashing about in the cold arctic waters. They are strong but slow swimmers, rather clumsy in

Polar Bear

the water, and find it hard to get a living out of the sea. Their main food is Seal which they capture by strategy. When sighting a Seal resting on an ice floe, a Polar Bear will swim underwater for long distances toward his prey. When close, he will raise himself out of the water and with a blow from one of his great paws he will crush the Seal's head, killing him instantly.

At times the Polar Bear will sit for hours at a "breathing hole" in the ice, waiting for a Seal to come up for a breath of air. He waits like a Cat watching for a Mouse to come out of a hole.

In the winter the female Polar Bear seeks out a cave or if a cave cannot be found she will curl up on a bed of rock and let the snow drift over her to keep her warm. The warmth of her body soon makes a hollow space under the snow. It is here that the cubs are born. The cubs have milk from the mother Bear but the mother has nothing to eat until the rays of the spring sun rouse her from her winter's sleep. By spring the little ones are strong enough to follow their mother out into the world.

With few exceptions, the old male Polar Bears are the only ones of the native Bear Family who do not hibernate during the winter months and dare to face the hardships of outdoor life when the ground is frozen and the sea locked with ice.

Genus *Thalarctos* means sea Bear (Greek *thalassa*, the sea, and *arktos*, a Bear).

Chapter IX
On Land and Sea

THE FIN-FOOTED
(order *Pinnipedia*)

This group of mammals is closely related to the *Carnivora*, the Flesh Eaters. They are descended from land ancestors but now spend most of their lives in the sea. Their bodies have become streamlined, their legs modified into flippers for swimming. Their feet are webbed and paddlelike. Although unlike the Whales they can still walk on land, their movements ashore are very awkward.

The appropriate group name, order *Pinnipedia*, comes from two Latin words, *pinna* meaning fin and *pes, pedis* meaning foot.

There are three families of the Fin-footed. They are the Walrus Family, the Eared Seal Family, and the Earless or Hair Seal Family.

The Mammal with Ivory Tusks

WALRUS
SEA HORSE
(genus *Odobenus*)

The Walrus Family
(family *Odobenidae*)

Everyone is familiar with the appearance of the large, hulking sea animals with long ivory tusks and rather small, whiskered, caterpillar faces. Few people see them alive. They are animals of the far north. The name Walrus comes from a Scandinavian word meaning Whale Horse. Unlike a Whale, Walrus have flippers which may be used for walking on land. Their hind legs, unlike those of the Hair Seals, rotate forward, making it possible for them to waddle clumsily around on ice cakes. They swim with all four flippers.

Full-grown male Walrus have huge shoulders. They weigh from a ton to a ton and a half and are from ten to twelve feet long. Females are much smaller. Walrus hide is yellowish brown in color, warty, wrinkled, and nearly an inch thick. It is covered with scant reddish hair. Under the skin is a thick layer of fat which keeps them so warm that they enjoy sitting on ice cakes. This fat makes such a good blanket that even after twelve hours of floating in icy water the dead body of a Walrus is warm.

Both the male and the female Walrus have ivory tusks which they use as hooks to help them climb out on ice sheets and to dig mollusks in the shallow waters of the sea. They swallow clams, shells and all, with a few stones at the same time. They also like sea snails. The tusks of the female are slenderer than those of the male. They curve inward at the ends and bow in the middle. The tusks of the male weigh from six to nine pounds and are from fourteen to twenty-six inches long, sometimes reaching three feet.

Walrus are rather mild-tempered. They let man approach close to them but if their young are in danger they fight fiercely, using their tusks as weapons. When a hunter comes near, a sentinel gives a loud bellow and they all dive into the sea.

They are social animals. They rest crowded so close together on an ice floe that sometimes those nearest the edge are pushed into the water by the tusks of their companions or the ice floe may break under the weight of many tons of Walrus, dumping all in the Arctic Ocean.

Only two species of Walrus exist, the Atlantic and the Pacific. In the spring when the ice of the arctic breaks they follow the ice packs north in herds. The Atlantic Walrus lives in the Arctic Sea and in the North Atlantic, ranging south to the coast of Labrador. The Pacific Walrus spends the winter in the Bering Sea and near the Siberian coast. During the months of May, June, and July they drift north on the ice floes. On their way north they breed. One young is usual.

The female Walrus are devoted mothers. The baby rides on the mother's back, holding tight with his flippers as she swims through the waves. When the mother dives, the baby Walrus rides in her wake until she returns to the surface. It takes two years for the tusks of the young one to grow three or four inches long, big enough to dig mollusks from the floor of the sea. Therefore, it is probable that the mother suckles her young for nearly two years.

These large sea animals have three powerful enemies. Polar Bears take their young. Their worst native enemy is the Killer Whale, Wolf of the sea. When one of these ferocious Whales sees a mother Walrus with a baby riding on her back, he dives and comes up underneath the mother and bumps the unfortunate young Walrus into the sea where the young one is easily caught.

The third enemy, man, has been responsible for reducing the herds. In the year 1881 it was estimated that one herd on the arctic coast of Alaska contained tens of thousands. During the great whaling period in the north, Walrus were taken for their oil, ivory, and hides in such numbers that they were threatened with extinction. Today Walrus are scarce but now that large-scale whaling has shifted to the southern hemisphere, these animals are holding their own in spite of the fact that from a thousand to fifteen hundred are still caught by the natives of the north each year. The people of the Straits Islands store one or two years' supply of Walrus meat and blubber in caves for their own use and for meat for their Dogs. The Eskimos use the hide to make line for their harpoons. They make the fine ivory tusks into harpoon tips.

The genus name *Odobenus* and the family name are derived from the two Greek words *odon* (tooth) and *bainein* (to walk). This refers to the fact that Walrus drag themselves out onto the ice with their tusks.

EARED SEAL FAMILY
(family *Otariidae*)

Members of this family have furry bodies and external ears. Their hind legs, like those of a Walrus, are fully webbed but rotate forward so that these animals are more active on land than are the Hair Seals. Their scientific family name is based on the Greek word *ous, otos,* an ear. There are four genera (groups) of American Eared Seals. They are the Alaskan Fur Seals, the Guadalupe Fur Seals, the California Sea Lions, and the Stellar (northern) Sea Lions.

The Valuable Seal

ALASKAN FUR SEAL
SEA BEAR
(genus *Callorhinus*)

Eared Seal Family

The Fur Seal, unlike a Hair Seal, has fine soft fur under the long guard hairs of his coat. This makes him a valuable fur animal.

The life of a Fur Seal is remarkable. The females, their young pups, and the young males spend the winter in the temperate waters as far

Walrus

south as the coast of southern California. In spring they make a long migration in order to breed. They swim north 3000 miles. After this great swim through calm seas, through heavy storms, they never fail to find the passage through the Aleutian Islands and land on the small rocky Pribilof Islands in the Bering Sea, 200 miles from the coast of Alaska! According to a report of the United States Fish and Wildlife Service this is thought to be the only land the Fur Seals touch.

On these remote islands teeming with breeding sea birds, the old bull Fur Seals are waiting for the arrival of the hordes of females. The males winter south of the Aleutians or in the Gulf of Alaska. By the time the females return from the south, the bulls have chosen their ground and begun the fight for a harem. For three months these hulking sea bulls battle. They do not leave their chosen ground even to eat. Their necks swell greatly during the breeding season. Their shoulders are powerful. Much larger than the females, the bulls weigh from 300 to 500 pounds and reach a length of over six feet.

During the desperate fights over the females, these big bulls wound each other severely with their teeth. Their coats become torn and bloody. One strong male may fight fifty battles and win each one. Covered with festering wounds he may continue. Others have to retire to rest and some die. The huskiest old bulls succeed in getting a harem of forty females. The government survey reports that one may win over seventy.

Soon after arrival at the Pribilof Islands each female Fur Seal gives birth to a black pup. Then they breed again. They spend the remainder of the summer feeding on squid and surface fish and caring for their newborn pups. The mothers go to sea, sometimes for two days at a time. When they return they find their own complaining babies among the thousands of other young Seals, apparently picking out their own by the tone of their calls. The babies suckle for six to eight weeks. They turn grayish in color at about six weeks.

Adult females are grayish with reddish under parts. The bulls are black on their backs, under parts brownish, with some gray on their shoulders.

By early August all the mothers have had pups and the breeding season is finished. The hungry, gaunt, battle-scarred old males return to the sea to feed. The females stay with their young on the Pribilofs until early November. Then their pups are large enough to make the long swim south. After spending the winter in southern waters, the urge to migrate comes to the females. With their large pups and the young males they turn again north to the Pribilof Islands to give birth to another young one and to breed once more. The remarkable yearly migrations of these swimming mammals remind one of the flights of migratory birds.

Because of their importance in the fur market, Fur Seals are of great interest to the United States government. Because Seals are aquatic like Whales, they have been pursued by people of many nations. Sealers from Russia, Japan, Great Britain, and the United States used to capture large numbers of them from boats during the yearly migration. This practice was costly. Many Seals were killed and lost, and mother Seals were slaughtered at the breeding grounds, leaving the pups to die of starvation on the rocky Pribilofs. The herds were greatly reduced. An international treaty and a government patrol has saved them.

The American herd includes about eighty per cent of all the Fur Seals in the world today. In the year 1910 the herd had been reduced to less than a hundred and fifty thousand. By 1940 the herd had increased to well over two million!

The Pribilof Islands belonged to Russia until the purchase of Alaska by the United States. Now these islands are a reservation belonging to the American government. Unless stranded in a storm, no one is allowed to land there except by special permission from the Secretary of the Interior. On their remote islands the American Fur Seals are now allowed to breed and raise their pups in peace. Each year the government agents

Alaskan Fur Seal

select those which are to be used for Seal coats.

The three-year-old males are the only ones killed. Bull Seals do not mature until they are seven or eight years old and until then they herd together. Since one old male may breed with from forty to seventy females, fewer males are needed. The killing of the males also reduces the fierce fighting during the breeding season. The females are carefully guarded. They have their first pup when they are three years old.

An average Fur Seal coat is made from six or eight skins. The skins are dyed black or brown. Today the yield of the islands is enough to make about 8000 coats a year without decreasing the herd. The skins are made ready for shipment by the Aleuts, natives placed on the Pribilofs by the Russians when Alaska belonged to that nation. The skins are processed in Saint Louis and sold at auction, the money going into the treasury of the United States.

To protect the mothers and pups on their yearly migration, a patrol was posted. By inter-national treaty between Russia, Great Britain, the United States, and Japan, the taking of Seals in the water was forbidden save to the natives of the north. This treaty also protected a Japanese Fur Seal herd of fifty thousand animals at Robben Island, the Russian herd of a little less than a hundred thousand animals at Commander Island, while fifteen per cent of the American take on the Pribilofs was sent to Japan and fifteen per cent to Canada to pay for loss of ocean sealing.

Until 1941 the mother Fur Seals swam safely north in the spring to the arctic breeding grounds and returned safely in the fall with their pups, by international agreement.

But in 1941 these great herds were again threatened. Japan canceled her treaty, the act taking effect in October of that year, and now no one can predict what effect the outbreak of war will have upon the lives of the Fur Seals.

The genus name *Callorhinus* comes from the Greek *kalos* (beautiful) *rhis* (nose).

GUADALUPE FUR SEAL
(genus *Arctocephalus*)

Eared Seal Family

These close relatives of the Alaskan Fur Seals were thought to be extinct in 1894. In 1928 they were found on Guadalupe Island, off Lower California. This may be the final appearance of a nearly extinct species or these southern Seals may again become numerous. The mounted specimen at the Natural History Museum in New York City has a blacker coat than the Alaskan Fur Seals.

The genus name *Arctocephalus* is derived from two Greek words *arktos* a Bear and *kephale* head.

Southern Sea Lion

CALIFORNIA SEA LION
(genus *Zalophus*)

Eared Seal Family

These cousins of the Fur Seals are the playful Seals frequently seen in zoos. Their native home is the Pacific Ocean off the coast from southern Mexico to northern California. Here herds of them swim with the joyous abandon of their kind. They feed on squid and octopus. In the zoo they are expert at catching and swallowing in one gulp fish tossed to them by the keeper.

Some authorities report finding stones in the stomachs of these Seals. Perhaps the stones help grind their unchewed food as shell or gravel in the crop grinds the food of a chicken.

The male Sea Lion is very large, has catlike whiskers. His neck and shoulders are hulking and thick. The full-grown bull may weigh 500 pounds and reach a length of over eight feet. One old male in the New York Aquarium reached 620 pounds. The females are smaller, slenderer.

Stellar's Sea Lion

Although awkward on land these Sea Lions are more active ashore than are the Hair Seals. They can bend their hind legs forward and waddle about quite fast when they haul out on rocks.

In the water they look sleek black in color. When dry their short fur is yellowish to reddish brown, sometimes darker, and sometimes with light gray about the head. They have a raucous demanding cry.

The one young Sea Lion soon learns to immitate his noisy parents.

The genus name *Zalophus* comes from two Greek words *za* (very) and *lophos* (crest). These words describe the prominent crests on the Sea Lion's skull.

Northern Sea Lion

STELLAR'S SEA LION
Northern Sea Lion
(genus *Eumetopias*)

Eared Seal Family

Stellar's Sea Lion is larger than the California Sea Lion. Males weigh from 1500 to 1800 pounds and reach thirteen feet in length. They live in the North Pacific from San Francisco, California, to Bering Strait.

Like others of this family they are polygamous. The males come ashore in May very plump. In June the females follow them to land to breed. The terrible fights between the bulls begin. Each male tries to gather a harem of from ten to fifteen females. The contests are so intense that no bull stops to eat for several months.

The one young pup is born in June and the mother nurses him and cares for him for at least a year.

In color these northern Sea Lions vary from dark brown to light yellowish brown.

The genus name *Eumetopias* comes from the Greek *eu* (true) and *metopon* (forehead).

EARLESS SEAL FAMILY
Hair Seal Family
(family *Phocidae*)

The members of this family are typical Seals with coarse short hair. They are more specialized for life in the water than are their cousins, the members of the Eared Seal Family. The Hair Seals have little hidden ears which close under water. While Eared Seals can use their hind flippers for moving on land, the Earless Seals cannot rotate their hind legs forward and are therefore very awkward, almost helpless ashore.

The root of the scientific family name for Hair Seals is the Latin word *phoca* which means a Seal.

There are five genera, groups, of these Seals found off American shores. The first genus includes the Common Seal, the Harp Seal, and the Ribbon Seal. The other four groups are the Hooded Seals, the Elephant Seals, the Gray Seals, and the Bearded Seals.

The Common Seal

HARBOR SEAL
Common Seal
Hair Seal
Leopard Seal
(genus *Phoca*)

Hair Seal Family

This is a small Seal which never goes far from shore. He lives about harbors or bays or off rocky points along the Atlantic coast from the arctic to the Carolinas. Another species with several

Harbor Seal

subspecies is found on the Pacific coast from the Pribilof Islands, breeding ground of the Fur Seals, into Mexican waters. Sometimes they wander up the Saint Lawrence and the Yukon Rivers.

This typical Seal is formed like other members of his family. He is unable to rotate his hind legs forward and while ashore he can only drag himself about with his front flippers. In the water the fully webbed hind feet act like tail fins of a fish. They serve to send him through his element, the water.

Harbor Seals are small, reaching but five feet in length. They are of a more slender build than the Sea Lions. Their coarse, rough fur has no value except to the Eskimos who hunt the Harbor Seals in the north when the animals come up to breathe through ice holes. They eat the meat and use the hides for clothing and to make rawhide lines. Out of the membranes of the intestines they make waterproof parkas.

The young Harbor Seals are white but the adults are spotted like Leopards and vary in color from dark brown, spotted with yellow, to yellowish spotted with dark brown.

Like all Seals the Common Seals have very sharp cusps on their premolar teeth which help them grasp slippery fish. The western Harbor Seal eats herring, sculpins, hake, cod, flounder, tomcod, pollack, and shiners and a few crustacea and squid.

These Seals do not swim in great herds as do some Seals. They rest on shore in small groups.

The genus name of the Harbor Seal is *Phoca*, the Latin word for Seal. *Phoca* is the root word of the family name *Phocidae*.

Seal-Oil Seal

HARP SEAL
GREENLAND SEAL
SADDLEBACK SEAL
(genus *Phoca*)

Hair Seal Family

The Harp Seals are large and abundant. Males may weigh 600 to 800 pounds and reach seven feet in length. Females are much smaller.

Like Bats and birds these sea mammals are driven by some strange instinct to migrate twice a year. Their migrations follow a set route which parallels that of the Hooded Seals for part of the long swim. Both species winter and grow fat in the waters around the Grand Banks off Newfoundland and near Sable Island. Some winter

Harp Seal

in the Gulf of Saint Lawrence. In early February they start for the breeding and whelping grounds. They swim north to the Strait of Belle Isle which lies between Labrador and Newfoundland. Near there they breed. Here too the white pups are born, one to a family. The nursery is a big, thin sheet of ice through which the mother makes a trapdoor. She dives through the trapdoor into the sea to feed, leaving her pup on the cold ice cake. The young do not learn to swim until they are almost two weeks old.

Sometimes a mother will be gone all day hunting. Yet she has no trouble in finding the floating nursery. While she is feeding, the ice sheet may drift but witnesses say that the roar and cries of the herd may be heard several miles. Home again the mother has no difficulty in picking out her own crying baby in the midst of thousands of other baby Seals.

At Belle Isle the main herd is joined by the Seals which spent the winter in the Gulf of Saint Lawrence. Soon the migration continues. The Hooded Seals leave the Harps off Cape Farewell and go to the east coast of Greenland for the summer. The Harp Seals follow the west coast of Greenland into Baffin Bay where they stay until the ice of late September warns them that it is time to start south again. Once more they meet the Hooded Seals near Cape Farewell. Then they all turn again toward the Grand Banks, the Harp Seals keeping to the inside lane, paralleling the shore, the Hooded Seals swimming in the outer lane.

The Harp Seal is the important Seal in the industry on the Atlantic coast. For many years sealers set out from Saint Johns, Newfoundland, to meet the Harps on their migration to the breeding grounds. Men returned with cargoes of Seal oil and hides. The oil of the Harps is of good quality. The hide is also good. In former years nearly a million Harp Seals were killed each breeding season. By 1928 it was estimated that there were 300,000 left in the herd which wintered in the Saint Lawrence Gulf and 500,000 in the larger herd. Occasionally Harps are reported as far south as Long Island.

Today the industry has declined but the oil is still valued as a lubricant. Modern ships aided by airplane and radio locate the remnants of the herds drifting on the ice sheets during the breeding season.

The hair of the adult Harp Seal is coarse and not of good quality but the fine white skins of the baby Seals are dyed and used today for women's coats. As the Seal grows older his white coat is replaced with a spotted brown one. Full-grown males have dark-gray hair marked with a harp-shaped band of brown. This distinctive marking may be absent in the female. The under parts are white. According to Robert A. Bartlett, the brown spots do not disappear until the Seals are five years of age. They do not breed until four.

Closely related to the Harbor Seal, they belong to the same genus of true Seals, genus *Phoca*, which is Latin for a Seal.

RIBBON SEAL
(genus *Phoca*)

Hair Seal Family

This rather small, strikingly marked Seal is rare. Its home is in the remote arctic region from the Aleutian Islands off Alaska, north to Bering Strait as well as on the Asiatic shores.

Formerly the hide was used by fur traders in the arctic. The skin was kept whole, save for a slit in the belly. After it was tanned it was laced tightly together and used as a waterproof bag to take on dog-sled trips. These Seal pokes are still used by Eskimos to hold oil or as floats on harpoon lines to keep a captured prey from diving.

The Ribbon Seal is strikingly marked with light tan or yellowish ribbons over a brown ground color. A rather solitary animal, he does not appear in large herds as do many others of his family.

He is the third member of genus *Phoca*, the genus of true Seals.

Ribbon Seal

RINGED SEAL
(genus *Phoca*)   **Hair Seal Family**

This is a close relative of the Common Seal but he has different markings. On the dark-brown body color are blotches or rings of yellowish. He is a Seal of the far north. He lives in polar seas ranging south to Labrador on the Atlantic coast, to Bering Sea on the Pacific. He is medium-sized.

He is another member of the genus of true Seals, genus *Phoca*, which is the Latin word for Seal.

Hooded Seal

HOODED SEAL
(genus *Cystophora*)   **Hair Seal Family**

Male Hooded Seals have bags of muscular tissue on the upper side of their faces. They can blow them up when they want to. These hoods are secondary sexual characteristics, like the beard of a man. Females have no hoods. The males often inflate theirs when they are angry.

These Seals are herd animals but travel in smaller groups than their cousins the Harp Seals. Like the Harps they migrate and some of their route parallels that of the Harps. The Hooded Seals summer off the east coast of Greenland. When the ice begins to form in early September they turn southward, reach the Strait of Belle Isle between Labrador and Newfoundland in about two months. About halfway between their summer grounds and the strait they bear in close to the mainland where they meet the southbound Harps. As they continue their migration they keep to the outer lane, the Harps remaining on the shore side. At the Strait of Belle Isle some of the Seals turn into the Gulf of Saint Lawrence. Most of them go to the Grand Banks, some to Sable Island. In the near-by waters they feed and spend a fat winter. Near the end of February they are back at the Strait of Belle Isle again. The pups are born on a heavy ice hummock. This is their nursery until they are able to swim well. They stay on the ice approximately two weeks but are more active than the baby Harps, probably venture into the water to try their flippers soon after birth. Robert A. Bartlett reports that the young one is colored gray on his back, white on his belly, and that his hair has a bluish tinge. "It does not have a white fluffy coat like a Harp Seal, but from the remnants of such a coat found after birth on the ice, we know that it passes through a similar stage."

The full-grown Hooded Seal is larger than the

Harp. Males reach from seven to nine feet long. In color they are dark bluish gray, blotched with brown. Their under parts are white. Their short hair is not valuable, but they are hunted by sealers for their oil which is inferior to that of the Harps. The dark coats of the growing pups are used for trimmings for women's and children's coats.

When the pups are able to swim long distances, they follow the ice pack northward with the herd. The retreating ice edge brings them to waters off the eastern coast of Greenland in early summer. In winter they are occasionally reported as far south as the coast of Long Island. They have never been as abundant as the Harps.

The bag on the upper faces of the males is the basis for their genus name *Cystophora,* which is formed from the two Greek words *kystis* (bladder) and *phorein* (to bear).

Northern Elephant Seal

Most Grotesque

NORTHERN ELEPHANT SEAL
SEA ELEPHANT
(genus *Mirounga*)

Hair Seal Family

This is one of the most grotesque mammals living today. A large hulking Seal, the largest of the family, the bull has a long pendulous nose. The nose looks like a short, fat Elephant trunk but contains an air chamber and can be inflated. It is frequently scarred by battles over the cows. Big, bulging eyes add to the ludicrous picture.

Like all members of their family Sea Elephants are specialized for sea life. Their hind legs stretch out into nailless flippers behind. They are of no use as legs because they do not rotate forward. The animals can only drag themselves about with their front flippers and never go far from the shore. They haul out in groups to rest on rocks by the edge of the sea during the day.

They flip sand over their enormous bodies and look very lazy but are probably quite active at night. Since some of their food is found at a depth of from fifty to one hundred and twenty fathoms it is thought that the animal must be a deep diver. His nostrils contain valves which can be shut underwater. He is known to be an excellent swimmer. He feeds upon squid, ratfish, skates, and sharks.

Many animals which are specialized grow very large. This is true of the Elephant on land and also of the Sea Elephant. The bodies of bulls are ponderous and may reach a length of eighteen feet and weigh two and a half tons. The females are half the size of the males and their noses are small, more like protruding upper lips.

On land these big animals are not only helpless but foolish and stupid. They seem to have no fear of men. They will permit people to come close enough to touch them, merely rumbling in their throats as protest. Consequently they have been nearly exterminated. They were not hunted for their walruslike, almost hairless, dirty-brown hides, but for their oil which is considered superior to whale oil as a lubricant. One bull may yield as much as 210 gallons. In the early days whalers found no difficulty in slaying these stupid beasts by the hundreds of thousands. Today the bones of the animals strew the island beaches.

Once very common, they are reduced to a herd of a few hundred. That these still live is largely due to the efforts of the Mexican government. The Mexicans established a refuge on Guadalupe Island off the coast of southern California. If they continue rigidly to protect these strange beasts they may be seen once again swimming along the coast as far north as Point Reyes, just above San Francisco. This used to be the northern limit of their range.

One gray-colored pup is common.

This huge Seal has a cousin in the antarctic, the Southern Sea Elephant. The genus name *Mirounga* is taken from *miouroung*, native Australian name of a species of Seal.

Uncommon Seal

GRAY SEAL   Hair Seal Family
(genus *Halichoerus*)

This large Gray Seal reaches a length of from ten to twelve feet. His color varies from a light gray to nearly black, is usually heavily blotched. He is uncommon on the American coast but is sometimes seen in the Atlantic from Greenland to Nova Scotia, occasionally south to Long Island. His genus name *Halichoerus* comes from two Greek words *hals, halos,* the sea, and *choiros,* a Pig.

BEARDED SEAL   Hair Seal Family
(genus *Erignathus*)

This is a polar Seal found south as far as Newfoundland. A large gray or yellowish Seal, he reaches from ten to twelve feet in length and has bristles on his face. When he comes up between fissures in the ice he is much sought by the Eskimos.

The genus name *Erignathus* comes from the Greek *eri,* a strengthening prefix, and *gnathos,* a jaw.

Chapter X

Sea Cow

THE SIRENS
(order *Sirenia*)

The Sea Cows are a small, queer group of aquatic mammals so adapted to life in water that they can no longer exist on land, nor can they even go ashore. Their hind legs have disappeared, their front legs are modified into flippers which remind one of Whales. But Sea Cows are quite different from the Whale Group. They have a curious lip development perhaps most nearly resembling the development of an Elephant's trunk, and authorities believe that the Sea Cows and the enormous hairless land mammals, the Elephants, are descended from a common stock.

The group is represented by the Dugongs of Asia, the extinct Stellar's Sea Cow, and one native American, the Manatee of Florida.

The group name, order *Sirenia,* is derived from the Latin word *siren,* meaning a mermaid. In the early days when sailors believed in sea dragons and sea serpents and mermaids, they mistook the Manatee for one of the latter. The scientific name was chosen because the breasts are located in the chest region.

MANATEE
FLORIDA SEA COW
(genus *Trichechus*)

Manatee Family
(family *Trichechidae*)

The Manatee Family contains one native American species, the Florida Sea Cow. This queer mammal has a fat hairless body, a head somewhat like a Seal's, a rough skin somewhat like a Walrus, and a unique tail which is un-forked, round, and flat like a paddle. His face has numerous whiskers. Individuals sometimes reach fifteen feet in length and a weight of 1500 pounds but are usually smaller.

The Manatee is a tropical animal, never goes north of the Indian River in Florida. He is close cousin to the Manatee of the Amazon in South America. He frequents rivers and estuaries and never goes very far out to sea. Buoyant, able to suspend himself at any depth in his river home, he is well adapted for river life. Manatees live among a multitude of fishes, yet they never prey upon them. They eat grass. Their taste has given them the name of Sea Cow. In captivity they do not usually live long, often refuse to eat anything but lettuce which they consume to the extent of from a quarter to a half bushel a day. In the wild state they eat quantities of water grasses which they pluck from the bottom of rivers. They may remain submerged for from two to six minutes but they must rise to the surface to breathe. They respire so loudly that they may be heard a half mile away. Often they graze along the river banks, swimming with their nostrils just out of water, sometimes with their whole heads and shoulders above the surface.

Manatees have rather weak teeth but their lips are extraordinarily strong, well developed, and mobile. They cannot stick out their tongues but the bristles on their inner lips and cheeks and the fibrous papillae on the roof and floor of their mouths aid chewing.

In temperament the Manatees are placid and lazy. They float along the warm rivers, grazing as peacefully as a family Cow. They are not streamlined, not built for swift swimming. They have no claws or other weapons of defense. One wonders how they have survived their cousins, the extinct Stellar's Sea Cows. They have few enemies except man, but man nearly exterminated the Florida species. Formerly the Manatees used to swim about in herds of from twelve to fifteen. They were indifferent or fearless. They were easily shot for the sport and for their meat. Today they are protected by law, a fine of $500 is imposed on anyone caught shooting this rare mammal.

The Manatee has one important enemy besides men. This is the weather. Even though covered with a heavy layer of fat similar to the insulation which protects a Whale, the Manatee cannot stand the cold. Frosts occasionally come to Florida, blight the citrus crops, take the lives of many Sea Cows.

Legend says that early navigators mistook Manatees for mermaids. How men saw the image of a mermaid in this strange ugly creature is a matter for conjecture. Two suggestions have been offered. When Sea Cows feed they use their flippers to push the grasses into their mouths. Perhaps at a distance this action was mistaken for a mermaid combing her hair. The sailors might also have seen a mother Manatee with her offspring. Manatees are fond of their young. They have one, sometimes two calves. When the babies are born, the father helps the mother hold the little ones out of water so that they won't drown.

Manatees suckle their young as all true mammals do. While the little one feeds, the mother remains upright in the water, with head and shoulders exposed, clasping the baby to her with her flippers. In this attitude she looks human and perhaps from a distance through an ancient spyglass sailors were convinced that the mother Sea Cow was a mermaid holding her child.

The genus name *Trichechus* and the family name are taken from two Greek words, *thrix, trichos* (hair) and *echein* (to have) and refers to the animal's bristling whiskers.

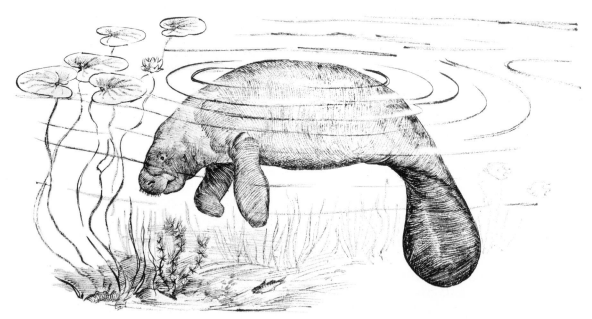

Manatee

Chapter XI
In the Sea

WHALES
(order *Cetacea*)

The members of this strange group of mammals look like fishes but have true lungs and must hold their breath while swimming underwater and come to the surface to breathe. Contrary to the common belief that water is ejected through the nose, the spout of a Whale is the condensed moist breath of the animal which becomes heated while the Whale is submerged. On a quiet day the metallic sound of a large Whale blowing may be heard a half mile away. Each Whale has a characteristic spout which is quickly recognized by whalers.

Unlike most mammals, Whales are hairless save for a few bristles on the heads of some species. Others have no hair. Their smooth bodies are adapted for swift swimming. Many Whales are very fishlike in form; they have little or no visible necks. But while fish are cold-blooded creatures, Whales are warm-blooded. Underneath the skin lies a thick layer of blubber. The blubber contains the oil so valuable to commerce. To the living Whale this fat gives insulation for their naked bodies against the cold of water, taking the place of hair. It also serves as a reservoir when food is scarce. Even the bones of Whales are spongy and full of oil.

Although they are well adapted for life in water they are no doubt descended from an ancestor which walked on land. They have the vestiges of all the organs of land animals but they can no longer exist on shore. All that remains of their hind legs are two small internal bones. Their forelimbs are modified into flippers, their tails are forked but spread out sidewise, not vertically like a fish's. The loose skeletal formation offers no support on land and stranded creatures soon suffocate from their own body weight on their lungs.

Other important but less clearly understood changes have taken place in the body of Whales. Their external ears have almost disappeared. In a Whale sixty feet long the opening into the inner ear is only large enough to admit a matchstick! The inner ear is greatly and curiously developed. From certain tests it is thought that Whales respond to sound waves under water. A sudden change in a boat's speed is echoed to them and frightens them.

A Whale's eye is minute, extraordinarily small considering the size of his body. He has lost power to weep. His tear glands have ceased to function, the water of his home replaces the soothing eyewash of a tear. Sweat glands have likewise disappeared.

The group name, order *Cetacea*, is from the Greek *ketos*, a Whale. There are many different forms within this group. They fall naturally into two distinct types and have therefore been subdivided into two suborders, the Toothed Whales and the Toothless or Whalebone Whales.

TOOTHED WHALES
(suborder *Odontoceti*)

These Whales all have teeth. Some species have a full set of ivory in both jaws, others have but two teeth and there is one species with a single tusk. Another distinguishing characteristic of this group is their noses. There is but one opening and all the spouting is through a single hole.

There are four families of Toothed Whales. They are the Sperm Whale Family, the Pygmy Sperm Whale Family, the Porpoise and Dolphin Family and the Beaked Whale Family.

The suborder *Odontoceti* comes from two Greek words, *odon,* a tooth, and *ketos,* a Whale.

The World's Biggest Nose

SPERM WHALE
Cachalot
(genus *Physeter*)

Sperm Whale Family
(family *Physeteridae*)

The Sperm Whale was called Cachalot by the Gascon whalers from the word *cachau,* a tooth. The lower jaw of this animal is shorter than the upper and long and narrow. In the underjaw are many formidable teeth made out of the finest ivory. These teeth are often eight inches long. The upper jaw is toothless. In the upper jaw are sockets where the teeth of the lower jaw rest.

The Sperm Whale is one of the most important Whales commercially. An enormous creature, the biggest of the toothed Whales, the males average sixty feet in length and have been known to reach eighty-four feet, which places them second in size in the Whale group. One of the toothless Whales is larger.

Like most mammals, the female Sperms are considerably smaller than the males, seldom exceeding half the size of the bulls.

In color this great sea animal is black above, lighter on the sides, silvery gray on the breast and sometimes on the sides of the head. Piebald Sperms have been reported. Members of this family have no dorsal fins but a series of bumps appear near their tails.

These enormous Whales have the distinction of having the largest noses in the world. Their noses form the greater part of their immense heads, and their heads equal a third of their total length! Of this mass there is very little lower jaw, the greater part is an adjustment of the nose.

It is certain that this mammal which spends his entire life in water does not use his weighty nose for smelling although its true purpose is not clearly understood.

The general formation of the nose is as follows. Immediately over the creature's upper jaw is the "junk," fibrous tissue surmounted by a great cavity toward the right side of the head. This cavity is filled with a granulated substance, the spermaceti. When the case is tapped, a colorless liquid oil flows out and turns to a waxy substance when exposed to the air. This is called sperm oil because it was formerly thought to contain the Whale's sperm cells. Through this mass of spermaceti runs the nasal passage which has but one opening to the outside. When the Whale rises he spouts a diagonal low column of condensed breath through this single nostril.

It is certain that this spermaceti organ with the surrounding muscular tissue helps close the nose while the Whale swims underwater. It is also thought that it may have something to do with equalizing the pressure when the Whale dives to depths of a thousand feet or more. The Sperm Whale is known to go very deep, some say that he can sound a mile! Even at a much shallower depth the pressure is enormous and would crush normal animals.

The bone formation as might be expected is heavy. The cavity supporting the spermaceti resembles a wheelless coach or sleigh and this it is called by early whalers.

Sperm Whale

The oil extracted from the head of a Sperm is the finest whale oil known. Since the head of one of these Whales may contain as much as fifteen barrels, and since the blubber is over a foot thick in places and has a high oil content, the creature is very valuable, has been extensively hunted.

The head oil is prized for lubrication of fine machinery. The spermaceti matter is used in making candles, in certain medicines, and in dressing fabrics. The blubber oil is used for the same purposes as other whale oil.

The Sperm Whale is perhaps best known for his ambergris. This rare and valuable substance comes from the Whale's intestines, is probably produced by a diseased condition. Sometimes it is taken from a dead Whale. It is lighter than water and sometimes floats ashore where it is often mistaken for greasy waste from boats. The lucky finder of real ambergris will receive a high price for it. The product is used today as a base of certain perfumes.

The Sperm Whales are formidable creatures. When attacked, the bulls are savage. These Whales have been known to smash whale boats with a flick of their great tail flukes. They may also crush the small boats with their powerful jaws and there are records of Sperm bulls charging and wrecking the whaling ships themselves. When undisturbed they swim at three or four knots an hour but are capable of making ten or twelve. When the ferocious animals are finally conquered, their dead bodies float. This makes salvaging easy for the whalers.

The prey of the Sperm Whale is worthy of his strength. Descending to great depths he seeks the giant squid and octopuses. The giant octopus may reach a length of thirty feet. Marks of battle, the imprint of squids' tentacles, are found on the jaws of harpooned Whales and testify to the fierce fights between the big sea mammals and their squirming prey.

These Whales also eat fish. There is a case on record of a ten-foot shark being found in the stomach of a Sperm. The shark had been swallowed whole which might be of interest to students of biblical history. Sperm Whales are found in the Mediterranean Sea and this could well have been the Whale that Jonah met.

A member of this family is capable of staying under water an incredibly long time. Eyewitnesses have reported that Sperm Whales may remain submerged from fifty minutes to an hour and a quarter and it must not be forgotten that all this time the animals are holding their breath. When they return to the surface they protrude their largest bump on their tails first. Sometimes they will shoot nearly out of water, landing with a tremendous splash which whalers say is visible ten miles away! Whalers are likewise responsible for the story that the spout can be distinguished from a distance of from three to five miles. They blow from sixty to seventy times before going under again.

When a Sperm Whale descends, he lobtails, or slaps the water with his flukes, unless alarmed, when he will sink suddenly down from a horizontal position without going through the usual process of rounding out and turning his flukes.

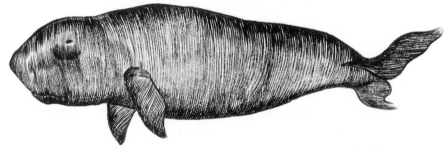

Pygmy Sperm Whale

The calves, usually one, sometimes twins, are born very large. At birth they are from twelve to fourteen feet long. The mother Sperm takes good care of her young. Captain Scammon describes her method of suckling her calf. She turns half on her side, exposing the upper part of her body above water, and the young one seizes one of a pair of teats situated near her tail. The little one seems to succeed in getting its milk in the sea as well as a four-legged calf does on land.

The range of the Sperm Whale includes all of the great oceans. He prefers warm zones, being found in greater numbers in temperate and tropical waters. According to old whaling charts he was most frequently taken between 35 degrees north and south latitude.

His genus name *Physeter* and his family name both come from a Latin word meaning a kind of Whale. This in turn is derived from the Greek *physeter* from *physan*, meaning to blow.

PYGMY SPERM WHALE
(genus *Kogia*)

Pygmy Sperm Whale Family
(family *Kogiidae*)

Closely related to the giant Sperm Whale is the Pygmy which is comparatively small, averaging from ten to fifteen feet in length, and often smaller than the newborn calf of his big cousin. Like the big Whale, the little Sperm has teeth in his lower jaw only and a single blowhole; but unlike the larger creature the Pygmy has a dorsal fin. His general appearance would seem to link him more with the Dolphins. His head is small,

equaling but one sixth of his total length but it contains a fully developed spermaceti organ.

The Pygmy Sperm Whale is a rare species but widely distributed, appearing on either coast of the Americas and far afield. He is said to eat crabs and cuttlefish. He has no commercial value and little is known of his habits.

The genus name Kogia is thought to be the Latinized form of the word "codger."

DOLPHIN AND PORPOISE FAMILY
(family *Delphinidae*)

To this family belongs a large number of comparatively small members of the Whale group. Two of the larger members, the Killer and the Beluga, are called Whales, and some are known as Dolphins or Porpoises. There is confusion among the common names of the smaller members, the word Porpoise and Dolphin being frequently used interchangeably. Strictly speaking, the name Dolphin should be applied to those

members of the family whose snouts are projected into beaks and the name Porpoise reserved for the smaller, beakless members.

Dolphins and Porpoises have the single blowhole characteristic of all of the toothed group. The majority have dorsal fins.

The family name *Delphinidae* comes from the Latin *delphinus* which means a Dolphin.

Wolf of the Sea

KILLER WHALE
ORCA
(genus *Orcinus*)

Dolphin and Porpoise Family

This is a giant Porpoise, the males reaching twenty feet in length, the females fifteen. The name Killer is deserved. They have sharp teeth in both jaws. They are very swift, and, according to whalers, overtake other Porpoises and Dolphins, swallowing them alive.

Handsome Whales, they are dashingly marked with white upon black. They hunt much as land

Wolves do, in small packs, scouring the waters of the temperate zone and the arctic, going up rivers, feared by all others of their kind and also by Seals and Walrus, by salmon and even the larger Whales. They appear in herds of less than a dozen, swimming in almost military fashion, their high, daggerlike fins cutting the surface of the water, spreading terror among other creatures of the sea.

Walrus mothers crawl up onto ice floes with their babies when Killers come. If they are caught at sea they attempt to protect their young by letting them ride on their backs, whereupon the Killer will come up underneath the mother and bump the helpless little one off into the water.

These creatures have voracious appetites. They are ravenous, tearing their victims apart and destroying more than they can eat. As a rule they confine their chase to smaller prey but have been known to attack the large Baleen Whales, pull them under the water where they tear out their tongues. They frequently attack the Gray Whales which are so terrified that they sometimes run aground to escape.

The Eskimos hunt the Killers for their meat and oil. They believe that these Whales are really Wolves in fish form. Their legends say that the Killers have the power to change themselves back into land Wolves whose habits they imitate.

The females and young may be distinguished by their shorter fins. In very large old males the dorsal fins reach six feet in height.

The common name Orca and the genus name *Orcinus* come from the Latin *orca*, a kind of Whale.

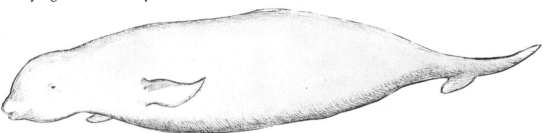

White Whale

Only White Sea Mammal

WHITE WHALE   **Dolphin and Porpoise Family**
BELUGA
(genus *Delphinapterus*)

Unique among Whales is this animal with the odd, spoonlike mouth, high forehead, and creamy white skin. The Beluga is the only completely white sea mammal known. Beluga is the Russian word for White Whale. His tiny eyes are the only color spots on the bodies of adults. The young are dark slate-colored, turning first mottled, then yellowish, before they attain the pure white stage at four or five years.

These are small Whales, averaging ten or twelve feet in length, sometimes reaching eighteen. They have no dorsal fins but a very slight ridge near their tails. They have teeth in both jaws and unlike their cousins they appear to have a slight constriction or neck between head and body.

White Whales are circumpolar, living in the far north, the Arctic Ocean, the seas of Okhotsk and Bering, coming south to Quebec. Their coloring reminds one of the color of many arctic land mammals, the Arctic Fox, the Polar Bear, the Lemming, and the Arctic Wolves and Foxes. They make a striking picture, swimming with an undulating movement into the shallows beneath

Killer Whale

the twilight of the northern lights, pursuing flounder and halibut and other bottom fish. They move in herds of from five to ten, advancing two or three abreast or in single file, showing little above the water, spouting irregularly and, according to Captain Scammon, when they do come to the surface to breathe, they make a sound like ". . . the faint lowing of an ox; but the strain is not so prolonged."

In the spring the White Whales come up the Saint Lawrence River as far as Quebec and they are hunted by natives for their oil which is used for lubricating watch springs. Their skins are the Porpoise skin of commerce.

Their genus name *Delphinapterus* comes from two Greek words, *delphis*, a Dolphin, and *apteros*, wingless. The White Whale is among the few members of the Dolphin and Porpoise Family which lack dorsal fins.

Blackfish

BLACKFISH   **Dolphin and Porpoise Family**
Pilot Whale
Ca'ing Whale
Grindhval
(genus *Globicephala*)

This is a large member of the Dolphin and Porpoise Family, the adults reaching as much as twenty-four feet in length. Their foreheads bulge over their blunt, saucerlike beaks. They are social, going about together in herds of from ten to many hundreds. The North Atlantic species which ranges from the Gulf of Mexico along our coast to the shores of Greenland is typical of this genus. He is black all over, giving the name of Blackfish. A species off the European coast usually has small white chin markings and sometimes white marks along the middle of the belly.

These Whales rise and fall less when they swim than do their cousins, and sometimes progress swiftly with heads and part of bodies out of water. Whale men used to call this swimming "eye out." The Blackfish's low spout reaches but two or three feet, issues straight up through the one nostril.

These polar Whales migrate south to breed during the northern winter. When the European species pass the Orkney and Shetland and Faroe Islands off the coast of England, fishermen set out in boats to capture them. The fat at the base of the jaw yields fine Porpoise oil, valued by watchmakers. The Blackfish are stupid, have a follow-the-leader instinct which reminds one of Sheep. When one is wounded, the fishermen chase him toward shore, whereupon all of the other Blackfish follow blindly. This has gained the creatures the name of Pilot Whales.

They have teeth in both jaws and feed on cuttlefish.

Their genus name *Globicephala* comes from the Latin word *globus,* meaning a ball and the Greek *kephale,* meaning a head.

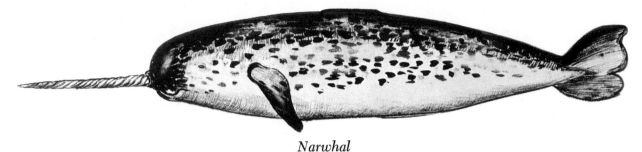

Narwhal

NARWHAL
(genus *Monodon*)

Dolphin and Porpoise Family

The queer Narwhal has only one tooth but it is a beautiful one, spirally curved, slender. This tusk has earned the creature the name of Sea Unicorn. It is usually found only in males and normally appears on the left-hand side of the upper jaw, growing to a length of nine feet and being made of the finest ivory. The tooth on the opposite side is buried under the gum.

Imbedded in the upper jaw of the females are two teeth but these generally remain hidden and useless.

Narwhals are rather small, inoffensive animals growing up to sixteen feet in length, not including tusk. Their heads are blunt, with small mouths, their bodies are streamlined and colored slate gray above, with tiger spots of black and gray on the sides and white on the abdomen. Like their cousins the White Whales, they have no dorsal fins and the tuskless young may often be mistaken for the Belugas.

Narwhals are arctic animals. They travel in small herds near the ice edge. Their food is squid and small fish which they swallow whole, having no teeth with which to chew.

There are theories about the purpose of the lance. There are stories of Narwhals ramming boats with their tusks but no authentic cases on record. Since the tooth is limited to the male, there is little likelihood that it has anything to do with gathering food. The most reasonable explanation seems to be that it is a weapon, like the antlers of Deer, used primarily when the males fight over the females during mating season.

Whatever use the animal makes of his fine tusk during life, it is greatly prized by the Eskimos. They wait by the breathing holes in the ice on arctic bays, knowing that the White Whales and the Narwhals will have to come up and breathe. When the Narwhals begin to break up the ice to enlarge the hole they are trapped by the Eskimos who use the tusks as harpoon heads and spears, their oil for moss lamps, their intestines for clothing and lines, their meat for food.

Although the Narwhal seems to be a harmless species, the natives of Siberia hold him in superstitious dread. According to Captain Scammon, natives of Asia who saw a Narwhal would kill themselves. The unfortunate one ". . . becomes a prey to evil forebodings which ultimately bring the poor victim to an untimely end."

The genus name *Monodon* comes from the Greek *monos,* meaning one, and *odon,* meaning tooth.

Common Porpoise

COMMON PORPOISE
HARBOR PORPOISE
(genus *Phocaena*)

Dolphin and Porpoise Family

This is the common member of the round-headed or Porpoise group on our coast. He is one of the smallest of the Whales, reaching from but a hundred to a hundred and twenty pounds in weight. Stockily built with a triangular back fin, he is black in color on the back, white underneath. He has teeth in both jaws and feeds on cuttlefish, fish, crustacea. He is frequently seen in harbors or along the coast near shore where he swims in schools, often jumping clear of the water as if in play.

The adults never reach more than six feet in length. The babies are about half the length of the parents. They are born in the spring. The mother Porpoise is said to suckle her young as she swims along lying on her side so that the baby's nose is out of water.

Phocaena, the genus name, is derived from the Greek *phokaina,* meaning a Porpoise.

COMMON DOLPHIN
STRIPED DOLPHIN
(genus *Delphinus*)

Dolphin and Porpoise Family

This is the playful Dolphin most frequently seen by travelers to Europe in the North Atlantic. He has a long beaked Dolphin nose, a dark-gray upper body with lighter gray stripes on the sides blending into white on the abdomen. The Common Dolphin grows to a length of a little over eight feet and feeds on small fishes. He has small teeth in both jaws.

This is the Dolphin which in mythology is sup-

posed to have rescued Arion of Lesbos when he was cast overboard by sailors jealous of his wealth, on a journey from Corinth to Sicily. A herd of Common Dolphins were following the boat listening to the poet play on a cithara. They carried him ashore.

The genus name of this group comes from the Greek *delphis* and means a Dolphin.

BOTTLENOSE DOLPHIN
(genus *Tursiops*)

Dolphin and Porpoise Family

This is the largest of our Dolphins, reaching ten feet in length. Instead of having a long beak

like the Common Dolphin he has a bottle-shaped, rather blunt nose. He has a back fin and teeth in

Common Dolphin

Bottlenose Dolphin

both jaws. In color he is gray on the upper body, white on chin and belly.

Widely distributed and common in the Atlantic, he is frequently called a Porpoise. Schools of them go about together looking for small fish.

They are netted by the Porpoise hunters for their hides and oil.

Genus *Tursiops* is taken from the Latin word for a Dolphin or a Porpoise, *tursio*.

Spotted Dolphin

SPOTTED DOLPHIN
Spotted Porpoise
(genus *Prodelphinus*)

Dolphin and Porpoise Family

This is a beaked-nose member of the Dolphin and Porpoise Family with a dark-gray back and a spotted underbody and sides. He has a back fin and numerous small teeth in both jaws. The prefix *pro* in genus *Prodelphinus* means in place of, and suggests another form of *Delphinus*.

Right Whale Dolphin

RIGHT WHALE DOLPHIN
STRIPED PORPOISE
(genus *Lissodelphis*)

Dolphin and Porpoise Family

These Dolphins have no back fins. In this respect they are unlike most of their family and like the Right Whales whose name they have acquired. They live in the North Pacific, in color are black above, lighter on the abdomen, with a band of white on their sides. They have distinct, short beaked noses, and foreheads which rise in a gradual curve. They are slender in form.

Lissos is Greek for smooth and when combined in the genus name *Lissodelphis* it aptly describes the smooth finless back of this creature.

Striped Dolphin

STRIPED DOLPHIN
(genus *Lagenorhynchus*)

Dolphin and Porpoise Family

This Dolphin grows about nine feet long. His beak is short and not prominent, his back fin is rather high and sharp. His body is marked with conspicuous oblique stripes. He is found in waters off the American coast in the Atlantic as far south as Massachusetts.

The genus name *Lagenorhynchus* comes from the Greek *lagenos* (bottle) and *rhynchos* (snout).

GRAMPUS
(genus *Grampus*)

The Grampus appears much like the Blackfish but his head is less globe-shaped. His back fin is high and sharp. In color he is blackish or dark gray on his back. His under parts, head, and forebody are light gray and frequently scarred with irregular marks which are thought to be the result of wounds. He grows about twelve feet long.

He is found in all the seas of the world except near the Poles but is rarely reported off the American coasts.

The genus name comes from the Latin *crassus pisces,* meaning fat fish, or from the French words, *grand poisson,* big fish.

FALSE KILLER
(genus *Pseudorca*)

The False Killer reaches eighteen feet in length. He differs from the true Killer in build. He is more slender, has a shorter back fin and more pointed flippers. In color he is black. Specimens have been reported on both coasts of America.

His genus name *Pseudorca* comes from the Greek stem *pseudes,* meaning false, and *orca,* the species name of the true Killer.

BEAKED WHALE FAMILY
BOTTLENOSED WHALE FAMILY
ZIPHIOID FAMILY
(family *Ziphiidae*)

The members of this family are rare on the North American coasts. They are comparatively small, ranging in size from fifteen to thirty feet. They have dorsal fins and like the Sperm Whale they have teeth in the lower jaw only, but these teeth are quite small and usually only two break through the gums in the mouth of an adult male. The young males and the females appear to be toothless because their teeth remain imbedded in their gums. Sometimes a pair of teeth in an old female will erupt.

The family is distinguished by long, bottle-shaped or beaked jaws. There are two grooves on the throat and but one blowhole, a characteristic of all Toothed Whales.

The root of the family name is the Greek *xiphos* meaning a sword and describing the form of their jaws.

BOTTLENOSED WHALE
(genus *Hyperoodon*)

This is a polar species. The forehead bulges more with increasing age in the male. Within this bulge is a reservoir of spermaceti similar to that of the Sperm Whale. A comparatively small species, the males reaching thirty feet in length, the females only twenty-four, he was hunted by whalers after the Right Whales became scarce and before the Rorqual industry had started.

Bottlenosed Whales are hard to capture since they dive with great speed. They are said to stay submerged for two hours.

They range the North Atlantic and the arctic seas in herds of from four to ten, feeding upon cuttlefish and herrings. In color they are dark gray or black on their backs, and gray or yellowish on their abdomens. They have no visible teeth but a pair of large teeth imbedded in the gums at the tip of the lower jaw sometimes appear in adults of advanced age. Sometimes there are two smaller teeth behind this pair. The other vestiges of teeth are buried in the gums of both jaws.

The genus name *Hyperoodon* is taken from two Greek words *hyperoios* and *odon* and means literally being above or over the tooth, and refers to the prominent crests on the upper jawbone.

CUVIER'S BEAKED WHALE
Z<small>IPHIUS</small> W<small>HALE</small>
G<small>OOSE-BEAKED</small> W<small>HALE</small>
(genus *Ziphius*)

Beaked Whale Family

Similar in appearance to the Bottlenosed Whale, Cuvier's Whale has a shorter beak, is smaller all over, reaching only twenty-six feet in length. The forehead is not prominent and the Whale has no commercial importance. Little is known of his habits, but he is widely distributed.

Unlike the toothless common Bottlenecked Whale, this Whale always has two front teeth in the male, two smaller ones sometimes breaking through the gums of the female. In color the creature is variable, some say he is dark above, light below, others reporting leopardlike spots along the female's side. His genus name *Ziphius* is taken from the same root as the family name.

True's Beaked Whale

COWFISH and TRUE'S BEAKED WHALE
(genus *Mesoplodon*)

Beaked Whale Family

This species has a pair of teeth usually located in the middle of the lower jaw. The teeth are rather large in males but often remain imbedded in the gums of females for life.

He is a deep-water species of the North Atlantic which reaches a length of sixteen feet. In color he is bluish black above, sometimes grayish on undersurface. His forehead recedes more than in any other Ziphioids but he has characteristic fins, flippers, flukes, and throat grooves.

One of these Whales captured in the year 1828 was kept alive for two days without water. According to Beddard in *A Book of Whales* he "... was offered soaked bread and other alimentary substances"; he "emitted a low cavernous sound like the lowing of a cow."

His genus name *Mesoplodon* comes from the Greek *mesos* (middle) plus *hopla* (arms) plus *odon* (tooth) and refers to the location of his teeth.

True's Beaked Whale is another species of this genus which has teeth at the very extremity of the jaw. They are not exposed in the female.

BAIRD'S WHALE
(genus *Berardius*)

This is a rare Beaked Whale which appears in the Bering Sea. He is similar in appearance to the Common Bottlenosed Whale but he grows larger, reaching a length of forty feet.

He has two rather large teeth in both sides of the lower jaw, the front pair being larger. In color the species is black above, light below.

The genus was named after M. Bérard, a naturalist.

WHALEBONE WHALES
Baleen Whales
(suborder *Mysticeti*)

Whalebone Whales are all very large, growing from thirty to one hundred feet in length. Strangely, these great sea creatures catch food to fill their enormous stomachs without the aid of teeth. Teeth are present in the unborn Whales but are lost before birth, leaving the adults without a tooth in their enormous mouths.

A Whalebone Whale can never chew his food but his mouth is peculiarly adapted for capturing minute prey. From the roof hang narrow plates of baleen, curious horny formations fringed on the front and bottom. These hairy-looking sheaths form screens on either side of the mouth so that when the animal opens his jaws and swims along the surface or under the water, the small sea life which abounds in the northern waters streams into the great scoop, is caught on the tongue while the water strains out again. The meal is swallowed alive through a rather small gullet.

Incidentally this baleen was the Whalebone which formed the stays in our great-grandmothers' corsets.

Like normal mammals the toothless Whales are equipped with two nostrils.

There are three families in this group which reach American shores. They are the Right Whale Family, the Gray Whale Family, and the Finback or Rorqual Family. The scientific family name *Mysticeti* is formed from two Greek words, *mystax,* meaning upper lip mustache, and *ketos,* a Whale. This describes the hairy-looking baleen which replaces teeth in this group.

RIGHT WHALE FAMILY
(family *Balaenidae*)

The members of this family are called Right Whales because in the very early days of whaling they were the only Whales hunted and thus came to be known as the Right Whales. There were three reasons for their popularity with early whalers. First, Right Whales are rich in oil and whalebone, one animal often yielding enough to pay the expenses of a trip to the hunting grounds. Second, these Whales are slower than others of their kind and do not remain under water as long.

Third, they are slightly lighter than water and float after death, making it easy for the whalers to handle their prey when they have succeeded in killing it.

The members of the Right Whale Family have no dorsal fins, no grooves on their chins, and are further distinguished by their enormous and curiously developed mouths.

The family name *Balaenidae* is derived from the Latin word *balaena,* which means a Whale.

Bowhead Whale

BOWHEAD
Great Polar Whale
Greenland Right Whale
(genus *Balaena*)

The most famous Right Whale is the Bowhead which is named for the pronounced arch of his upper jaw. He is a giant Whale, averaging sixty feet in length, occasionally reaching seventy, and fully one third of his total length is his head. Of his head by far the greater part is mouth, and of his mouth the greater part is lower jaw and enormous underlips.

From the roof of a Bowhead's mouth hang long, thin plates of baleen, the curious fringed whalebone which replaces his teeth. There are approximately 300 sheathes to a side. In the center the whalebone reaches ten or twelve feet, averaging from ten to twelve inches wide at the gum. A man could easily stand up in the mouth of a full-grown Bowhead, but the gullet is small, not suited for swallowing big prey.

The food of the great Bowhead is almost microscopic. He eats tiny, shrimplike animals found in masses in the polar seas and called brit by the American whalers. Armed with their great scooped mouths, Bowheads used to comb the polar seas in great numbers. The pioneer whalers pursued these Whales through the arctic fogs to their arctic home. Bowheads are called Ice Whales because according to early accounts they never traveled far from the arctic and in the summer hugged the ice edge, often coming up underneath and breaking a three-inch thickness of crust with a blow of their great heads. Their range includes Atlantic and Pacific Polar Seas south to 53 degrees north latitude.

When Bowheads were harpooned they often dove so deep that they pulled out all the line. The line had to be cut to prevent the boat and crew from being dragged down to the depths. One can well imagine the power of this stout sea giant and the struggle the whalers had to capture him before the days of steam whaling ships and bomb harpoons. But to catch a Polar Whale was worth great effort because this species sometimes yielded over 275 barrels of oil and 3500 pounds of whalebone.

In their cold homeland they must have presented a thrilling sight. Picture one raising his head a little above the surface of the water, then loudly blowing a spout which divided at the summit. The blowing was repeated from six to nine times, then he rounded out his back and up-ended, or as the whalers say "turned his flukes," and flipped them from six to eight feet clear of water, then he dove to stay under for ten or twenty minutes before he reappeared to blow again. Today this performance is rarely seen. The Bowhead is nearly extinct.

The families of these big Polar Whales are small, they do not increase fast. Usually one calf, sometimes twins, are born in February or March. The mother takes good care of her young, suckles it for nearly a year. Captain Scammon in his famous book on Whales pictures a Whalebone mother suckling her completely submerged twins; but other authorities believe that in this position the babies would get more salt water than milk, and perhaps the mother lies partly above water surface while the young take her milk.

In color the Bowhead is predominantly black with white or grayish undermarkings and a white area on the chin and front of the lower jaw. One early writer reports piebald specimens and some very large brown phases. However, the color of the big brown Whales was due to the scum of diatoms, minute algae which sometimes attach themselves to Whales.

The genus name *Balaena* is the root of the family name *Balaenidae* and is the Latin word for a Whale.

NORTH ATLANTIC RIGHT WHALE and
PACIFIC RIGHT WHALE
(genus *Eubalaena*)

These two species of the Right Whale Family are very similar to the Bowhead but their upper jaws are not as arched, their heads join their bodies in a straighter line, and their heads are smaller, equaling about a fourth of their total length. Their mouths contain proportionately shorter baleen, perhaps a foot or two shorter than the Bowhead's. One other distinguishing feature is the "bonnet," a small horny formation on the front part of the upper jaw which is infested with crustacea and other parasites. The Bowhead has neither the bonnet nor the parasites.

White patches do occur on the lower body of some specimens but there is never a white patch on the anterior end of the lower jaw, a characteristic of the Bowhead. There seems little reason to differentiate between the Atlantic Right Whale and the Pacific Right Whale except their range. The former lives in the waters of the Atlantic arctic in the vicinity of Hudson Bay and Baffin Island and the latter lives in the Kadiak Ground,

as the waters between Vancouver and the Aleutian Islands were known to early whalers.

Captain Scammon, an early authority on Whales, says that the Right Whale of the Kadiak Ground was met with singly, sometimes in pairs, and again in triplets until the last of the season when they appeared in gams (herds), at which time the giant creatures were seen ". . . scattered over the surface of the water as far as the eye could discern from the mast-head." After being struck by a harpoon these Right Whales bellowed like large bulls and according to the whalers were vicious.

Overhunted they became wild and wary. The average yield of oil from one of these Whales was 130 barrels. For this valuable product they, like the Bowhead, have been nearly exterminated.

The genus name of this group, *Eubalaena* comes from the combining Greek form *eu*, meaning true, and the Latin *balaena*, a Whale.

CALIFORNIA GRAY WHALE
Hardhead, Mussel Digger
Ripsack, Devilfish
(genus *Rhachianectes*)

The one species in this family is among the smallest of the Baleen Whales. It averages from forty to forty-four feet from nose to tip of flukes and its head is relatively small, the longest baleen being from but fourteen to sixteen inches which is short when compared to the Bowhead's from ten- to twelve-foot whalebone.

Like the Right Whales, the Gray Whales lack dorsal fins. They have two, rarely four, grooves in their throats and in the tail region eight or ten characteristic bumps. In color they are mottled gray, sometimes light, sometimes dark. The blubber is from six to ten inches thick and for their size they yield a large amount of oil, an average of twenty barrels per Whale.

Gray Whale Family
(family *Rhachianectidae*)

From November to May the Gray Whales are found off the coast of California where they enter the lagoons to bring forth their young. After the calves are born they swim north to the Arctic Ocean and the Okhotsk Sea where they spend the summer, returning to the coastal waters off California when fall comes. When the ice packs of the north are thickly jammed, the Gray Whales ram up through the fissures to breathe.

On their migrations they stay near land, often swimming among the kelp beds. When the water is calm they may frequently be seen in southern lagoons, resting in one spot for an hour or more while Sea Gulls and Cormorants alight on their bodies. They play in the shallow water, often turning over and thrusting their flippers out of water, then rising and splashing.

Their habit of staying near shore has brought about near extermination. Formerly during the calving season they appeared in such great numbers in lagoons that it was difficult to row a boat across without bumping into one. Occasionally the tide went out and left the adult Whales stranded in just enough water for the calves to swim in. The mother Whales seemed unexcited, waiting calmly for the tide to return and float them away.

The Gray Whales are troubled by parasites which infest their skin. They live in terror of the Killer Whale. But their real enemy has been man. Whalers took advantage of their shore-loving instincts. Like the Rorquals, the Gray Whales sink when dead but in shallow water it is easy to recover a body particularly if one waits for the decomposing gases to make it rise.

In the early dawn the whalers would hasten to the lagoons to catch the Gray Whales. The mother Whales were very fierce if their calves were injured. If a little one had difficulty in keeping up with the big Whales in the dash for escape, the mother would turn on the men, often upsetting the boats with a blow of her head or staving them with a turn of her powerful flukes. She would thrash about wildly, fighting for her young. She was wise and soon learned to stay farther offshore beyond the kelp beds.

Here, however, the Gray Whales were relentlessly pursued. When they left the whaling grounds of the white men and went north for the summer, the northern Indians met them in canoes. When they reached the icefields they would rise and blow so loudly that they could be heard for miles on a calm day. This was the signal for the Eskimos to give chase in their walrus-hide umiaks, armed with Stone Age implements, flint-pointed lances, bone-pointed spears. The Eskimos ate the meat of the Gray Whales, the fins and the lips and the flukes of the tails being especially prized. They sold the whale oil in skins of fifteen gallons each, one skinful being worth one Reindeer to the Reindeer men of the interior.

Needless to say, the number of Gray Whales rapidly decreased. As early as 1874 they were nearing extinction.

The genus name *Rhachianectes* comes from the Greek *rhachia* (surf) and *nektes* (swimmer).

Gray Whale

FINBACK FAMILY
RORQUAL FAMILY
(family *Balaenopteridae*)

To this family belongs the largest mammal which ever lived on land or in the water, the Blue Whale. Some other members are comparatively small but all Finbacks have dorsal fins as their name implies. This at once distinguishes them from the Right Whales and the Gray Whales. Another distinction is seen in the numerous grooves on the throat and chest of a Finback. None of the Right Whales have these grooves, the Gray Whales have at most but two or four. Finbacks also have smaller, flatter heads which contain shorter, more flexible baleen. Their flippers are long and tapering, not blunt and round like the Right Whales and when they spout they send up a single column, even though they have two blowholes. The condensed moisture of their breath unites to form one spout.

Their habits in many ways are similar to the habits of the Right Whales but because their whalebone is shorter, because they can swim faster and are less buoyant, sinking when killed, whalers did not catch many of their kind until the harpoon gun and modern methods of whaling were in general use.

Their family name *Balaenopteridae* comes from the Latin *balaena*, which means Whale, plus the Greek *pteron,* which means wing. The "wing" is the characteristic back fin.

There are three genera (groups) in this family. One is the Humpback. The second includes the Common Rorqual, the Piked Whale, Sei's Whale. The third is the enormous Blue Whale.

Humpback

HUMPBACK
(genus *Megaptera*)

This member of the Finbacks has all the characteristics of the family, a grooved throat, a dorsal fin, comparatively short baleen, but in other respects he is queer-looking. He has a small fin on his back near his tail and when he dives he makes an exaggerated hump with his back. This action gives him his name. His underjaw extends aggressively beyond the upper, the top of his head is bumpy, and he has very long, narrow flippers which are characteristically scalloped on the front edges.

In build this giant Rorqual is chunky. He sometimes reaches a length of seventy-five feet. In spite of his clumsy appearance, he is exceedingly graceful. He swims with swift, undulating movements. Whalemen observing Whales "under the rim of the water" recognize Humpbacks immediately by their frequent "roundings" and "turning of flukes," and their irregular course. They respire one to twenty times at a rising, spouting about twenty feet into the air.

In color the Humpback is black above, marbled

or sometimes pure white below. His blubber yields a quantity of oil, from ten to seventy-five barrels per animal, and he was one of the few species besides the Right Whales taken by primitive methods. Although like all Rorquals he is swift, and sinks when dead, he likes to stay rather near shore. As with the Gray Whales this habit made it easy for whalers to rescue the body which rose again to the surface when it became charged with gases after death. So he was frequently taken in the whaling grounds on the coast of Alaska and in Magdalena, Balaena, and Monterey Bays.

Early whalemen believed that the Humpbacks follow some sort of seasonal migration, journeying to the polar seas during the warmer months, to feed on "brit" and small fishes, returning south to warmer waters to breed in the winter and entering inland waters to have their young. They have been found in all the great oceans of the world.

The Humpback is extremely active and playful, particularly during the mating season. Sometimes he will lie motionless, then roll over and over, flapping his flippers in the air, making a commotion with his enormous body. He frequently leaps clear of the surface and lands with a tremendous splash. This is called "breeching" by the whalers, who also describe the way the creature spanks the water as lobtailing.

When showing off before a female, the bull turns upside down and waves his flukes slowly, then so fast that he spanks the water fiercely. Captain Scammon says that while mating they pat each other with their long flippers, and the sound may be heard at least a mile.

In spite of the activity of this Whale he seems unable to rid himself of the parasites which infest his skin, clinging to the bumps on his head and to other parts of his body.

One specimen of these odd Whales belonged in the circus side show among the two-headed calves. It aroused great interest among scientists. This was the Humpback which had legs! The creature was captured by a whaler off the west coast of Vancouver Island, British Columbia. He had two hind legs a little more than four feet long, covered with a half-inch thickness of blubber and ending in round knobs. These legs were, of course, of no use to the Whale and were thought to be an unusual case of reversion to a primitive type, the land animal from which Whales are supposed to be descended.

The genus name *Megaptera* comes from the Greek *megas* (great) and *pteron* (wing). The "wing" in this case refers to the very long flippers of the Humpbacks.

Greyhound of the Sea

COMMON RORQUAL   Finback Family
FINBACK
FINNER
RAZORBACK
(genus *Balaenoptera*)

This is the Whale most frequently seen by steamer travelers who are often drawn to the ship's rail at sight of the Finback's tall spout. This Whale prefers the temperate waters of both the Atlantic and the Pacific to the polar seas. He is immense, sometimes reaches a length of eighty-one feet. The average adult measures sixty-five from nose to tail, is streamlined in build, with a wedge-shaped head, a fairly high dorsal fin, and a ridge on the hind end of his back which accounts for the name Razorback. He is powerful, a swift swimmer, often being called the Greyhound of the sea, and like all of his family he sinks when killed. These two characteristics have favored his survival.

He feeds upon the small, shrimplike sea animals so popular with the Whalebone groups, but he also catches barrels full of herring and smelt at certain times of the year. In the antarctic, whalers have observed that Finbacks eat the adult shrimp-like sea animals. This is in keeping with their preference for prey slightly larger than tiny food taken by the Right Whales.

In color the Finner is light gray above, pure white below, and upon the head, jaws, and shoulders the white continues on the right side, is grayer on the left, making an unusual unbalanced pattern. This Whale is a herd animal, frequently seen in schools.

His genus name *Balaenoptera* is formed from the Latin *balaena,* a Whale, and the Greek *pteron,* a wing, probably refers to the winglike back fin and dorsal ridge.

SEI'S WHALE and the PIKED WHALE or LESSER RORQUAL
(genus *Balaenoptera*)

Finback Family

These are two comparatively small members of the Finback Family and the Rorqual genus. Although Sei's Whale does reach sixty feet sometimes, the Piked Whale does not exceed thirty-three, thirty feet being an average for an adult. In most respects both resemble the Common Rorqual. The Lesser Rorqual is stouter in build, and in color is blue gray above, white beneath. The larger Sei's Whale is not as stout as the Lesser Rorqual nor as slender as the Finner.

Both species are widely distributed but do not seem to frequent the coasts of North America as often as do other species. They feed upon the small, shrimplike sea animals and some small fish.

The Biggest Mammal in the World

BLUE WHALE
SULPHUR BOTTOM
(genus *Sibbaldus*)

Finback Family

This is the biggest mammal ever known to exist in the world. This is *the* enormous Whale. Specimens sometimes reach ninety-five feet in length and a weight of from 150 to 200 tons. The eyes are but pinpoints in this great mass.

The Blue Whale haunts the polar ice edge, sculling the cold seas in search of tiny sea animals. He scoops up barrels of the small shrimplike sea creatures in his enormous mouth and like the Right Whales he collects his food on his tongue, letting the water strain out again through the baleen, the whalebone sheaths within his mouth.

He is a world-wide traveler, appearing off the coast of California and Alaska, off the North Atlantic coast, and far away in African and Asiatic waters. When he rises, he blows a tall, dense spout.

Although this giant of the seas exceeds all other Whales in length, he is rather slender in build, not nearly as clumsily built as the Right Whales. The Blue Whale's head is but one quarter of his total length and flat on top, save for a small bump in the center ridge. He does not look so head-heavy. His bellylike chin merges without a sign of a neck into his body. His throat is deeply grooved. He has a combined mustache and beard of from twenty to forty hairs. His body color is slate blue with mottled white under parts. He received the name Sulphur Bottom from the film of diatoms, minute marine algae, which sometimes covers his skin, making his belly look brownish yellow. Some early writers believed that this was the natural color of his skin and incorrectly classified the Sulphur Bottom as a separate species.

The female Blue Whales look like the bulls, save for being a foot or two longer! The young may weigh eight tons at birth! The calves, one usually, sometimes twins, are immense, thus giving the Blue Whale another claim to giganticism. What other mammal can boast of a young one eight yardsticks long from nose to tail at birth? No land animal could carry such a large baby within its womb. Only the supporting element of the water makes this possible for the biggest Whale.

For all his size the Blue Whale is timid and shy in temperament, or perhaps merely wise. Whalers say that this great creature will take fright at the smallest noises. The shout of a man will put a Blue Whale into such a state of panic that no whaling boat can hope to overtake the fleeing animal once it begins to swim. He is a swift swimmer and less buoyant than the Right Whales. Like the Common Rorqual, these habits protected the greatest of all mammals until the invention of the harpoon gun and modern whaling methods.

The genus name *Sibbaldus* comes from the name of a Scottish scientist, Robert Sibbald.

Population of the Commercially Valuable Whales Today

The Right Whale Family
The Gray Whale Family

The Rorqual Family
The Sperm Whale Family

The range and population of completely aquatic mammals is difficult to determine. The native range of the once abundant families listed above has been noted under the family, being computed from whalers' charts. As has already been said, the Bowheads are practically extinct. They were the first to be exploited. In the year 1697 nearly two thousand of this species were taken by the hand harpoon methods off Spitsbergen.

Frequently today people think of whaling as being an industry which went out of date when coal oil was discovered, partially replacing whale oil for illumination. Unfortunately for the Whales, important uses for their oil were found even after the discovery of electricity. Today whale oil is extensively used in the manufacture of lard substitutes, margarine, and the like; also in soaps and in the making of high explosives. Other parts of the Whale are used for fertilizer.

In the years 1935-36, 45,000 Whales were killed! Considering the rate of increase in these mammals, there being usually but one calf at a time, one can readily understand what is happening to the population of the commercially important Whales.

The slaughter of the Rorquals began in the middle of the eighteenth century. The invention of the harpoon gun by a Norwegian, Sven Foyn, made it possible for whalers to capture the swift and less buoyant Finbacks and the enormous Blue Whales which they could not handle with primitive methods. This period spelled disaster for the ferocious Sperm Whales too.

However, the situation did not get completely out of control until the appearance of floating stations. Formerly whalers went ashore to boil the blubber and extract the oil. Recently with steam vessels of large tonnage, whalers have carried on the whole process at sea, catching the Whales, preparing them in floating factories aboard ships which sailed beyond the possible control of the law.

Repeated efforts, particularly on the part of the United States, were made to enlist the cooperation of governments in a program to save the big Whales. Discussion at a meeting of the League of Nations came to naught. But in 1937 an International Agreement for the Regulation of Whaling was signed at London by the United States, Great Britain, the Union of South Africa, the Argentine Republic, Australia, Northern Ireland and the Irish Free State, New Zealand and Norway.

This agreement forbids the killing of any Right Whales or Gray Whales; it forbid the killing of calves or females with young, in any species; in some species it defined the minimum length of a legal catch. No Finback could be taken under

Blue Whale

fifty-five feet, no Humpback or Sperm under thirty-five; no enormous Blue Whale under seventy!

To ensure enforcement of the laws, each country agreed to appoint and pay a government inspector to go with each factory ship. He was not only to enforce regulations but also to see that all parts of the Whale were properly used to avoid waste.

Large areas of the oceans were closed entirely to floating factories, and all oceans had a closed season for six months of every year, while the antarctic was closed to floating factories for nine months. These laws should lead to an increase in rapidly disappearing species. How the present war will affect the treaty which protects the world's largest mammals from extinction, time only will tell.

Appendix I
Immigrants from Foreign Shores

THE GNAWERS
(order *Rodentia*)

HOUSE RAT
NORWEGIAN RAT
WHARF RAT
(genus *Rattus*)

Old-World Rat and Mouse Family
(family *Muridae*)

This rather large Rat is neither pretty nor nice in his habits. His coarse fur is brownish or grayish on the back, grayish or dirty white below. One subspecies is almost black. The House Rat's tail is scaly, almost hairless. His ears are nearly naked, his nose is pointed.

In colonial days he came off the boats from Europe, swarmed over the wharves. Very hardy, resourceful, and prolific, he spread rapidly to every community settled by man and even invaded some of the country hideouts of our pretty native Rats, driving them out and giving a bad name to all that resembled him in form. He only shuns desert places and places where water can-

not be found.

Our native Rats are rather clean in habits, live in woodsy or other outdoor places, and eat clean food. The Norwegian Rat eats practically everything, including garbage, and often lives in sewers and other dreadful places. Not only is he destructive with his gnawing teeth, but he also eats quantities of stored grain and carries disease. He is host to the flea which brought bubonic plague to this continent.

The genus *Rattus* is medieval Latin for Rat, perhaps derived from *rodere*, to gnaw. The family name *Muridae* comes from the Latin *mus,* a Mouse.

House Rat

207

ROOF RAT
Alexandrine Rat
(genus *Rattus*)

This foreign Rat is not common in America. He is a typical form from Alexandria, Egypt. Rather small and slender, he is brown gray in color, white below, has large ears and a longer tail than the common House Rat. He is sometimes seen on the coasts in southern states and a specimen was recorded in New Mexico. He is not found as frequently in buildings as is the Norwegian Rat but often lives under trash piles.

House Mouse

HOUSE MOUSE
(genus *Mus*)

This little Mouse with its long, almost naked tail is perhaps among the best-known Mice on this continent. Yet he is not native. He came from Europe like the House Rat. He is now living in almost all parts of the United States and Canada where the country is settled. Not pretty like many of our native Mice, he is dull brownish in color with grayish under parts. He eats almost anything but is particularly fond of grain and while he likes house living he also frequently moves into meadows and lives like a wild Mouse until severe weather drives him to shelter.

Like the native Brown Lemmings of the arctic these Mice appear sometimes in incredible numbers. Even though not native to this continent, these Mice have thrived so that they are always pests wherever man goes and occasionally a scourge.

In 1925 there was a terrible outbreak of these Mice at the southern end of the dry bed of Buena Vista Lake in the San Joaquin Valley in California. This is an arid country, dry, and not cultivated to a great extent at this point, but thickly settled because of the oilfields.

The Mice suddenly began coming by the millions from the dry lake bed toward the communities where men lived. None of the little Rodents was less than three-quarters grown which indicates that overpopulation and lack of food stopped breeding. The masses already born were seeking new homelands. They swarmed over grain bins and haystacks. In one barn on oil property two tons of Mice were killed where the grain was stored. In a bin twenty feet square it was estimated that, including those on the rafters, there were over 3000 Mice in sight at one time. People found Mice in their clothing when they awoke in the morning. In places the highways became slippery with the dead Rodents.

These terrible outbreaks are uncommon but these little Mice are so hardy that they never seem to decrease under normal numbers no matter how much man attacks them.

HARES AND RABBITS
(order *Lagomorpha*)

EUROPEAN HARE
(genus *Lepus*)

Hare and Rabbit Family
(family *Leporidae*)

The typical European Hare is about two feet long, has grayish-brown fur mixed with reddish-white under parts, and the tips of his ears and the top of his tail are black. He weighs about eight or nine pounds.

He is so closely related to our common Varying Hares, Arctic Hares, and Jack Rabbits that he not only belongs to the same family but to the same genus *Lepus*.

Like most of his kind, this Hare has large families and several litters a season. Introduced to New England he has now become so abundant in western Massachusetts and Connecticut and the Hudson River Valley of eastern New York that he is a pest. Very injurious to crops and orchards, in the winter of 1915-16 he caused over $100,000 damage to the fruit orchards in a single New York State county. When the snows are deep these Hares invade the orchards, gnaw the bark on the trees.

MARSUPIALS
(order *Marsupialia*)

MURINE OPOSSUM
MOUSE OPOSSUM
(genus *Marmosa*)

Opossum Family
(family *Didelphiidae*)

Sometimes on banana boats from Central America this small Opossum comes to our shores. He remains hidden among the bunches of bananas until the boat docks.

Much smaller than the Virginia Opossum, specimens are about as big as common House Rats. They are yellowish or brownish in color and the females lack the marsupial pouches on their abdomens which gave the group its name. Their tails are like those of the Virginia Opossum, formed like a Monkey's for grasping.

HOOFED ANIMALS
(order *Ungulata*)

MUSTANG
(genus *Equus*)

Horse Family
(family *Equidae*)

Here is one of the group of odd-toed or single-hoofed animals, none of which are native to America. All American hoofed animals have cloven feet.

Wyoming was one of several places where the ancient ancestors of the Horse lived. Here are found the fossils of the Dawn Horse, *Eohippus,* a little foxlike animal. Later a real wild Horse roamed over the west but, strange to say, all of this species died out before men came to live on the American continent. The native Indians had no beasts of burden except Dogs.

Early Spanish explorers, De Soto, Coronado, and others, were the first to bring modern Horses to the New World. From time to time these European Horses escaped, fled to the mesas or the remote plains, and established wild herds. They had in them the blood of Arabian steeds and of the great Horses ridden by knights in armor in southern Europe. Rustling for their own food,

Mustang

enduring the hardships of life in the wilds, and interbreeding with smaller, inferior stock, they soon established a type, the Mustang, a rather small but sturdy pony, often piebald or painted in color, frequently buckskin with a faint trace of the dorsal and shoulder stripe common to the wild ponies of Asia.

Most of the wild herds have recently been rounded up so that the wild stallions will not breed with improved stock. But in the remote sections, among the wild mesas of the west, wild Horses may still be found.

Equus is the Latin word for Horse.

BURRO
(genus *Equus*)

Horse Family

Burro is the Spanish word for Donkey. The Spaniards introduced Donkeys to America during Spanish colonial days. Burros are small, strong, stubborn like their kind. Able to endure hardships that would kill an ordinary Horse, they have been the beasts of burden for prospectors in the desert. Here sometimes they escape, or wander off when their masters are killed, and establish little herds of wild Burros. They seem perfectly at home in some of the most arid wastelands such as Death Valley and the Painted Desert and thrive on the scant vegetation.

EUROPEAN BOAR
(genus *Sus*)

There are no members of the true Pig Family native to America. The piglike Peccaries are the nearest relatives and are sometimes called Pigs.

The true Wild Boar of Europe was introduced to North Carolina near the Tennessee border by a group of English sportsmen who hoped to establish the sport of Boar hunting in the states. A club was formed, a six-hundred-acre tract was enclosed, and within were placed Elk, Buffalo, Bear, and Wild Hogs. The club failed.

About one hundred Boars escaped from the enclosure and ran over the surrounding country. Here they and their descendants have lived ever since. Many bred with the domestic Pigs which were running loose but a few remained pure-blooded. They increased until 1932 when many died of the Hog cholera.

These southern Wild Boars avoid people, are not found where Bears live. Like all of their kind they live near wallows. In the early summer they range up in the shaded cover on the mountains. When the blackberries ripen they drift down, then back to the huckleberry slopes. In the fall they seek apples and acorns and root for bulbs, are fond of fungi but will eat meat.

The Tennessee Wild Hog is powerfully built, stands over three feet high at the shoulder, may weigh as much as four hundred pounds. Like his European ancestor which is supposed to have come from the Hartz Mountain section of Germany, he has hulking shoulders, small rump, long, narrow snout, small hairy ears, and long tufted tail. The skin is thick and the grizzled-gray, woolly hair mixed with bristles. A mane runs from head to rump. The young are striped lengthwise.

The Wild Hogs are very shy but have great strength and are ferocious when attacked. The Boars have strong tusks which they use with fierce energy. They charge recklessly, are dangerous opponents. The sport of hunting Boars is wild and rugged. It is very popular in British India where the animals are killed from horseback with lances.

In the last big-game census it was estimated

Burro

that there were over 1600 Wild Hogs in the United States, most of them in Tennessee and North Carolina, a few in Mississippi, New Hampshire, and California. The sport of Boar hunting has not become popular in America.

The genus *Sus* is from the Latin word *sus*, a Pig.

REINDEER
CARIBOU
(genus *Rangifer*)

Deer Family
(family *Cervidae*)

The Laplanders have tamed their native Caribou (Reindeer), use them as beasts of burden. Although the Barren Ground Caribou of our arctic wastes are closely related to the Lapland Caribou they have never been tamed.

Recently Laplander Reindeer have been imported to Alaska for the Eskimos and Indians to use as pack animals and sledge pullers. The wild Lapland Caribou is uniform in color, the domestic Caribou is any variation between black and white. The tamed animals are easy to handle but they often wander off with the wild herds. In Alaska the native Caribou have to be killed where the foreign species is introduced. This prevents the mingling of the herds.

Frequently the coast natives have lost interest in the imported Reindeer when they have wandered away from the villages. The natives often prefer to fish. Undoubtedly many of the tame Reindeer are now with the closely related wild herds of America.

Wild Boar

Appendix II
Classification Key

Listed below are the order, family, and generic names of every mammal native to North America, north of Mexico. These are the key names to the maze of suborders, subfamilies, species, and subspecies which appear on the charts of specialists.

Occasionally you will find that the names of certain animals have been changed since their first classification. For example, the Red and Hoary Bats used to be placed in genus *Nycteris*. Now they are generally placed in genus *Lasiurus*. We have used the earlier form save in the very few cases such as these Bats where the change has come into general use.

1. INSECT EATERS (order *Insectivora*)
   Shrew Family (*Soricidae*)
   Pygmy Shrew (genus *Microsorex*)
   Common Shrew (genus *Sorex*)
   Short-tailed Shrew (genus *Blarina*)
   Water Shrew (genus *Neosorex*)
   Little Shrew (genus *Cryptotis*)
   Gray Shrew (genus *Notiosorex*)
   Mole Family (*Talpidae*)
   Brewer's Mole (genus *Parascalops*)
   Common Mole (genus *Scalopus*)
   Star-nosed Mole (genus *Condylura*)
   Oregon Mole (genus *Scapanus*)
   Gibbs' Mole (genus *Neürotrichus*)

2. THE BATS (order *Chiroptera*)
   Common Bat Family (*Vespertilionidae*)
   Little Brown Bat (genus *Myotis*)
   Pipistrelle (genus *Pipistrellus*)
   Big Brown Bat (genus *Eptesicus*)
   Twilight Bat (genus *Nycticeius*)
   Big-eared Bat (genus *Corynorhinus*)
   Red Bat and Hoary Bat (genus *Lasiurus*)
   Large Pale Bat (genus *Antrozous*)
   Silver-haired Bat (genus *Lasionycteris*)
   Yellow Bat (genus *Dasypterus*)
   Jackass Bat (genus *Euderma*)
   Free-tailed Bat Family (*Molossidae*)

Common Guano Bat (genus *Tadarida*)
California Mastiff Bat (genus *Eumops*)
Leaf-nosed Bat Family (*Phyllostomidae*)
   California Leaf-nosed Bat (genus *Macrotus*)
   Fruit Bat (genus *Artibeus*)

3. THE STRANGE-JOINTED (order *Xenarthra*)
   Armadillo Family (*Dasypodidae*)
   Nine-banded Armadillo (genus *Dasypus*)

4. THE GNAWERS (order *Rodentia*)
   Squirrel and Marmot Family (*Sciuridae*)
   Tree Squirrels (Red, Gray, Fox, Kaibab, Abert) (genus *Sciurus*)
   Flying Squirrel (genus *Glaucomys*)
   Eastern Chipmunk (genus *Tamias*)
   Western Chipmunk (genus *Eutamias*)
   Ground Squirrel (Striped Ground Squirrel, Columbian Ground Squirrel, Desert Ground Squirrel) (genus *Citellus*)
   Golden Mantled Ground Squirrel (genus *Callospermophilus*)
   Rock Squirrel and California Ground Squirrel (genus *Otospermophilus*)
   Antelope Ground Squirrel (genus *Ammospermophilus*)

Prairie Dog (genus *Cynomys*)
Woodchuck and Hoary Marmot (genus *Marmota*)
The Beaver Family (*Castoridae*)
Beaver (genus *Castor*)
Mountain Beaver Family (*Aplodontiidae*)
Mountain Beaver (genus *Aplodontia*)
Porcupine Family (genus *Erethizontidae*)
Porcupine (genus *Erethizon*)
Pocket Gopher Family (*Geomyidae*)
Western Pocket Gopher (genus *Thomomys*)
Eastern Pocket Gopher (genus *Geomys*)
Chestnut Pocket Gopher (genus *Cratogeomys*)
Pocket Mouse Family (*Heteromyidae*)
Pocket Mouse (genus *Perognathus*)
Kangaroo Rat (genus *Dipodomys*)
Dwarf Pocket Rat (genus *Microdipodops*)
Spiny Pocket Rat (genus *Liomys*)
Jumping Mouse Family (*Zapodidae*)
Jumping Mouse (genus *Zapus*)
Woodland Jumping Mouse (genus *Napaeozapus*)
Native Rat and Mouse Family (*Cricetidae*)
Common Field Mouse (genus *Microtus*)
Pine Mouse (genus *Pitymys*)
Red-backed Mouse (genus *Clethrionomys*)
Muskrat (genus *Ondatra*)
Round-tailed Muskrat (genus *Neofiber*)
Brown Lemming (genus *Lemmus*)
Collared Lemming (genus *Dicrostonyx*)
Bog Lemming (genus *Synaptomys*)
Lemming Mouse and Red Tree Mouse (genus *Phenacomys*)
White-footed Mouse (genus *Peromyscus*)

Grasshopper Mouse (genus *Onychomys*)
Harvest Mouse (genus *Reithrodontomys*)
(No common name) Mouse (genus *Baiomys*)
Wood Rat or Pack Rat (genus *Neotoma*)
Cotton Rat (genus *Sigmodon*)
Rice Rat (genus *Oryzomys*)

5. HARES AND RABBITS (order *Lagomorpha*)
Hare and Rabbit Family (*Leporidae*)
Snowshoe Hare, Arctic Hare, Jack Rabbits (genus *Lepus*)
Cottontail Rabbit and Marsh Rabbit (genus *Sylvilagus*)
Idaho Pygmy Rabbit (genus *Brachylagus*)
Pika Family (*Ochotonidae*)
Rocky Mountain Pika (genus *Ochotona*)

6. MARSUPIALS (order *Marsupialia*)
Opossum Family (*Didelphiidae*)
Common Opossum (genus *Didelphis*)

7. HOOFED ANIMALS (order *Ungulata*)
Cattle Family (*Bovidae*)
Bison (genus *Bison*)
Musk Ox (genus *Ovibos*)
Mountain Sheep (genus *Ovis*)
Rocky Mountain Goat (genus *Oreamnos*)
Pronghorn Antelope Family (*Antilocapridae*)
Pronghorn Antelope (genus *Antilocapra*)
Peccary Family (*Tagassuidae*)
Peccary (genus *Tagassu*)
Deer Family (*Cervidae*)
Mule Deer and Black-tailed Deer and White-tailed Deer (genus *Odocoileus*)

Wapiti or Elk (genus *Cervus*)
Moose (genus *Alces*)
Caribou (genus *Rangifer*)

8. FLESH EATERS (order *Carnivora*)
   Weasel Family (*Mustelidae*)
      Weasels, Mink, and Ferret (genus *Mustela*)
      Common Skunk (genus *Mephitis*)
      Spotted Skunk (genus *Spilogale*)
      Hog-nosed Skunk (genus *Conepatus*)
      Martens and Fishers (genus *Martes*)
      Wolverine (genus *Gulo*)
      Badger (genus *Taxidea*)
      River Otter (genus *Lutra*)
      Sea Otter (genus *Enhydra*)
   Raccoon Family (*Procyonidae*)
      Raccoon (genus *Procyon*)
      Coatimundi (genus *Nasua*)
   Ring-tailed Cat Family (*Bassariscidae*)
      Ring-tailed Cat (genus *Bassariscus*)
   Dog Family (*Canidae*)
      Timber Wolf, White Wolf, Coyote (genus *Canis*)
      Red Fox and color phases Black Fox, Silver Fox, Cross Fox; and the Kit Fox (genus *Vulpes*)
      Gray Fox (genus *Urocyon*)
      Arctic Fox and color phase Blue Fox (genus *Alopex*)
   Cat Family (*Felidae*)
      Cougar, Jaguar, Ocelot, and Jaguarundi (genus *Felis*)
      Canadian Lynx and Bobcat (genus *Lynx*)
   Bear Family (*Ursidae*)
      Black Bear and the color phase Cinnamon, and the Glacier Bear and Kermode Bear (genus *Euarctos*)
      Grizzly Bear and Alaskan Brown Bear (genus *Ursus*)
      Polar Bear (genus *Thalarctos*)

9. THE FIN-FOOTED (order *Pinnipedia*)

Walrus Family (Odobenidae)
   The Walrus (genus *Odobenus*)
Eared Seal Family (*Otariidae*)
   Alaskan Fur Seal (genus *Callorhinus*)
   Guadalupe Fur Seal (genus *Arctocephalus*)
   California Sea Lion (genus *Zalophus*)
   Stellar's Sea Lion (genus *Eumetopias*)
Earless or Hair Seal Family (*Phocidae*)
   Harbor Seal, Harp Seal, Ribbon Seal, Ringed Seal (genus *Phoca*)
   Hooded Seal (genus *Cystophora*)
   Northern Elephant Seal (genus *Mirounga*)
   Grey Seal (genus *Halichoerus*)
   Bearded Seal (genus *Erignathus*)

10. THE SIRENS (order *Sirenia*)
   Manatee Family (*Trichechidae*)
      Florida Manatee (genus *Trichechus*)

11. THE WHALES (order *Cetacea*)
   TOOTHED WHALES (suborder *Odontoceti*)
   Sperm Whale Family (*Physeteridae*)
      Sperm Whale (genus *Physeter*)
   Pygmy Sperm Whale Family (*Kogiidae*)
      Pygmy Sperm Whale (genus *Kogia*)
   Dolphin and Porpoise Family (*Delphinidae*)
      Killer Whale (genus *Orcinus*)
      White Whale (genus *Delphinapterus*)
      Blackfish (genus *Globicephala*)
      Narwhal (genus *Monodon*)
      Common Porpoise (genus *Phocaena*)
      Common Dolphin (genus *Delphinus*)
      Bottlenose Dolphin (genus *Tursiops*)
      Spotted Dolphin (genus *Prodelphinus*)
      Right Whale Dolphin (genus *Lissodelphis*)
      Striped Dolphin (genus *Lagenorhynchus*)
      Grampus (genus *Grampus*)
      False Killer (genus *Pseudorca*)
   Beaked Whale Family (*Ziphiidae*)
      Bottlenose Whale (genus *Hyperoodon*)

Cuvier's Beaked Whale (genus *Ziphius*)
Cowfish and True's Beaked Whale
(genus *Mesoplodon*)
Baird's Whale (genus *Berardius*)
WHALEBONE WHALES (suborder *Mysticeti*)
Right Whale Family (*Balaenidae*)
Bowhead (genus *Balaena*)
North Atlantic Right Whale and North
Pacific Right Whale (genus *Eu-
balaena*)

Gray Whale Family (*Rhachianectidae*)
California Gray Whale (genus *Rhachi-
anectes*)
Finback or Rorqual Family (*Balaenop-
teridae*)
Humpback (genus *Megaptera*)
Common Rorqual and the Piked Whale
and Sei's Whale (genus *Balaenop-
tera*)
Blue Whale (genus *Sibbaldus*)

Classification
Mammals Introduced

1. THE GNAWERS (order *Rodentia*)
Old-World Rat and Mouse Family (*Muri-
dae*)
House Mouse (genus *Mus*)
Norway Rat (House Rat) and Roof Rat
(Egyptian Rat) (genus *Rattus*)

2. HARES AND RABBITS (order *Lagomor-
pha*)
Hare and Rabbit Family (*Leporidae*)
European Hare (genus *Lepus*)

3. MARSUPIALS (order *Marsupialia*)
Opossum Family (*Didelphiidae*)
Murine Opossum (genus *Marmosa*)

4. HOOFED ANIMALS (order *Ungulata*)
Horse Family (*Equidae*)
Mustang (genus *Equus*)
Burro (genus *Equus*)
Pig Family (*Suidae*)
Wild European Boar (genus *Sus*)
Deer Family (*Cervidae*)
Reindeer (Lapland) (genus *Rangifer*)

Index

ARCTIC

OCE

C A N A D A

U. S

PACIFIC

OCEAN

MEXICO